THE BIBLE AND CHRIST

the BÍBLE and chRíst

he unity of the two testaments

By leopold saBouRín, S.J.

ALBA · HOUSE   NEW · YORK

SOCIETY OF ST. PAUL, 2187 VICTORY BLVD., STATEN ISLAND, NEW YORK 10314

Library of Congress Cataloging in Publication Data

Sabourin Leopold.
 The Bible and Christ

 Bibliography: p.
 Includes Index.
 1. Bible. N.T.—Relation to the Old Testament.
 2. Typology (Theology) I. Title.
 BS2387.S23   220.6   80-14892
 ISBN 0-8189-0405-4

Nihil Obstat:
Daniel V. Flynn, J.C.D.
Censor Librorum

Imprimatur:
Joseph T. O'Keefe, Vicar General
Archdiocese of New York
April 20, 1980

Designed, printed and bound in the United States of
America by the Fathers and Brothers of the
Society of St. Paul, 2187 Victory Boulevard,
Staten Island, New York 10314, as part of their
communications apostolate.

---

1 2 3 4 5 6 7 8 9 (Current Printing: first digit).

PREFACE

The correlation of the Jewish Bible and of the New Testament writings may be observed by an agnostic. The reason is quite simple: the second part of the parallel, the New Testament, is entirely centered on the message of a Jewish believer who surrounded himself with Jewish apostles who shared the same faith and the same tradition. We know from the texts that this man, Jesus of Nazareth, constantly affirmed that he did not want to destroy the traditional faith of Israel, but to fulfill it, to accomplish it.

The correspondence of both Testaments can also be studied by a believing Christian. When it is seen from that point of view, the correspondence acquires a greater density and a greater complexity. In fact, if Jesus, who lives at the heart of the New Testament, is truly Son of God and Savior, it becomes normal that he should be at work from the very beginning of the Bible and that He himself inspires it. At the same time, the correspondences become a project, conceived from the beginning, even if they become visible only later on. The correspondences suggest more than one meaning, when they anticipate Christ, the Church, the final realization of the Kingdom. All in all, these correspondences reveal to us the deep roots of Christ in creation, time and history.

Father Leopold Sabourin, who is well known for important studies of both parts of the Christian Bible, adopts this second point of view. He brings to this study his vast erudition and his long familiarity with the texts and with the scientific literature that surrounds it. He also brings to it the warmth and enthusiasm of a believer who marvels at the huge biblical fresco that unfolds for more than a millenium and reveals its many connections, once the structural main-lines have been detected.

The reader will particularly appreciate the simplicity and coherence of the work and the rich bibliographies.

The Harmony of both Testaments has interested many of the best minds from the beginning of Christianity till now, from Tertullian to Leonard Goppelt! Sabourin is well conscious of depending on them all. But he brings us a refreshingly new reading and a new light on an ancient theme. He deserves our gratitude for this well structured presentation of an immense literature on a fundamental theme. I wish him a well deserved success.

Julien Harvey, S.J.
Jesuit Faculties
Montreal, Canada

CONTENTS

INTRODUCTION

As the title indicates, this work intends to demonstrate that the unity of the two Testaments rests in Christ. In no other way, can the unity of the Bible be defended and the thrust of its trajectory be discovered and verified. A consensus of Christian scholars agrees with this global solution to the unity of the Testaments. However, within this solution lie many options regarding particular problems. In examining these options, several aspects of biblical theology will be treated, particularly the facets of biblical thought that demonstrate a *continuum* between the Old and New Testaments. The main problems relating to the unity of the Bible, together with the proposed solutions and their Scriptural basis will be presented here.

The work is addressed to both scholar and general reader alike. It is thoroughly documented to aid the reader in further study and reflection. The bibliography at the end of the work contains no more than about one fifth of the studies referred to throughout the book. The Biblical quotations are usually cited from the *Revised Standard Version*.

When Christians write on the unity of the Bible, they generally have in mind the unity of the two Testaments. The non-Christian Jewish readers do not acknowledge the term "Old Testament" which they consider to be purely a Christian designation for what they believe to be the only authentic scriptures. Therefore, to speak of the unity of the two Testaments does not make much sense to them. The problem is further complicated by the fact that the Jewish collection of scriptures does not correspond exactly to the canonical "Old Testament" of the Catholic Church.

Through a process that is not altogether clear to the historians, the Jewish doctors themselves reached a consensus on the books to be regarded as sacred and divided them into the Law, the Prophets and the writings (i.e. Psalms, Job, Ruth, Canticles, Qohelet, Lamentations, Esther, Daniel, Ezra-Nehemiah, Chronicles). The Law, of course, refers to the Pentateuch, while some of the "historical books" are grouped as the "former" prophets: Joshua, Judges, Samuel, Kings. Before the Reformation, the Christian Church generally recognized as equally inspired other books including some originally composed in Greek. These deutero-canonical Writings include Tobit, Judith, Wisdom of Solomon, Wisdom of Jesus the Son of Sirach (Ecclesiasticus), Baruch, Maccabees and some passages of other books. At the time of the Reformation, however, the Protestant churches decided to adopt the Jewish canon of sacred books for the Old Testament and not to count as truly inspired the deutero-canonical writings which they refer to as "apocrypha." It is comforting to note that recent editions of the Bible within the Reformed traditions also include these writings at least in the appendix. This is an acknowledgment of the special role these works have played in the history of Christianity and must be considered a step forward in the ecumenical spirit of our era. At times, the first and second books of Esdras will be included in these collections of "apocrypha"; however, unlike the books of Ezra and Nehemiah these are not considered inspired by the Catholic Church though they too were often appended to certain Vulgate (Latin) editions of the Bible.

Although most Christian scholars defend the unity of the Bible, they understand in a variety of ways the unity of the two Testaments. They readily admit that a certain unity exists already from the fact that God is the principal author of the whole Bible, since the whole Bible is rightly held to be the Word of God. Thus the Bible represents *one Revelation*. In the following chapters we will examine the various types under which the unity of the two Testaments can be affirmed with regard to their *contents*. We will begin with the divine dispensation or economy. It has appeared to us possible to group under this heading reflections on the one God of both Testaments, on Law and Grace, and on the Kingdom and its phases. We shall then investigate particularly important areas, where the unity of the two Testaments is involved, namely the various covenants and the promise-fulfilment theme. Leaving behind what belongs rather to the field of concepts, we will then concentrate our attention on the personal key to the unity of the Bible, Christ himself, whose advent, we maintain, was prepared by the Old Testament and prefigured in it. This will involve a study of prophecy, of the biblical notion of history, and of the main christological figures. With the overall view of the features of unity in mind it will be possible in the last chapter to see how the Scriptures have evolved according to a God-inspired pattern and how they should be read, if we are to grasp their full and deepest meaning.

It cannot be denied that the NT authors have considered the Old Testament—the only existing "Scripture" available to them—as the Word of God. Although Jesus disputed several points of the traditional Jewish interpretation, he has not positively abrogated any statement contained in the Old Testament; but he knew that the time of the old law would soon elapse, leaving only its permanent values to survive. Christ himself quoted the Old Testament as the Word of God (see Mt 15:4), and he upheld the validity of the Law, of the Decalogue in particular, against the antinomians, the false prophets, who apparently claimed for themselves charisms that would place them above the Law (Mt 7:21). In fact, Jesus asserted that he came not to abolish the Law and the Prophets, but to fulfil them (5:17), in this way implying that the Law was prophetic.

In spite of this positive attitude of Jesus and of the New Testament authors towards the Old Testament, some Christian writers, ancient and modern, have expressed negative judgments on the OT in the light of the Christ-event. As Anderson puts it, Marcion was expelled from the church at Rome about 144 A.D. mainly for proposing in his no longer extant work, the *Antitheses*, a list of "genuine" Christian writings which excluded the Old Testament. For Marcion the God of the Old Testament is another God, inferior to the God of Jesus Christ. He held that there was a *radical discontinuity* between flesh and spirit, law and gospel, the God of Israel and the Father of Jesus, between the Old Testament and the New Testament. He followed his theory through to its logical conclusion and eliminated from his Bible the Old Testament, together with unacceptable parts of the New Testament (cf. Baker 45). Justin Martyr rejected dualism in the second century and argued for the unity of God's revelation, stating that the OT itself looks forward to the Messiah and the New Covenant. Tertullian, a little later, systematically refuted Marcion's dualism, showing that Marcion's own version of the Bible presented a Christ who was the fulfilment of the Law and the Prophets. Other ancient writers have successfully defended the unity of the two Testaments and the continuity of the divine Revelation from one to the other. They argued that the *Logos* had already spoken to the Patriarchs and the Prophets (*see* J. Fischer), using almost the same assertions as those in the beginning of the Epistle to the Hebrews. Adolph Harnack adopted more or less Marcion's views in his book *Marcion: Das Evangelium vom fremden Gott*. For him the attempt to perpetuate the OT in the Christian canon is the sign of "a religious and ecclesiastical paralysis." Although Rudolph Bultman in a way opposed Marcion (*see* Michalson), he also depreciated the value of the Old Testament.

That a bond exists between the two Testaments can hardly be denied. Recently, several authors have discussed the relationship that connects them both, and they tend to agree that the promise-fulfilment category, rooted in history and prophecy, constitutes the best framework in which this relationship can be explained and established. This supposes that the meaning of "Testament" and "Covenant" is first clarified, together with the important notion of "people of God." A few scholars take a view radically opposed to that of Marcion, and claim, as Arnold Van Ruler does, that the essential Bible is the OT, the NT being its interpretative glossary (on this view *see* Baker 97-120). But a large majority of Christian scholars find rather that the NT brings to the OT its *necessary complement*, as the roof completes a building. There exists such a unity and continuity between the two Testaments, J. Leclercq explains (p 174), that one cannot be understood without the other. The OT must be studied in the light of the New, and also the NT in the light of the Old (*see* Lyonnet).

General Bibliography on the Unity of the Two Testaments

BAKER, D.L. *Two Testaments, One Bible: A Study of some Modern Solutions to the Theological Problem of the Relationship between the Old and New Testaments* (Leicester, G.B., 1977).

BEAUCHAMP, P. *L'un et l'autre Testament. Essai de lecture* (Paris 1976).

DANIÉLOU, J. "L'unité des deux Testaments dans l'oeuvre d'origène," RevSR 22 (1948) 27-56.

DELGADO, A. *"La unidad de las Escrituras,"* Scripta Theologica 4 (1972) 7-82, 279-354.

DIEM, H. *"Die Einheit der Schrift,"* EvT 13 (1953) 383-405.

FILSON, F.V., "The Unity of the Old and New Testaments: A Bibliographical Survey," *Interpretation* 5 (1951) 134-52.

GAEBELEIN, F.E. "The Unity of the Bible," in C.F.H. Henry, ed., *Revelation and the Bible: Contemporary Evangelical Thought* (London 1959) 387-401.

GALBIATI, E. *"L'ui•à del due testamenti,"* in T. Ballerini, ed., *Introduzione alla Bibbia*, vol. 2 (Turin 1969) 8-12.

GLEN, J.B. "Jesus Christ and the Unity of the Bible," *Interpretation* 5 (1951) 259-67.

LESTRINGANT, P. *L'unite de la Bible. Fondement théologique et religieux de la Réforme,"* in J. Boisset. ed., *Le problème biblique dans le Protestantisme* (Paris 1955) 45-69.

LUBSCZYK, H. *"Die Einheit der Schrift: Zur hermeneutischen Relevanz des Urbekenntnisses im Alten und Neuen Testament,"* in F. Hoffman, u.a. eds., *Sapienter Ordinare*, Festgabe für E. Kleineidam (Leipzig, 1969) 73-104.

MC CASLAND, S.V. "The Unity of the Scriptures," JBL 73 (1954) 1-10.

MILDENBERGER, F. *Gottes Tat im Wort. Erwägungen zur alt-testamentlichen Hermeneutik als Frage nach der Einheit der Testamente* (Gütersloh 1964).

MOYTER, A. "Bible Study and the Unity of the Bible," in J.B. Job, ed., *Studying God's Word: An Introduction to Methods of Bible Study* (London 1972) 11-23.

ROWLEY, H.H. *The Unity of the Bible* (Philadelphia 1953).

SCHMIDT, L. "Die Einheit zwischen Altem und Neuem Testament im Streit zwischen Friedrich Baumgartel und Gerhard von Rad," *Evangelische Theologie* 35 (1975) 119-39.

SCHMID, H. "Die Einheit der Testamente," *Judaica* 21 (1965) 150-66, which discusses mainly Mildenberger.

SHIH, D.P. *The Unity of the Testaments as a Hermeneutical Problem* (Dissn., Boston 1971, see Diss. Abstr. Intern. vol. 32, p. 2186A).

SIEDL, S. "Das Alte und das Neue Testament. Ihre Verschiedenheit und Einheit," *Theologie-praktische Quartalschrift* 119 (1971) 314-24.

THOMAS, T.G. "The Unity of the Bible and the Uniqueness of Christ," *London Quarterly and Holborn Review* 191 (1966) 219-27.

WRIGHT, G.E. "The Unity of the Bible," *Interpretation* 5 (1951) 504-17.

Bibliography on the Relationship between the Two Testaments

DEQUEKER, L. "Old and New in the Bible. Guidelines for a Better Understanding of the Relationship between the Old and New Testaments," *Louvain Studies* 3 (1971) 189-205.

RIDDERBOS, N.H. "De Verhouding van het Oude Testament en het Nieuwe Testament," *Gereformeerd Theologisch Tijdschrift* 68 (1968) 97-110.

SCHNIEWIND, J. "Die Beziehung des Neuen Testaments zum Alten Testament," *Die Zeichen der Zeit* 20 (1966) 3-10.

VAN ZYL, A.H. "Die verhouding van die Ou en Newe Testament," in *Fs. E.P. Groenewald* (Pretoria 1970) 9-22.

VERHOEF, P.A. "The Relationship between the Old and the New Testaments," in J.B. Payne, ed., *New Perspectives on the Old Testament* (Waco, Texas/London 1970) 280-303.

WOLF, E. *Die Einheit des Bundes: das Verhältnis von Altem und Neuem Testament bei Calvin* (Neukirchen 1958).

Further Reading

ANDERSON, B.W. "The Old Testament as a Christian Problem," in *Id., The Old Testament and Christian Faith* (New York 1969) 1-7.

BULTMANN, R. "The Significance of the Old Testament for the Christian Faith," in B.W. Anderson, *op. cit.* 8-35.

FISCHER, J. "Die Einheit der beiden Testamente bei Lactanz, Victorin von Pettau und deren Quellen," MüTZ 1 (1950/3) 96-101.

JENSON, R.W. "Die Kontinuität von Altem und Neuem Testament als Problem für Kirche und Theologie heute," in H. Zeddies, ed., *Hoffnung ohne Illusion: Referate und Bibelarbeiten* (Berlin 1970).

LECLERCQ, J. "L'éxègese médiévale de l'Ancien Testament," in P. Auvray, ed., *L'Ancien Testament et les chrétiens*, (Paris 1951) 168-82.

LYONNET, S. "Le Nouveau Testament à la lumière de l'Ancien. A propos de Rom 8, 2-4" NRT 87 (1965) 561-87.

MICHALSON, C. "Bultmann against Marcion," in B.W. Anderson, *op. cit.*, 43-63.

SANDERS, J.A. *Torah and Canon* (Philadelphia 1972).

VAN RULER, A.A. *The Christian Church and the Old Testament* (Grand Rapids, Mich. 1966). On Van Ruler's views *see* J.J. Stamm, "Jesus Christ and the Old Testament," in C. Westermann, ed., *Essays on Old Testament Hermeneutics*, tr. and ed. by J.L. Mays (Richmond, Virg. 1963) 200-10.

VOIGT, D.G. "Worin besteht das Continuum der beiden Testamente?" *Pastoralblätter* (Stuttgart 1967) 68-78. The "Continuum" he finds in *Heilsgeschichte*, "salvation-history," with other authors.

ABBREVIATIONS

AmEcRev	American Ecclesiastical Review
BAC	Biblioteca de Autores Cristianos
BibTB	Biblical Theology Bulletin
BJRL	Bulletin of the John Rylands Library (Manchester)
BZAW	Beihefte zur Zeitschrift für die Alttestamentliche Wissenschaft
CanJT	Canadian Journal of Theology
CBQ	Catholic Biblical Quarterly
EstBib	Estudios Biblicos
et al.	*et alii* (and others)
E.T.	English Translation
ETL	Ephemerides Theologiae Lovanienses
Evt	Evangelische Theologie
ExpT	Expository Times
FRLANT	Forschungen zur Religion und Literatur des Alten und Neuen Testaments
Fs.	Festschrift (publication for birthday celebration
HTR	Harvard Theological Review
ibid.	*ibidem* (same work)
id.	*idem* (same author)
JB	Jerusalem Bible
JBL	Journal of Biblical Literature
JerBC	Jerome Biblical Commentary
JEvTS	Journal of the Evangelical Theological Society
MüTZ	Münchener Theologische Zeitschrift
NAB	New American Bible
NEB	New English Bible
NRT	Nouvelle Revue Théologique
NT	Novum Testamentum
NTA	New Testament Abstracts

op. cit.	*opus citatum* (work already quoted)
OTS	Oudtestamentische Studiën
RB	Revue Biblique
RecSR	Recherches de Science Religieuse
RevSR	Revue des Sciences Religieuses
RTLouv	Revue Théologique de Louvain
RHPR	Revue d'Histoire et de Philosophie Religieuses
RSPT	Revue des Sciences Philosophiques et Théologiques
RSV	Revised Standard Version
RT	Revue Thomiste
RThPh	Revue de Théologie et Philosophie
ScEcc	Sciences Ecclésiastiques (now called Science et Esprit)
ScotJT	Scottish Journal of Theology
SDB	Supplément au Dictionnaire de la Bible
TDNT	Theological Dictionary of the New Testament
ThZ	Theologische Zeitschrift
TLZ	Theologische Literaturzeitung
TOB	Traduction Oeucuménique de la Bible
TS	Theological Studies
T.U.	Texte und Untersuchungen
VT	Vetus Testamentum
ZAW	Zeitschrift für die Alttestamentliche Wissenschaft
ZTK	Zeitschrift für Theologie und Kirche

The Unity of the Two Testaments

The Unity of the Two Testaments

CHAPTER ONE
THE DIVINE DISPENSATION

For "divine dispensation" or "divine economy" could be substituted the expression "divine rule," but the former formulations are better, since they point not only to God's government of the world, but also to the beneficial effects this divine rule has among men and in the universe, resulting in what Teilhard de Chardin called "le milieu divin." In the present chapter we will consider the unity of the two Testaments under the viewpoint of revelation found in Scripture; in chapter 2 we will consider this unity under the aspects of the institutions involving the people of God.

We wish to present here a few remarks on the notion of *revelation*. It is important in the first place to distinguish revelation from inspiration. By inspiration we mean the charism, or grace, which moved the sacred authors to write, and assisted them until their work was completed. It is not possible to discuss here the different theories on inspiration. A consensus is developing around P. Benoit's proposal that inspiration has to be understood analogously. While it applies fully to the sacred author, it also affected in various degrees all those who mediately contributed to his work, including the people of God, the leading figures in biblical history, and even later the authorized interpreters of holy writ. The relationship between the main author of the Scriptures, God himself, and the human author will be discussed in ch. 4 with the senses of Scripture.

While scriptural inspiration consists in the dynamic impulse of the Spirit leading to the production of a sacred writing, *revelation* is the manifestation of the Word founded on the divine communication of truths and on the supernatural judgment which the human mind can express with divine certitude under divine illumination. The charism of inspiration, on the other hand, animates and directs the actual communication of the truths obtained through revelation. A sacred book normally results from the interaction of revelation and inspiration. Revelation is closely connected in the Bible with prophecy, and in the New Testament with Jesus and the apostolic age. Catholic theology commonly holds in fact that revelation came to an end with the death of the last apostle. This does not mean that *inspiration* also ceased then. So the writing of an inspired book could take place even in the post-apostolic period, as was probably the case for the Second Epistle of Peter, composed very likely around 125 A.D.

Though the concept of revelation is central to the whole of Old Testament piety, there was as yet no settled term for it (Oepke 577). In the Greek Bible the word *apokalyptein* took on theological significance when Yahweh was the subject, as in Is 52:10, where it translates the Hebrew *hasaf*, "uncover:" "The Lord has revealed his holy arm in the sight of all the nations." It is again in the later sections of Isaiah that we find another good illustration of the use of *apokalyptein*, this time as translating the Niphal (passive) of *gālâh*, "reveal:" "My salvation is close at hand, my (saving) justice is about to be revealed" (56:1). The distinctiveness of OT revelation is most clearly expressed in its reference for the future (Oepke 576). Also in the New Testament the true *locus* of revelation is in eschatology, as when Paul speaks of the future revelation of Jesus Christ as the glorious Lord (1 Cor 1:7; 2 Th 1:7). Christ himself praised God in his hymn of jubilation for having revealed to the little ones the secrets of his transcendental life with the Father (Mt 11:25-27), and in the Fourth Gospel he speaks mostly as the Revealer. In connection with his parables Jesus told the disciples: "To you it has been given to know the secrets of the kingdom of heaven, but to them it has not been given" (Mt 13:11). This statement is probably literarily dependent on Dn 2:22f: "There is a God in heaven who reveals mysteries . . . The Revealer of mysteries (*ho apokalyptôn mystēria*) disclosed to you what is to take place."

For Paul the possession of salvation rests on hope, for John the evangelist, hope rests on possession (Oepke 588). In the Book of Revelation *apokalypsis* again looks to the future. This writing intends to strengthen the Church which, as the bearer of revelation, is bound to preserve it and convey its contents to all generations.

The fact that the religion of the Bible is founded on an historical revelation distinguishes it from other religions that cannot seriously claim to be revealed. Besides, the origin of the biblical revelation is not lost in hermetic speculations, as in gnosticism, or in vague experiences of the mystery cults, but can be traced to mediators that are generally identified and whose credentials can be verified. Biblical revelation does not rest on the teaching of a single founder, but the divine word spans the ages and is connected with the development of history. In chapter 3, we will discuss if and how prophecy can incarnate in history, making the transcendental experience of God the vehicle of divine revelation in his people.

The main subject of the Vatican II constitution *Dei Verbum* is revelation. In revelation God manifests himself, his intentions, and his interventions, in the framework of a large pattern of divine rule set forth in salvation history. Vatican II has developed the christocentric bearing of revelation, more so than Vatican I, which emphasized rather the theocentric aspects (*see* R. Latourelle). According to *Dei Verbum* there is only one source of revelation, with two modes of transmission, written and oral, as previous Councils had already noted. "Hence there exist a close connection and communication between sacred tradition and sacred Scripture. For both of them, flowing from the same divine wellspring, in a certain way merge into a unity and tend toward the same end. For sacred Scripture is the word of God inasmuch as it is consigned to writing under the inspiration of the divine Spirit. To the successors of the apostles, sacred tradition hands on in its full purity God's word, which was entrusted to the apostles by Christ the Lord and the Holy Spirit. Thus, led by the light of the Spirit of truth, these successors can in their preaching preserve this word of God faithfully, explain it, and make it more widely known. Consequently, it is not from sacred Scripture alone that the Church draws her certainty about everything which has been revealed. Therefore both sacred tradition and sacred Scripture are to be accepted and venerated with the same sense of devotion and reverence" (*The Documents of Vatican II*, W.M. Abbott, ed., p. 117). *Dei Verbum* also acknowledges that "there is a growth in the understanding of the realities and the words which have been handed down" (p. 116). J.H. Walgrave has recently restated with clarity what Catholic theology has to say on the development of revelation.

a) The God of Israel and the Father of Jesus Christ

The most prominent feature of the *continuum* that binds the Old with the New Testament is, of course, the main author of the Bible, God Himself, whose self-manifestation constitutes the principal contents of the whole Scripture. Most Christian scholars accept as evident also from Scripture that the heavenly Father of Jesus Christ is no other than the God of Israel. Marcion had few followers in his claim that the God of Jesus Christ is different from and superior to the God of the Old Testament. Bultmann does, however, limit their identity with regard to us, where he pretends that the God who spoke to Israel no longer speaks *to us* in the time of the new covenant, that for the Christian the Old Testament is not revelation, but is essentially related to God's revelation in Christ as hunger is to food or despair to hope (*see* B.W. Anderson 227f). Thus, for Bultmann, the Old Testament would be for Christians only indirectly the word of God (Baker 187), inasmuch as it constitutes a presupposition for an understanding of the New Testament.

In the introductory chapter of a recent collective work on the *Old Testament* notion of *God*, Joseph Coppens brings out quite clearly some central points examined in the subsequent studies. He underlines the fact that to his people, Yahweh appeared as a personal God, living and transcendent. God's very transcendence, the aloofness of his "holiness," tended to distance him excessively from man. To preclude the danger of relegating God to a majestic solitude, the inspired writers also recalled that man had been created in the likeness of God, and God himself was described with human attributes, such as father, spouse, shepherd and others. God's solitude was further reduced by imagining him surrounded by a council of heavenly beings. Among the sapiential writers some, like the author of Wisdom, insist on the perfection of the divine plan, reflected in creation, while others, such as Job and Qohelet, considering more the human destiny, expressed criticism before falling into the submission of an anguished faith. The psalmists generally overcome this tension by a sort of mysticism in which blind trust in God's love removes the obstacles of a reasoning faith. The apocalypticists saw a solution to the problem of retribution in the belief that God will at the end triumphantly establish his reign and call the just to eternal life.

It is legitimate to ask ourselves if the true God can be the God of one book, be it the Bible, or the God of one culture, be it that of the Israelites, or the God of one religion, be it that of the Christians. Van der Veken has addressed himself to that problem, hoping to "shed some light upon the tension between the particularity of the religious language of Israel and the God who revealed Himself to that people, and the obvious fact that if the expression 'true God' is to have any meaning at all, it points to the fact that the true God is necessarily the God of all men, the only true God there is" (p. 431). He goes on to say that there is no God in general, but only a God that religions worship, a God of a particular religious tradition, and in most cases the God of a Holy Book. It is striking, he adds, how the growth of the belief in the true God of Israel accompanied the awareness of his uniqueness *and* universality. The only real revelation of God is historical and concrete. This was already the case in Israel; it is outstanding and definitive in the revelation of God found in Jesus Christ. It can even be said that "the only true God there is, is the God who reveals himself in personal encounter, in history" (p. 439). To say that the only true God is the God revealed in and by Christ is a belief, a matter of Christian faith; it does not rely on rational proof. Finally, Van der Veken makes a statement, which invites reflection, perhaps controversy, as the reader may judge for himself: "That the true God has revealed himself in a particular history need not imply that this particular revelation of God is the only revelation of the true God there is" (p. 443).

The Old Testament religion is often characterized as monotheistic, and this is true. But OT monotheism was not an abstract metaphysical conception, such as deists would produce. Metaphysical thought construes its monotheism from a reflection on the world, showing that its ultimate foundation has to be a spiritual, transcendental being, and even a personal God. The way to God in the Old Testament runs in the opposite direction. The starting point is the experienced intervention of a personal God in the affairs of the world. It is the self-manifestation of God to his servants, telling them his name, Jahweh, and who he is (Ex 3:6). On the basis of such historical experiences a more elaborate conception of God was worked out, but in the OT it never comes to a vague and abstract metaphysical concept. The OT God is always a concrete person, with traits which he himself manifests, and which generally have a manwards direction. The OT God is a covenant God, the God of his chosen people. The basic formula of OT monotheism is not "there is only one God" but "Jahweh is the unique God" (see K. Rahner 32-35).

When we pass to the New Testament, God becomes even more a concrete person. According to Rahner, the expression *ho Theos* designates almost always in the NT the person of the Father, and not the divine being common to the three Persons of the Holy Trinity. In the Latin way of proceeding, followed by St. Augustine and the later Scholastics, the point of departure is rather the divine essence, from which the reasoning went to the Persons. Not so in the Greek oriental tradition, which first considered the Father and the Son engendered by him, and finally the Spirit. Besides, in the NT view, all Christian knowledge of God the Father is through the Son. Christ himself said: "No one knows the Son except the Father, and no one knows the Father except the Son and any one to whom the Son chooses to reveal him" (Mt 11:27), and John recalls this when he writes: "No one who denies the Son has the Father" (1 Jn 2:23). The Christian prayer then is Trinitarian; it is not addressed to the God of natural theology or to be the divine essence, but to the Father of our Lord Jesus Christ; this often occurs in the Christian version of the Jewish formula of blessing (see 2 Cor 1:3; Ep 1:3; Col 1:3; 1 P 1:3).

It is noteworthy that Jesus almost always said "Father" when addressing God. Furthermore, he has not taught his disciples an abstract doctrine on God, but he has led them to live in a new way their relation with God and thus discover anew who God is, namely their Father (Giblet 234). In his study on the NT use of *Pater* for God, G. Schrenk poses the question: "Did Jesus think of God as the Father of all men?" He observes: "According to Mt 5:43-45, His goodness as Creator extends to all. But this is not fatherhood" . . . "The word 'father' is for those who accept the teaching of Jesus about 'your Father' " (TDNT 5, pp. 990f). With regard to God's intervention in the world the vision of Jesus is less historical than that of the OT prophets who saw the course of history in relation to Israel. The God of Jesus is more universal, and at the same time more related to each person in particular. Jesus did not obtain his knowledge of God through philosophical reasoning or even through a prolonged spiritual experience. He appears to be in full possession of it from the very beginning. Jesus lived conscious of God's presence in a unique manner, and conformed his life to the divine will without hesitation, teaching his disciples to do the same: "Be perfect, as your heavenly Father is perfect" (Mt 5:48).

Although his writings are obviously christological, *Paul* shows he possessed also a strong sense of the Father's role in the economy of salvation. For him it is God who raised Christ from the dead (1 Th 1:10; Rm 4:24), and through this action the Father of Jesus Christ manifested himself as the God of the living, and perfected his work of creation. Christ himself is the power and the wisdom of God (1 Cor 1:24). It is on the cross of Christ that God showed himself to be the God of love (Rm 5:8). The Father sets in motion eschatological life in everyone by the gifts of the Spirit, which he bestows to the believers through his Son. At the end Christ will deliver the Kingdom to God the Father after destroying every power of the enemy (1 Cor 15:24).

Of all the NT writings, only in *Hebrews* is God named at the very beginning. Vanhoye believes that the author has deliberately avoided naming any creature before the holy name of God. The letter, a written sermon, also ends with several mentions of God. Besides, no attribute accompanies God's name, for the author of Hebrews does not pretend to present God, as he does Jesus Christ, for there exists no point of reference prior to God. The *Theos* of Hebrews usually has the article, because he is the *God*, the only God. Besides, the article refers to a being already known: the God of Christian belief is the same God whom the Old Testament revealed, he who "spoke of old to our fathers by the prophets."

If one should wish, writes Vanhoye, to express the most distinctive feature of the notion of God in Hebrews, it would be that God appears as someone who establishes a relation with men by instituting a mediation. This allows God's self-communication to men and permits them to enter into relation with God in spite of his utter transcendence. It is remarkable that the initiative comes from God, who sent a mediator for a better covenant (8:6). According to Hebrews, God is henceforth known as he who made perfect through suffering the pioneer of our salvation (2:10). In fact, it is through his sacrifice (5:10) and through his resurrection from the dead (13:20) that Jesus became the perfect high priest.

John also has underlined the primacy of God the Father in the work of salvation. All the saving initiatives belong to him (Jn 3:16). For he gave his Son to the world so that men may through him receive eternal life (Jn 3:16; 4:10), and he leads everyone to his Son so that all who believe may receive resurrection from him (Jn 6:44). For John the union between the Son and the Father is so close that God is totally revealed in Jesus: "He who has seen me has seen the Father" (Jn 14:9). It is not possible to see God (Jn 1:18; 1 Jn 4:12), but what God the Father is appears in his Son and the Son's works: to know the Son is to know the Father (Jn 14:7). In the Book of Revelation, God the Father retains his primacy. In several passages, he appears gloriously enthroned; his name is that revealed at the burning bush (Ex 3:14); he receives the acclamation of the Isaian seraphim (Is 6:3); he is the creator and the ruler of the world (Rv 4:1-11).

But in Revelation, even more than in the Fourth Gospel, Christ shares the glory and the power of God the Father (Rv 5:11-14). As Giblet observes (p. 243), the Johannine writings place within the Holy Trinity itself the presentation of the relations between the Father and the Son. F. Porsch has initiated an exegetical discussion on the vaster problem of the relation of the Spirit with the Word, and with the Godhead. A Christian theology of the Trinity was worked out very early, also to combat heresies. It led to the Nicene creed, which was soon developed into a full doctrine by St. Augustine, St. Thomas Aquinas, and other scholastics, not to mention a very elaborate speculation still current. This speculation finds only indirect support in Scripture, which speaks of the acts of God rather than of his being. On the other hand, the New Testament conception of God does not repudiate its connection with the beginning of OT religion, but its ties are much closer to the later prophetical and post-prophetical developments (Eissfeldt 46). The New Testament speaks of the same God as the OT does, but he is better known through the person, the work, and the revelation of Jesus Christ.

b) The Mosaic Law and the Law of Christ

We will compare here briefly the Old Testament with the New under one particular aspect, a central one, which concerns the role of the law in the economy of salvation. Is salvation bestowed as a reward for obedience, or is it offered as a pure gift of God, in Christ? Due to the importance of what is involved, it is not unusual to distinguish, even to oppose, the economy of the law and the economy of grace. This distinction may be basically correct, but it has to be well understood, and we hope the lines that follow will contribute to this (see Grelot 260-65).

In the Hebrew Bible "law" is called *torah*, a term which is broader in meaning and less juridical than its Greek equivalent *nomos*. For *torah* designates a divine "instruction" given to men to regulate their conduct. The term is *primarily* applied to that body of legislation which the OT tradition associates with Moses. With this meaning in view, Rm 5:20 states: "Law came in, to increase the trespass; but where sin increased, grace abounded all the more."

The law, then, was the rule of life given to man through the inspired word. This revealed law incorporated many rules of conduct already followed through the indications of *the law of nature* (Rm 2:14), but it made these more explicit and added precepts which were either unknown or no longer observed. Besides, this law had public implications: in Israel religious law became civil law and it imposed a particular stamp on the national institutions as well.

Paul's view of the role of the law is particularly important for our purpose. When he says that the law was "custodian" (*paidagôgos*) until Christ came (Gal 3:23), he underlines its provisional character. Positively it had a beneficent educative influence, as Deuteronomy (cf. 4:5-8) and several psalms indicate, especially the long Ps 119. By making the precepts explicit, without providing the strength to observe them, the law made man conscious of his sinfulness and kept alive the need of a Savior. Thus could Paul say that the law was given "in view of the transgressions" (Gal 3:19), "to increase the trespass" (Rm 5:20), that "through the Law comes knowledge of sin" (Rm 3:20), not the grace to overcome its power. In this sense the law served to prepare humanity for the salvation to be offered by Christ, and the old economy was shaped with reference to the new. In fact, until the coming of Christ men "were by nature children of wrath" (Ep 2:3) and stood under God's judgment (Rm 1:18; 4:15). Already the OT, especially Deuteronomy, linked man's afflictions to the unobservance of the law (Dt 8:20; 11:16f), and natural calamities, like the great Flood, were seen as a punishment for the spread of sin (see also Gn 18:20f). And of course the prophets saw the day of Yahweh as a divine judgment against defiant iniquity. Because of the law, man's existence was thus seen in a clearer light and the need of redemption deeply felt.

The killing of Jesus has been the extreme sin of the world: "Now is the judgment of this world, now shall the ruler of this world be cast out" (Jn 12:31). The whole Jewish religious institution, as involved in the refusal and rejection of Jesus by the Jewish leaders, in his condemnation by the Sanhedrin, underwent judgment and received its death sentence. For Paul, Christ who in his death took upon himself the curse of the law (Gal 3:13), brought it to an end (Rm 10:4; Ep 2:15), and with it the temporal condition of sinful humanity virtually ceased because of God's judgment: "The law of the Spirit of life in Christ Jesus has set me free from the law of sin and death" (Rm 8:2). Through the grace of Christ (Jn 1:17) an absolute newness changed religiously the lot of humankind: it introduced the promised eschatological existence already characterized by the prophets (Jr 31:33; Ezk 36:25f) as life under the Spirit. The old economy of the law has come to an end; it is replaced by the economy of the Spirit, in grace and freedom.

In the passages where Paul is exalting the newness of the life in Christ, he tends to accentuate the fact that the economy of the law is a bypassed reality, and this is the truth. However, it should not be understood as contradicting what Jesus said in the Sermon on the Mount: "Think not that I have come to abolish the law and the prophets; I have come not to abolish them but to fulfill them" (Mt 5:17). The Mosaic economy has elapsed with the advent of Christ, but the permanent values of the law as the expression of God's will remain fulfilled in the commandment of love (Mt 22:40), as Paul himself recognized: "Love is the fulfilling of the law" (Rm 13:10). This law fulfilled is no longer, however, a reality of the old economy: it is in a way "the law of Christ" (1 Cor 9:21).

Against the overall background just given we can now examine more closely one of the key texts, in which Paul states that Christ "is the end of the law" (Rm 10:4). In the old dispensation most people faced a very difficult situation. Obliged to observe the law, but hardly capable of doing so, they had to live under the rule of sin. According to Paul "the scripture consigned all things to sin, that what was promised to faith in Jesus Christ might be given to those who believe" (Gal 3:22). For Jeremias, Rm 10:4-5 "opposes the righteousness of works which Moses proclaimed (Lv 18:5) to the righteousness of faith" (*TDNT* 4, p. 870). For the believer, in Delling's view, the law is set aside as a way of salvation by the Christ event. In Rm 10:4, he thinks, *nomos* corresponds to man's own righteousness, which the pious Jew seeks, and God's righteousness stands in contrast with the *nomos*: this is the righteousness which God creates, his justifying work. In Rm 10:4 he understands *nomos* as especially the law whose observance makes one just before God. "This possibility of justification before God is abolished by Christ's cross. *Nomos* and *dikaiosunē* in Rm 10:4 denote the

Jewish way of salvation which is set aside in Christ. The two are mutually exclusive for Paul" (*TDNT* 8, p. 56).

In line with the proposed interpretation it is appropriate to quote another text where law and grace are set again in contrast: "I do not nullify the grace of God; for if justification were through the law, then Christ died to no purpose" (Gal 2:21). Later, Paul writes that the law is not against the promises of God: "for if a law had been given which could make alive, then righteousness would indeed be by the law" (3:21). A closer look at the context suggests to G.E. Howard that in Rm 10:4 Paul wishes to affirm mainly this: Christ is the goal of the Law to everyone who believes because the ultimate goal of the law is that all nations are to be blessed in Abraham. Did Christ put an end to the law by taking upon himself the curse of the Law? Gal 3:13 seems to suggest precisely this (*TDNT* 9, p. 545), but other interpretations of the verse are also proposed. What Christ himself taught on the Mosaic law should not be left out, if we wish to remain in the proper perspective.

Christ's most explicit teaching on the meaning and value of the Mosaic law is found in Mt 5:17-20. The proper interpretation of these verses has to take into account the prophetic nature of the law, which is also expressed in Mt 11:13: "For all the prophets and the law prophesied until John." For Matthew in fact the Old Testament as a whole has prophesied Christ: the prophets, more particularly his person and activity; the law, his teaching. With Christ's coming everything is fulfilled: what therefore has been prophesied is not abolished, it is realized. The law finds again in Christ its initial role, that of giving life. There is, besides, in Christ a total surpassing, for the life he procures is eternal life. But it is a surpassing in continuity, for it had been prophesied as belonging to the new economy.

These concepts apply also to Mt 5:18, which at first sight appears as a difficult verse, containing two coordinate propositions: "For truly, I say to you, till heaven and earth pass away, not an iota, not a dot, will pass from the law until all is accomplished." In our view the first proposition is a temporal one, which can be referred to v. 19: it underlines *the duration* of the law. It will last, forever, with all its prescriptions. This is easier to understand if by law we understand mainly the Decalogue, the ten commandments, perhaps with Dt 4:44, where this meaning seems to be indicated. Furthermore, for Jesus all the law and the prophets depend on the two commandments of the love of God and of neighbor (Mt 22:40). To obey these commandments is to accomplish God's will as expressed in the law. The second proposition of Mt 5:18, "until all is accomplished," refers, we think, to the *total fulfillment* of the law, and to remove ambiguity should be perhaps translated, according to its meaning, "but all will be realized." Here it is the *prophetic role* of the law which is envisioned and the proposition looks back to v. 17, where this is particularly stressed. For Matthew, Jesus did not have to replace the Mosaic law with a code of rules of his own; the rule of life he intended would be realized in discipleship, and for this reason his last words to his closest followers were: "Go, therefore, make disciples of all the nations (28:19). For the New Testament God's will is fulfilled in the following of Christ.

The Mosaic law continues in its permanent features, insofar as Christ assumed it, to perpetuate its initial force and value as the expression of the divine will. It is possible, in this sense, to speak of "the law of Christ." Thus Paul writes: "Bear one another's burdens, and so fulfill the law of Christ" (Gal 6:2), and he also states that he finds himself "not without law toward God but under the law of Christ" (1 Cor 9:21). However, for Paul the law of Christ has close connections with the law of the Spirit, since he can write in Rm 8:2: "For the law of the Spirit of life in Christ Jesus has set me free from the law of sin and death." From other texts it can be deduced that Paul considers himself under the law of Christ because he imitates him in his own life (1 Cor 11:1) and lives of Christ's life (Gal 2:20).

As Paul suggests in Rm 8:2 the new law gives life, just as the Spirit of the Lord called back to life the dry bones of the valley in Ezekiel's vision (Ezk 37). This prophecy has connections with the promise that God would give to his people "a new spirit," an inward spirit to change their hearts. Thus will it be possible for everyone to observe God's will, his "statutes" (Ezk 36:26f). This change of heart will accompany the making of "a new covenant" (Jr 31:31). Feil advises correctly that we speak of the "law of Christ" mainly, as Paul does, when it is set into contrast with the Mosaic law. If Paul calls the life in Christ a "law" in Rm 8:2, it is because he is contending with those for whom the law was the mediator of all justification as the positive and external expression of the divine will (Lyonnet). In addition, had not Jeremiah himself spoken of a new inward "law" in connection with the future covenant (31:33)?

To conclude, the role of the Mosaic law as the custodian until Christ, and its replacement by the law of the Spirit in the new economy also shows the interrelation of the two testaments. The provisional character of the law indicates that the whole Mosaic institution pointed towards another dispensation, which it was meant to prepare. At the same time, without the background the OT texts provide, it would hardly be possible to understand a large part of the NT, and even the exact nature of the redemption Christ brought to us. The law of God does therefore provide in a way a *continuum* from the Old Testament to the New, and not only in the sense that one law of God is involved, proposed and observed differently in harmony with the different manner of looking at God himself. Since God, as we have seen, appears in the NT rather as Father, it should be no surprise that a radical change takes place. It is not by observing more laws that the disciples will surpass in righteousness the scribes and the Pharisees (Mt 5:20), but by observing them differently, animated by love for God and with God's love, as children of the Father. Or, as R.S. McConnell puts it, the Torah is given a heart of love (p. 50).

c) The Kingdom of God and its Phases

The Kingdom of God in the teaching of Christ is best defined as the divine economy of salvation. On the other hand, the present section belongs to a chapter titled "the divine dispensation." While "economy" in our context refers to the divine way of implementing the salvation in Christ, the term "dispensation" evokes rather the divine order in which this or that economy of salvation is carried out. Although they have received special emphasis in the teaching of Jesus the concept and the reality of the Kingdom of God belong to the whole Bible and are thus particularly relevant in a study on the unity of the two Testaments.

The idea of the kingdom of God was initially connected with Yahweh's kingship. This kingship is affirmed in numerous passages of the Old Testament. But the conception, in McKenzie's view, is strangely lacking in unity, and it can be asked whether the kingship of Yahweh was a basic element of Israelite belief (*Dictionary of the Bible* 476). According to old texts, Yahweh is king of Israel (1 S 8:7); later he is said to rule over all nations (Ps 22:29), and elsewhere he is simply called king (Ex 15:8), or king as savior of individuals (Ps 74:12) and of Israel (Ps 145:11-13). Perhaps dependently on a deutero-Isaian proclamation (Is 52:7), a series of psalms are specifically dedicated to the kingship of Yahweh (Pss 47 and 96 to 99). The notion of divine kingship may have been borrowed from elsewhere. In Israel it was apparently connected with the ark of the covenant, the throne of Yahweh (*see* 1 Ch 28:5), with his eschatological saving deeds, and with the covenant festival. Considered at first as the king of Israel, Yahweh became later the king of all nations, while his cosmic kingship was a later development.

Although it reflects the OT conception of the kingship of Yahweh, *the idea of kingdom* is rarely connected *explicitly* with Yahweh. However, we read in Ps 109:19: "The Lord has established his throne in the heavens, and his kingdom rules over all," and in Dn 3:33, Nebuchadnezzar asserts of the Most High that his kingdom (*malkût*) endures from generation to generation (4:34). But in Dn 7:14-27 the kingdom is given to the Son of man and to the saints. Later Jewish writings, in which attributes are often substituted for the divine name, occasionally use the expression *malkût haššamayyim*, or in Aramaic *malkuta' dišmayya'*. Jesus has canonized the expression by using it, and Matthew rendered it literally in Greek with his frequent *basileia tôn ouranôn*. While Italian, following the Latin *regnum*, has only one word *regno* to translate *basileia*, we are confronted in German and English with different possibilities: *Königtum*, "kingship," *Herrschaft*, "Lordship," "reign," and *Reich*, "kingdom." The term "kingship" will preferably be reserved for texts where God is explicitly described as king (mainly in the Old Testament), while "reign" (cf. Lc 1:33) could be the regular term in the New Testament, leaving "kingdom" to denote the domain over which the reign of God, in its final phase, is perfectly exercised. Such a *basileia* groups all the souls who accept the reign of God over them. Thus one will normally say "to enter the kingdom," as in Mk 9:47, Jn 3:5, while Mk 10:15 seems to state: "Truly, I say to you, whoever does not receive the reign of God like a child shall not enter into the kingdom." Schweizer notes that Jesus "spoke frequently of one's *entering* the kingdom . . . so 'realm' would be a better translation" (*The Good News According to Mark* 45f).

In connection with the messianic kingship it has to be said that *directly* the historical kings are meant in the royal psalms. But the successful reigns can have indicated the pattern of a reign properly messianic. Besides, by some traits the figure of the Davidic kings mentioned in the psalms appears as prophetic in the strict sense, even attaining beyond the level of typology. This could be verified especially in Pss 2, 45, 72, 110 (also perhaps 20 and 21). In Pss 132 and 89 the confirming and restoring of the messianic dynasty could be intended. Additional revelation has made it possible to discover in previous texts "a fuller sense" than that which had been apprehended even by the writer himself. The king's divine sonship, his "priestly" prerogatives, his role as judge, his spectacular victories, even over all the nations, the "eternity" of his reign, these were preparations for the definitive conceptions of messianism. Some conventional expressions of the extravagant court-style were to be used as patterns to formulate beliefs related to Christology.

Apart from the traditions centered on the royal messiah or the prophet of end time (cf. Dt 18:15-18), there existed what has been called "messianism without a Messiah." This biblical tradition carried a more general hope, that of the coming of God himself to establish his rule and to ensure the effective recognition of his royalty. A psalmist, for example, invited the heavens, the earth and its inhabitants to exult "before the Lord, for he comes; for he comes to rule the earth. He shall rule the world with justice and the peoples with his truth" (Ps 96:7-9). Hope in God's coming was kept alive for a long time, until it found its accomplishment in the incarnation of the Emmanuel, which means "God-With-Us."

The *basileia* was certainly the central theme of the public proclamation of Jesus. This is apparent from Mk 1:15, and from the phrase *kērussein* (proclaim) *to euaggelion tēs basileias* in Mt 4:23 (9:35), which Luke combines differently when he speaks of *euaggelizesthai tēn basileian* (4:43; 8:1). In the *Kaddish*, a "holy" Jewish liturgical prayer, which Jesus certainly knew, the wish is expressed that God's great name be exalted and that he rule his kingdom (or dominion). This may seem surprising to many, but it is quite impossible to determine with certainty what for Jesus *basileia* represented and when it would be inaugurated. The difficulty is due in part to the fragmentary character of the Gospel reports of what Jesus said and to the reinterpretation his words received before and when they were given their fixed form in writing.

It is quite certain though that Jesus saw the kingdom as essentially a *future* reality. This is implied in the second petition of the *Pater*, "thy kingdom come" (Mt 6:10; Lk 11:2). It is also suggested in the promise of Lk 12:32: "Fear not, little flock, for it is your Father's good pleasure to give you the kingdom." Assuming that Lk 22:15-18, apart from the mention of the passover, actually says no more than Mk 14:25, it is very probable that here Jesus declares that he will not drink wine any more until he can partake of the messianic meal with his disciples, that is, until the coming of the kingdom in the near future. The kingdom of God also appears as a future reality when admittance to it is said to depend on the outcome of the judgment (Mt 25:34). The future judgment and admittance to the kingdom are linked in the judgment scene (Mt 25:31-46) and elsewhere (*see* Lk 12:8f). The futurity of the kingdom is also clearly stated in Mt 8:11: "Many will come from east and west and sit . . . in the kingdom of heaven."

According to the theory of "realized eschatology," with the public appearance of Jesus the eschatological Reign of God has actually entered into history: the Kingdom of God has come: "The *eschaton* was moved from the future to the present, from the sphere of expectation into that of realized experience" (C.H. Dodd 40f). It must, however, be held that "the Reign of God awaits consummation somewhere beyond the bonds of history" (R.H. Fuller 20). On the other hand, the final interruption of the kingdom is certainly related in some way to the historical event of Jesus' life. The death and exaltation of Jesus constituted a necessary prelude to the coming of the kingdom. It is shortly before his death that he said, using a covenantal phrasing: "I appoint (*diatithemai*) unto you a kingdom, even as my Father appointed (*dietheto*) unto me" (Lk 22:29). Other texts place a connection between the public ministry of Jesus and the coming of the kingdom. Two are prominent: "If it is by the finger of God that I cast out demons, then the kingdom of God has come upon you" (Lk 11:20); "Behold! the kingdom of God is in the midst of you" (Lk 17:21).

Features of the Kingdom and a Definition

Jesus relates the kingdom to the eschatological rule of God, but the effect of this rule is anticipated, since its advent is connected with the present moment, for decisions for or against the kingdom are taken now. However, the constitution of the kingdom rests exclusively on God's action, seed, growth, and harvest (*see* Mk 4:25-29). Although conditions have to be fulfilled to qualify for the kingdom, it is received by men as a supernatural and gratuitous gift. Human effort can do nothing to accelerate or to prevent its coming.

Another important feature of the kingdom is that it means *salvation*. The OT prophetic threats and the revengeful overtones of Jewish apocalyptic, Qumran included, have almost entirely disappeared in Christ's teaching. Those who interiorly resist the offer of salvation will indeed "perish" (Lk 13:3, 5) and Jesus uses traditional imagery, like "hell of fire" (Mt 5:22), to accentuate what it means to be excluded from the kingdom (Lk 13:28). But the point of the message on the kingdom is salvation. Jesus himself stressed this when he quoted Isaiah in his inaugural message at Nazareth, "He has sent me . . . to proclaim the year of the Lord's favour," while he omitted what follows immediately: "and the day of vengeance of our God" (Is 61:2). What Jesus told Zacchaeus, "today salvation has come to this house" (Lk 19:9), is typical of his teaching about the kingdom.

In the definition we will propose of the kingdom we have in mind the kingdom of God and not the kingdom of the Son of man, which is different. Matthew alone speaks quite clearly of a *kingdom of the Son of man*, which seems to be the messianic community here on earth, perhaps to be equated with the Church. In the explanation of the parable of the weeds we are told that, at the time of the harvest, "the Son of man will send his angels, and they will gather out *of his kingdom* all causes of sin, all evildoers" (13:41). Elsewhere Jesus says: "Truly, I say to you, there are some standing here who will not taste death before they see the Son of man coming in his kingdom" (Mt 16:28). In other NT texts it is unclear if the *basileia* of Christ represents in fact the same reality as the Father's kingdom. For the intermediate period, between the resurrection of Christ and his parousia, it is permissible to speak of the messianic "reign of Christ," which will come to an end with the perfect establishment of God's reign (cf. 1 Cor 15:24f). Only 1 Tm 4:18 (cf. 4:1) speaks of the Lord's (Christ's) "heavenly kingdom," while a similar notion appears in 1 P 1:11 (*see* Col 1:13). Paul speaks at one point of those who have no "inheritance in the kingdom of Christ and of God" (Ep 5:5). Jesus himself foresaw that the disciples would "eat and drink at my table in my kingdom" (Lk 22:30). Again in Luke the repentant criminal asks Jesus: "Remember me when you come in your *basileia*" (23:42), and, according to John, Jesus told Pilatus: "my *basileia* is not of this world" (18:36).

In the various attempts made to define the Kingdom, proper attention is given to its "dynamic" aspect, which is meant to explain that the kingdom can be both present and future. What is generally lacking is a clear idea of the nature itself of the Kingdom. It is usually described as reign or rule of God, but this is both tautological and not comprehensive enough, since it hardly applies to texts in which the kingdom appears as a place or state into which one enters. Besides, the providential rule of God has always been operative. The kingdom proclaimed by Jesus must involve a specific newness, it must be a distinctive reality. Before proposing our own definition we wish to make the observation that although the term *basileia* is etymologically connected with the notion of "reign" or of "kingship," it does not have to mean precisely this in the Gospel context, for terms are known to carry meanings that are only vaguely connected with their etymology. Thus, for example, the term "economy" etymologically refers to "household management," but has taken with time many other meanings. Besides, God is not presented as king in the gospels, especially in Matthew— explicitly only in Mt 5:35 in a clear reference to Ps 48:2 or Is 66:1—but as the Father. In this sense the word "economy" is strikingly appropriate: God governs mankind as a father presides over his household.

In our view the Kingdom of God of the gospels is *the divine economy which unfolds dynamically and gradually in the actualization of God's paternal rule in and through Christ, with man accepting it in faith now, in anticipation of its future transcendent manifestation.* We employ here *divine economy* not precisely in the sense usually given by dictionaries, "a form of divine government," a "dispensation (as the old or the new dispensation)" but in a broader sense, which encompasses both divine rule and the situation which derives for men from its actualization in the world and in everyone. It is very close in meaning to what Teilhard de Chardin called "le milieu divin" in his book of that name. With the advent of the kingdom a *milieu de vie divin* for men becomes a reality, of course in the full sense only in the other world. How does this divine economy become a reality? To say it briefly, it is brought about through God's paternal rule, which does not impose itself, as in the apocalyptic dream, by a spectacular and terrifying display of vengeful and annihilating power, but through the redemptive work of Jesus Christ and the saving grace of a merciful Father. Of course the kingdom grows of itself (Mk 4:26-29), just as salvation is a free gift of God, but it becomes operative when through God's grace it is fully received by men, whose contribution here is analogous to that of faith in Pauline thought.

The advent of the kingdom is *gradual*, because it is a dynamic reality: the coming of Jesus initiated a new era of God's dealing with men, one in which God's fatherly love and mercy was visibly manifested in Jesus Christ, whose person, teaching and work appeared as a challenge to men, and also as a call and the assistance needed to transform their lives into that of true children of the heavenly Father and of brothers in the great family of mankind. Not all will qualify for the kingdom. Only after the final judgment will the kingdom be fully established. Although the fate of the material world remains obscure, shrouded as it is in traditional imagery, there is no doubt it will in some way share in the fate of human society (Rm 8:22f). Jesus foresaw for the end a regeneration (*paliggenesia*), a new beginning (Mt 19:28), which in the apocalyptic language appears as "new heaven and new earth" (Rv 21:1). Everyone has to strive, with God's grace, to enter into this divine economy which contains all the blessings: "Seek first the kingdom and its righteousness, and all the rest shall be yours as well" (Mt 6:33).

In his basic observations on the conception of *basileia* in Matthew, Kretzer notes that in the expression "Father in the heavens" the communication line is from above downwards, as the descent of the dove at Jesus' baptism suggests. The fact that the plural *ouranoi*, "heavens," occurs so frequently (51 times) in the Septuagint, especially in the Psalms, is particularly significant for the use of "kingdom of heavens" in Matthew, which is known to reflect partly a liturgical background. For Matthew the importance of *ouranios*, "heavenly," seems to lie in the universalist notion it conveys, in line with the idea current in antiquity of "the unity of heaven and earth." Besides, "heaven" is a *theion*, a divine reality. All this would serve well Matthew's understanding of the *basileia*: God's overall rule coming earthwards from above and achieving the salvation of man. God's lordship (*Herrschen*) over the world and his rule (*Walten*) over men are rooted in his fatherly care and his gracious interest for the created world. This should not be seen as conflicting with the other image of him as the stern judge (Mt 7:21-23) concerned to have his lordship recognized and his will accepted as a norm for man's behaviour.

It is not difficult to find a continuity between the two Testaments from the viewpoint of the kingdom. The same God rules over the world in the Old as in the New Testament, although the manner of his rule receives a different emphasis. Besides, the purpose of

God's rule in both Testaments is the redemption of man, as a definition proposed by Ladd suggests: the kingdom of God is "the *redemptive* reign of God dynamically active to establish his rule among men . . . which will appear as an apocalyptic act at the end of the age" (p. 214). Also in both Testaments the reign of God implies "a personal relation between God and the individual . . . It is a standing claim made by God on the loyalty and obedience of man... When the sovereignty of God is . . . accepted, the kingdom becomes a present reality to those who are the subjects of the king" (T.W. Manson, *The Teaching of Jesus* 135 f). According to Perrin, "the Kingdom is the sovereign power of God breaking into history and human experience" (p. 177). "In the apocalyptic literature, in the Qumran texts and in the teaching of Jesus, the Kingdom of God is his kingly activity, and the coming of the Kingdom is, in fact, the decisive eschatological intervention of God in the affairs of men whereby he exercises his royal power on behalf of his subjects" (p. 95).

The comprehensiveness of the notion of kingdom appears especially in its absolute use, without a determinative like "of God' or "of heavens." This absolute use proves, especially in Matthew, that the concept has become a central doctrine of Jesus' proclamation, object of faith and of teaching, principle and purpose of moral life, a compendious formula which epitomizes the whole new reality of salvation. In connection with Matthew again, it is worth noticing that in the first Beatitude the kingdom of God is promised to the poor in spirit, while in the third the meek are told that they will inherit the land. This suggests there is a continuity between the "land" and the "kingdom." Reviewing Brueggemann's book, Craghan writes that the "land embraces the whole history of both Old and New Testaments." It can be affirmed, I suppose, that the "land" conception once spiritualized or idealized has gradually been taken over by the concept of kingdom, which in turn went through different phases before reaching the more specific meaning which we have tried to determine.

Bibliography on Revelation

ALFARO, J. "Encarnación y Revelación," *Gregorianum* 49 (1968) 431-59.

ALONSO-SCHÖKEL, L. ed., *Concilio Vaticano II. Comentarios a la constitución Dei Verbum sobre la divina revelación,* BAC 284 (Madrid 1969); for details see NTA 14, p. 100.

BENOIT, P. "Révélation et inspiration: selon la Bible, chez Saint Thomas et dans les discussions modernes," *Revue Biblique* 70 (1963) 321-70, more briefly in *Concilium* (Engl.) 10 (Dec. 1965) 5-14.

DULLES, A. *Revelation Theology. A History* (New York 1969).

DUPUY, B.D. ed., *La Révélation Divine. Constitution Dogmatique "Dei Verbum,"* two vols., Unam Sanctam 70a and 70b (Paris 1968).

GRELOT, P. "La Tradition, source et milieu de l'Ecriture," *Concilium* 10 (1966) 13-29.

HENRY, C.F.H. ed., *Revelation and the Bible: Contemporary Evangelical Thought,* (London 1959) 387-401.

HILL, E. "Revelation and Gnosis," *Scripture* 17 (1965) 80-90.

HOLSTEIN, H. "Les 'Deux Sources' de la Révélation," RecSR 57 (1969) 375-434 (an historical study).

LATOURELLE, R. *Théologie de la Révélation* (Bruges 1963).

LENGSFELD, P. ed., *La révélation dans l'Ecriture et la tradition* (Paris 1969); see on this CBQ 1970, p. 613f.

LÉON-DUFOUR, X. ed., "Revelation," *Dictionary of Biblical Theology* (New York 1973) 499-505.

LIPINSKI, E. *Essais sur la révélation et la Bible,* Lectio Divina 60 (Paris 1970).

O'COLLINS, G.G. "Reality as Language: Ernst Fuch's Theology on Revelation," *Theological Studies* 28 (1967) 76-93.

OEPKE, A. *"Apokaluptô,"* TDNT 3 (1965) 563-92.

RAHNER, K. "Ecriture et tradition, à propos du schéma conciliaire sur la révélation divine," in *Ecrits théologiques* 7 (Bruges 1967) 77-93.

Idem., "The Death of Jesus and the Closing of Revelation," *Theology Digest* 23 (1975) 320-29.

SCHNACKENBURG, R. "Biblical Views of Revelation," *Theology Digest* 13 (1965) 129-34.

TRESMONTANT, C. *Le problème de la Révélation* (Paris 1969).

VOLTA, G. "La Rivelazione di Dio e la Sacra Tradizione secondo la Costituzione dogmática 'Dei Verbum' (I), (II), *Scuola Cattólica* 97 (1969) 30-52, 83-115.

WALGRAVE, J.H. *Unfolding Revelation: the Nature of Doctrinal Development* (Philadelphia 1972); on this *see* CBQ 1973, pp. 563f.

WIDMER, G.-P. "Quelques réflexions d'un point de vue réformé sur la Constitution conciliaire 'Dei Verbum'," *Irenikon* 42 (1969) 149-76.

Bibliography for Section A

ABEL, E.L. "The Nature of the Patriarchal God 'El Sădday'," *Numen* 20 (1973) 48-59.

BOOBYER, G.H. "Jesus as *'Theos'* in the New Testament," *Bull. J. Ryl. Libr.* 50 (1968) 247-61.

COPPENS, J. "La notion vétérotestamentaire de Dieu. Position du problème," dans J. Coppens, éd., *La Notion biblique de Dieu,* Bibl. ETL 41 (Gembloux 1976) 63-76.

DANTEN, J. "La révélation du Christ sur Dieu dans les paraboles," NRT 77 (1955) 450-77.

DENTAN, ROBERT C. *The Knowledge of God in Ancient Israel* (New York 1968).

DUESBERG, H. "Le Dieu de la Bible est notre Dieu," *Bible et Vie Chrétienne* 16 (1956) 33-43.

DUQUOC, CHR. "Jésus le Fils, visage humain de Dieu," dans *Jésus, homme libre. Esquisse d'une christologie* (Paris, 1974) 115-28.

EICHRODT, W. *Das Gottesbild des Alten Testaments* (Stuttgart 1956).

EISSFELDT, O. "Ist der Gott des Alten Testaments auch der des Neuen Testaments?" in *Geschichtliches und Uebergeschichtliches im Alten Testament* (Berlin 1947) 37-54.

GELIN, A. *The God of Israel, the God of Christians* (New York).

GIBLET, J. "La révélation de Dieu dans le Nouveau Testament," dans J. Coppens, éd., *La Notion* . . . 231-44.

IZCO ILUNDAIN, J.A. "El conocimiento de Dio entre los Gentiles según el Antiguo Testamento," *Eph. Th. Lov.* 49 (1973) 36-74.

JEREMIAS, J. "Die Bezeichnung Gottes als Vater Jesus," in *Abba* (Goettingen 1968) 33-67.

KLEINKNECHT, H. *et al., "Theos," TDNT* 3 (1966) 65-119.

KNIGHT, G.A.F. *A Biblical Approach to the Doctrine of the Trinity,* Scot. J. Th. Occ. Papers (Edinburgh 1950).

LABUSCHAGNE, C.J. *The Incomparability of Yahweh in the Old Testament,* Pretoria Oriental Series (Pretoria 1966).

LYONNET, S. "Dio nella Bibbia," *Civiltá Cattólica* 119/3 (1968) 371-80.

MAC KENZIE, R.A.F. "God: Power or Personality," in *Faith and History in the Old Testament* (Minneapolis 1963) 18-31.

MATHEW, K.V. "The Biblical Concept of God," *Indian Journal of Theology* 21 (1972) 38-51

MC KENZIE, J.L. "God and Nature in the Old Testament," in *Myths and Realities* (Milwaukee 1963) 85-132.

MICHAELI, FR. *Dieu a l'image de l'homme* (Neuchatel 1949).

OGIERMANN, S.J., H. " 'Existiert' Gott?" in K. Rahner-O. Semmelroth, *Theologische Akademie* 7 (Frankfurt a. Main 1970) 25-45.

PORSCH, F. *Pneuma und Wort. Ein exegetischer Beitrag zur Pneumatologie des Johannesevangelium* (Frankfurt a. Main 1974); cf. *Biblical Theology Bulletin* 6 (1976) 94f.

RAHNER, K. "Dieu dans le Nouveau Testament. La signification du mot 'Theos'," dans *Ecrits Théologiques,* vol. 1, (Bruges 1959) pp. 11-111.

RATZINGER, J. ed., *Die Frage nach Gott*, Qu. Disp. 56 (Herder 1973); cf. NTA 18, p. 119.

REHM, M. *Das Bild Gottes im Alten Testament* (Würzburg 1951).

ROBERTSON, JR., J.C. "Rahner and Ogden: Man's Knowledge of God," *Harv. Th. Rev.* 63 (1970) 377-407. (S.M. Ogden published *The Reality of God and Other Essays*, New York 1966).

SANDYS-WUNSCH, J. "The Old Testament 'Proofs' of God's Existence," ZAW 86 (1974) 211-16.

SCHILLEBEECKX, E. *God, the Future of Man* (New York 1968).

SCHMIDT, W.H. *Alttestamentlicher Glaube und seine Umwelt: zur Geschichte des alttestamentlichen Gottesverständnisses* (Neukirchen 1968).

SCHNACKENBURG, R. "Das Gottesbild des Neuen Testaments," in *Lebendiges Zeugnis* (Paderborn 1953) 17-32.

SCHWEIZER, E. "Was heisst 'Gott'?" *Evangelische Theologie* 25 (1965) 339-349.

SPARKS, H.F.D. "The Doctrine of the Divine Fatherhood in the Gospels," in *Studies in the Gospels. Essays in Memory of R.H. Lightfoot* (Oxford 1955) 241-62.

TANNER, R.G. "Jesus and the Fatherhood of God," *Colloquium* 3 (1969) 201-10.

VAN DER VEKEN, J. "Can the True God be the God of one Book? The Particularity of Religion and the Universality of Reason," in J. Coppens, Ed., *La Notion* 431-444.

VANHOYE, A. "Le Dieu de la nouvelle alliance dans l'épitre aux Hébreux," in J. Coppens, ed., *La Notion* . . . 315-30.

WINTER, H.J. "Der christologische Hoheitstitel 'Theos' im Neuen Testament," *Bibel und Liturgie* 42 (1969) 171-90.

Bibliography for Section B

BANKS, R. *Jesus and the Law in the Synoptic Tradition* (London 1975).

BEAUCHAMP, P. *L'un et l'autre Testament. Essai de lecture* (Paris 1976) 39-73.

BRING, R. "Das Gesetz und die Gerechtigkeit Gottes. Eine Studie zur Frage nach der Bedeutung des Ausdruckes *telos nomou* in Rm 10:4" *Studia Theologica* 20 (1966) 1-36; (*see* NTA 12, pp. 79f.).

Idem. Christus und das Gesetz. Die Bedeutung des Gesetzes des Alten Testaments nach Paulus und sein Glauben an Christus (Leiden 1969).

CAZELLES, H. "La Torah de Moise et le Christ Sauveur," *Concilium* 10 (déc. 1965) 51-67.

CHAMORRO, J.F. *La ley nueva y la ley antigua en Santo Tomás* (Avila 1967).

CORBIN, M. "Nature et signification de la Loi évangélique," RecSR 57 (1969) 5-48.

DAUBE, D. *Studies in Biblical Law* (Cambridge 1947).

DERRETT, D. *Law in the New Testament* (London 1970).

DODD, C.H. *Gospel and Law* (Cambridge 1951).

FEIL, E. "Erwägungen uber die Rede vom Gesetz. Zur Fragwürdigkeit juridischer Terminologie und Denkform als Verstehenshorizont in Glaube und Theologie," *Una Sancta* 22 (1967) 276-90.

FITZMYER, J.A. "Saint Paul and the Law," *The Jurist* 27 (1967) 18-36.

GRELOT, P. *La Bible, parole de Dieu* (Paris 1965) 259-65.

GUNTHOR, A. " 'Endziel des Gesetzes ist Christus' (Rm 10:4). Zur heutigen innerkirchlichen Gesertzeskrise," *Erbe und Auftrag* (1967) 192-205.

HAMEL, E. *Loi naturelle et loi du Christ* (Bruges-Paris 1964).

HOWARD, G.E. "Christ the End of the Law: the Meaning of Romans 10:4ff.," JBL 88 (1969) 331-37.

LARCHER, C. *L'actualité chrétienne de l'Ancien Testament d'après le Nouveau Testament*, Lectio Divina 34 (Paris 1962), 199-284.

LYONNET, S. "La loi de l'Esprit de la vie" in "Le Nouveau Testament à la lumière de l'Ancien. A propos de Rom 8,2-4," NRT 87 (1965) 565-71.

MC CONNELL, R.S. *Law and Prophecy in Matthew's Gospel . . .* (Basel 1969).

MC KENZIE, J.L. "Natural Law in the New Testament," *Biblical Research* 9 (1964) 3-13.

SABOURIN, L. "Matthieu 5,17-20 et le rôle prophétique de la loi (cf. Mt 11,13)," *Science et Esprit* 30 (1978) 303-311.

SAND, A. "Gesetz und Freiheit. Vom Sinn des Pauluswortes: Christus, des Gesetzes Ende," *Theologie und Glaube* 61 (1971) 1-14; cf. NTA 16, pp. 71f.

SCHNEIDER, E.E. "Finis legis Christus, Rom 10,4," *Theologische Zeitschrift* 20 (1964) 410-22.

STUHLMUELLER, C. "The Natural Law Question, the Bible never asked. A Bibliographical Study," *Cross Currents* 19 (1969) 55-67.

VAN DULMEN, A. *Die Theologie des Gesetzes bei Paulus.* Bibl. Monogr. 5 (Stuttgart 1968).

VERWEIJS, P.G. *Evangelium und neues Gesetz in der ältesten Christenheit bis auf Marcion* (Utrecht 1960).

In his doctoral dissertation on Freedom in Galatians, F. Pastor Ramos has exposed in great detail the Pauline conception of Freedom from the Law; *see* his *La libertad en la carta los Galatas* (Valencia 1977) 177-328, where he has also a chapter on Christ the Liberator. *See*, in addition, G. Bornkamn, *Das Ende des Gesetzes, Paulusstudien* (Munich 1952).

SANDERS, J.A., "Torah and Christ," *Interpretation* 29 (1975) 373-900; Sloyan, G.S., *Is Christ the End of the Law?* (Philadelphia 1978).

Bibliography for Section C

BRIGHT, J. *The Kingdom of God in Bible and Church* (London 1955).

DODD, C.H. *The Parables of the Kingdom* (London 1935).

FULLER, R.H. *The Mission and Achievement of Jesus* (London 1954).

GLASSON, T.F. "The Kingdom as Cosmic Catastrophe," in *Studia Evangelica* 3, TU 88 (Berlin 1964) 187-200.

JEREMIAS, J. *New Testament Theology*, vol. 1 (London 1971) 96-108.

KLEIN, G. " 'Reich Gottes' als biblischer Zentralbegriff," *Evangelische Theologie* 30 (1970) 642-70.

Idem, "The Biblical Understanding of 'The Kingdom of God'," *Interpretation* 26 (1972) 394-400.

KRETZER, A. *Die Herrschaft der Himmel und die Söhne des Reiches. Eine redaktionsgeschichtliche Untersuchung zum Basileiabegriff und Basileiaverständnis im Matthäusevangelium* (Würzburg 1971).

KUMMEL, W.G. *Promise and Fulfillment* (London 1957) 19-87.

LADD, G.E. *Jesus and the Kingdom* (London 1966).

LANGEVIN, P.E. "The Builders of the Kingdom. The Church in its Spiritual Dynamism," BibTB 4 (1974) 178-204.

LUNDSTROM, G. *The Kingdom of God in the Teaching of Jesus. A History of Interpretation from the last decades of the nineteenth century to the present day*, tr. by J. Bulman (Edinburgh 1963).

PERRIN, N. *The Kingdom of God in the Teaching of Jesus* (London 1963).

SABOURIN, L. *The Gospel According to St. Matthew* (Bombay 1980), ch. 5 of the Introduction and the commentary of Mt 13.

SCHMIDT, K.L. *"Basileia,"* TDNT (1964) 574-93.

SCHNACKENBURG, R. *God's Rule and Kingdom* (New York 1963).

THOMPSON, J.W. "Recent Studies on the *Basileia*," *Restoration Quarterly* 10 (1967) 211-16.

WALKER, JR., W.O. "The Kingdom of the Son of Man and the Kingdom of the Father in Matthew. An Exercise in *Redaktionsgeschichte*," CBQ 30 (1968) 573-579.

WEISS, J. *Jesus' Proclamation of the Kingdom of God* (Philadelphia 1971, Engl. tr. of a work first published in German in 1892).

WENZ, H. *Theologie des Reiches Gottes* (Hamburg 1975).

CHAPTER TWO

THE COVENANTS AND THE PROMISE

Examining the role of the law in the Christian economy of salvation, Paul explains that it came centuries later than the promise (*epaggelia*) to Abraham, but it did not annul a covenant (*diathēkē*) previously ratified by God, so as to make the promise void (Gal 3:17). Abraham had received great promises: he would have a land, he would become a great nation, and he would be for other peoples a mediator of blessings (Gn 12:1-3). Abraham's faith was put to the test, as the fulfillment of the promises was delayed, but they were later renewed and even sealed by a covenant (Gn 15). We have here the ratification of a promise by a covenant, through which God, as it were, obliges himself, if need be, to fulfill the promise. A promise contains the assurance that something will be done, while "covenant" is the biblical term designating an agreement or compact between various parties. The promise is a unilateral, gratuitous gesture, a covenant is usually bilateral, involving obligations.

a) The Old Covenants and the New Covenant

The covenant with Noah is the first to be mentioned in the Bible. It is unilateral on God's part and it involves the whole creation, under the sign of the rainbow (Gn 8:20-22). The covenant with Abraham embraces his descendants only and it has a sign in the flesh, circumcision (Gn 17). The Mosaic covenant of Mount Sinai is confined to Israel and carries an obligation, obedience to the law (Ex 19 and 24), with a special reference to Sabbath (Ex 31:16f). Recent scholars like to distinguish two main types of covenants. In the first, which they call "Covenants of divine commitment," God commits himself forever to a person and his descendants, out of pure choice or to reward meritorious behavior. To this type belong the covenants with Abraham and David. Since they were unconditional, Israel placed in them great hope and confidence. The other type has been called "Covenants of human obligation." It is represented in the Bible by the Mosaic covenant of Sinai. Israel accepted this covenant, with the obligation of doing what it prescribed (Ex 24:3). It gave Israel a conscience, in the sense that the people knew what was God's will. It lacked, however, the interiority that would have made it truly a principle of life in God.

Several scholars, mainly G. Mendenhall, K. Baltzer, and D.J. McCarthy, have recently developed or discussed the thesis that Israel has used an ancient non-biblical treaty structure to formulate its covenant with Yahweh. Salient features of such ancient treaties can be compared with OT texts, mainly from Deuteronomy: Introduction of the speaker (4:35), historical prologue (4:45-47), stipulation (6:5), document (27:8), curse and blessing (28:1, 2, 15). It is noted that *El-berit*, the "Covenant-God," was worshipped at Schechem long before that locality became an Israelite city. McCarthy has argued that in 1 S 12 is found the oldest evidence for the covenant formulary. There, as also in 2 S 23:5 and in 2 K 11 and 23, King and covenant are combined. Ex 19:3b-8 represents a step further, toward seeing the Mosaic covenant in terms of the covenantal formulation, the treaty genre (pp. 284-86). Whatever the origin of its formulation the covenant is a basic and recurring motif in the Old Testament. It urged the Israelites to observe the law (Dt 4:23); it threatened them with punishment if they didn't (Lv 26:15); it could be appealed to for obtaining assistance from God (Dt 7:9), reminding him to be merciful and forgiving (Dt 4:31).

Covenant and Testament

The word "covenant" translates the Hebrew *berit*, which was rendered in Greek by *diathēkē*. *Foedus* is a good Latin translation, but *testamentum* was also used, and because of this the two main bodies of Scripture are called by the Christians the Old Testament and the New Testament. "Testament" can, of course, mean also the (last) will ("testament" in French) left by the deceased, in which it is stated how their property is to be disposed of. According to *Traduction Oecuménique de la Bible*, the verb *diatithemai* in Lk 22:29 can signify both the concluding of a *covenant* and the formulation of a *testament*. For J. Behm, however, no testamentary disposition can be read in this verse, since the *diatithesthai* of Jesus corresponds to that of the Father, who is certainly not making his will (*TDNT* 2, p. 105). But Behm seems to exaggerate where he claims (p. 131) that even in Heb 9:15 *diathēkē* does not mean "testament," for the author of Hebrews does argue there from the double meaning of the Greek term, that of "covenant," as in the Septuagint, and that of "testament," as in ordinary language. So he writes: "Therefore he is the mediator of a new covenant, of a new Testament . . . For where a will is involved, the death of the one who made it must be established" (Heb 9:15f). Here, as in TOB, the single term *diathēkē* has been rendered by two words.

This seems to be the proper place to take a second look at the word "Testaments" used to denote the two great parts of Scripture. With the "Israelites" in view, Paul wrote to the Corinthians: "But their minds were hardened; for to this day, when they read the old testament, that same veil remains unlifted, because only through Christ is it taken away" (2 Cor 3:14). According to Behm, the *palaia diathēkē*, "old covenant," mentioned by Paul, is "the Mosaic Law as the epitome and basis (so here for the first time) of the old religion. In spite of the sharp dismissal of the old *diathēkē* in the whole passage (2 Cor 3:4-18), which reflects Paul's own experience, he still recognizes that it is God's *diathēkē*, that it has its own *doxa* ("glory") and that it is a historical declaration of the same God as the God of the new" (p. 130). For Carmignac, however, *palaia diathēkē* should be translated "old testament" and referred to Scripture, not to "covenant," because of the *reading* mentioned. In his authoritative *Novi Testamenti Lexicon Graecum* (Parisiis 1911), Fr. Zorrell expresses a similar opinion: "Per metonymiam 2 C. 3,14 *hē palaia diathēkē* vocantur libri Veteris Testamenti" (p. 126). A non-Christian Jew would never have thought of the Scripture as the Old Testament. What prompted Paul to use *palaia diathēkē* in this sense must have been his previous mention of *kainē diathēkē* in 2 Cor 3:6 which perhaps can be read as follows: "who has qualified us to be ministers of a *new testament*, which is not (only) a writing, but a spirit." This New Testament could have included some previous epistles of Paul and possibly the gospels of Mark and Matthew (Carmignac), if not other epistles, since early datings of James and Hebrews cannot be excluded. It is admitted that the Pauline epistles are called *graphē*, "Scripture," in 2 P 3:16 (*TDNT* 1, p. 757).

The New Covenant

In his words over the cup at the last Supper Jesus said, according to Luke: "This cup which is poured out for you is the new covenant of my blood" (Lk 22:20). Paul's formulation is very similar: "This cup is the new covenant in my blood" (1 Cor 11:24). This sacrificial significance of the eucharist is expressed probably in relation to the Sinai rite, where Moses used similar words: "Behold the blood of the covenant . . ." (Ex 24:8). The redemptive character of the Eucharist is explicit in the words according to Matthew: "For this is my blood of the covenant, which is poured out for many for the forgiveness of sins" (Mt 26:28). This can be related to the development found in the Onkelos Targum of Ex 24:8: "Moses took the blood and sprinkled (it) upon the altar to make atonement (*lkpr*) for the people."

Also in Heb 9:18-22 is the expiatory character of the Sinai rite underlined (cf. BibTB 1974, p. 252). The Luke-Paul formula quite certainly refers, besides, to the only OT *locus* where the expression *kainē diathēkē* is found, namely in Jr 31:31. The "words of the (old) covenant" (Ex 34:28) were engraved on tables of stone, on "the tables of the covenant" (Dt 9:9-11), but the new law, God told the prophet, I will put it within them, "I will write it upon their hearts" (31:33). This is echoed in Paul, where he writes that the Corinthians are "a letter from Christ . . . written not with ink but with the Spirit of the living God, not on tablets of stone but on tablets of human hearts" (2 Cor 3:3). Ezekiel will later develop Jeremiah's oracle by attributing to the Spirit of God this transformation of the human heart (Ezk 36:26f). Being a priest, concerned with ritual purity, he does not fail to add that purification will be an outstanding fruit of the Messianic grace. As for Jeremiah, he stressed that in the economy of the new covenant everyone will be instructed directly by God, and will know him. Jesus must have thought of this when he quoted Is 54:13 to explain that henceforth "they shall all be taught by God" (Jn 6:45).

Also Jesus' words at the Last Supper, "a new commandment I give to you" (Jn 13:34), can be referred to the theme of the new covenant. For Paul, as we have seen, the disciples of Christ are the letter of the new covenant (2 Cor 3:33). The mysterious *presence of Christ with the disciples* is particularly underlined in the Johannine discourse of the Last Supper. One spirit animates this presence: it is the spirit of love, which is "the new commandment" or a *new law*, since it is an interior principle, moving hearts from within. The epithet "new" is part of the distinctive vocabulary of NT eschatology, and it characterizes the condition of the last times in a multitude of expressions: new teaching (Mk 1:27), new wine (Mk 2:22), new garment (Lk 5:36), new covenant (2 Cor 3:6), new commandment (Jn 13:34), new dough (1 Cor 5:7), newness of life (Rm 6:4), newness of spirit (Rm 7:6). Paul says it explicitly: "Therefore, if any one is in Christ, he is a new creation, the old has passed away, behold, the new has come" (2 Cor 5:17). Having quoted Jr 31:31-34, the author of Hebrews concludes: "In speaking of a new covenant he treats the first as obsolete. And what is becoming obsolete and growing old is ready to vanish away" (Heb 8:13). The prophecy of Jeremiah had prepared the transition from the old covenant to the new. Interiority and personal relation would mark the passage from one to the other. This became possible through

Christ, who carried in his own person and in his work the whole source of all the newness which characterized the center of salvation history and its last phase.

The Essenes of Qumran believed themselves to be "the people of the New Covenant." They celebrated annually the renewing of this New or "Eternal" Covenant, no doubt recalling Jeremiah's prediction of a new covenant. They understood, writes Fr. M. Cross, this New Covenant "to be at once the 'renewed (old) covenant' and the 'eternal covenant' to be established at the end of days, i.e. precisely in the New Testament sense" (*The Ancient Library of Qumran* 219). Generally speaking, however, their "new" covenant was not radically new, since it was based essentially on the observance, within the community, of the Mosaic Law correctly interpreted by the Righteous Teacher. Jeremiah (31:31-34) proposes, on the other hand, a new model of covenant, which will rest on God's initiative in changing the hearts of men. In addition, the author of Hebrews stressed that this new covenant has a new liturgy, "the greater and more perfect tent," centered on the sacrifice of Jesus the High Priest, offered once for all, through which he entered the sanctuary (Heb 9:11f). The new covenant has its own mediator, the new high priest, who redeems from the transgressions that occurred "under the first covenant" (Heb 9:15), and leads the pilgrim people to its place of rest (Heb 4:11, 6:20).

In spite of the absolute newness of the Christian economy, a *continuum* exists from the old to the new covenants, since in God's own plan the first dispensation was meant to be temporary. Heb 8:5 underscores the imperfection and ungenuiness of the Mosaic institution. It rose as an *hypodeigma*, a "model," an imperfect figure, a defective indication of what was forthcoming; it was only a *skia* "shadow," a "draft" of the definitive reality expected, which Moses saw in advance as *typos* (Heb 8:5), a God-made "pattern" of the future heavenly things connected with the liturgy of Christ the High Priest. While this *typos* was perfect, its earthly expression, worked out by Moses, could only be imperfect and inadequate. Thus we are introduced to the proposition that the old cultus was earthly and figurative and was bound to be replaced, for models and drafts lose their *raison d'être* when the reality they announce is an accomplished fact: "He removes the first to establish the second" (Heb 10:9). A *continuum* can be found from another viewpoint as well. In B.W. Anderson's words, we find in Jeremiah's oracle "that the relation between the old and new covenants is characterized by both discontinuity and continuity . . . The new covenant will not be a reactualization of the Mosaic past. Its newness will mark a deep discontinuity with Israel's history of the broken covenant. At the same time, however, Jeremiah indicates ways in which the new covenant will be 'like' the Mosaic covenant, for it will fulfill God's purpose intended in the original covenant" (pp. 238f).

b) Promise and Fulfillment

It is probably true that promise/fulfillment constitutes the most relevant category in which the unity of the two testaments can be defended (cf. Murphy 356). It includes other categories, like prophecy/fulfillment, preferred by some (Bultmann, Childs). In the words of W. Zimmerli, "when we survey the entire Old Testament, we find ourselves involved in a great history of movement from promise toward fulfillment" (pp. 111f). We have already noted how the themes of promise and covenant are interrelated. It has been observed, for example, that in Gn 17:6-8 (Priestly Document) the covenant overshadows the description of the renewal of the promise to Abraham (R. Murphy 350). Significantly, F.C. Fensham can write: "The important question now is whether we can trace this influence of covenant-promise and hope through to the New Testament, or not" (p. 90). In C. Westermann's view, the real significance of Jr 31:31-34 lies in the fact that here the (new) covenant is included in the promise: "According to its original meaning a covenant can only be concluded, it cannot be promised. With the inclusion of the covenant in the promise the nature of the covenant was radically changed: it now means the end of the previous history of God with his people" (p. 219).

God's Dynamic Presence in the History of Israel

It is God's presence in both Testaments which assures from above their unity. This presence is both dynamic and dialectical through the category promise/fulfillment. The promise which moves history futurewards is too vast to be realized fully in the limited space of human contingencies. Falling short of its aim it has to be continually relaunched towards a new horizon. For Proulx it is possible to analyze all biblical history in terms of dialectic relation and dynamic tension between promise and fulfillment (p. 202). Thus were the contents of the Israelite hope and the narratives related to it continually amplified to incorporate the patriarchal experience, the liberation from Egypt, the sojourn in the desert, the gift of the land, the story of David, the building of the temple, the creation of the world, the constitution of a cultic community around the *Torah*, the expectation of a new world, and finally of the Kingdom of Heaven.

In contrast with what took place outside the biblical world, past events in the life of Israel had an epiphanic dimension, since they revealed the dynamic of God's intervention and the pattern of the new world lying in the future. Thus Israel's past was never a burden weighing down the present, but it nourished its aspirations and hopes for a better, even grandiose future. The expectations were kept alive and enhanced by the recorded realization that divine intervention could alter the course of events and render unpredictable the trajectory of Israel's future.

Israel's temptation has always been to try and contain the promise in human institutions, to reduce it to a temporal dimension, geographic (the land), political (monarchy), religious (the temple-cult), or to confine it to a language, to formulations, sometimes borrowed from other cultures. The prophets reacted to this temptation, and represented God as not bound, as promising a future that would not be contained in any concrete realization of this world. It is distinctive of the promise to have unlimited horizons. The Babylonian exile spelled for Israel the loss of the three realities in which it tried to incorporate the effects of the promise: land, king, and temple. Liberated from all these limiting impediments, reduced to the nothing of its origins, Israel could through its prophets look again at the promise with a pure eye. Second-Isaiah saw that the promise meant nothing less than a new creation, as if nothing had happened before (Is 43:18f). Not surprisingly Second-Isaiah has been called "the chief witness about creation" (G. von Rad, *Old Testament Theology*, vol. 1, p. 137). However, creation, for him, is a saving event, for Jahweh created also Israel: he is both creator and redeemer (Is 44:24). The Priestly Document, which describes creation out of chaos (Gn 1:1-2:4a), is also a writing elaborated out of the experience of the exile. The same could be said of Ps 74:12-17. The pushing back to creation itself of saving history was only possible because creation was regarded as a saving work of Jahweh. Besides, by setting creation in a sequence of time the biblical writers removed it from the realm of myth, this "timeless revelation taking place in the natural cycle" (G. von Rad 139).

Promise/Fulfillment and History

According to Pannenberg, the tension between promise and fulfillment makes history. History is "event so suspended in tension between promise and fulfillment that through the promise it is irreversibly pointed toward the goal of future fulfillment" (p. 317). Like Proulx, Pannenberg observes that the horizon of the historical consciousness of the Old Testament writers becomes ever wider, the length of time spanned by promise and fulfillment becomes ever more extensive. In the Jahwistic presentation, after the introductory statement of the pre-history, Genesis 12 opens with the promise to Abraham. The J document ends in the book of Joshua with the fulfillment of the promise through Israel's reclaiming the land. Deuteronomy attaches a qualification to the promise, the fulfillment of the law. Along with the promise, the law comes to be the power which determines the course of history. Because of the ever-growing guilt of the people, history has worked negatively for Israel: it lost the monarchy and the land which God had promised and given. Noting that the deuteronomist wrote when the land was already Israelite possession, Beauchamp observes that for Deuteronomy, God's promise was not that the people be nourished, but that he nourish himself (Dt 26:1f) as regards the earthly goods, and that he learn to *formulate* the word of truth: "the promise, finally, it is the presence of man to the gift and to the word, the exit from the state of childhood" (p. 61).

Jewish apocalypticism completed the extension of history so that it covered the whole course of the world from creation to the end. For the writers of this later trend it is an eternal law which is the unchangeable ground of all world history. In other words, an eternal election precedes the course of history (Pannenberg 320). For the author of the Book of Daniel God is the revealer of mysteries, and he has made known what will be in the latter days (2:28). Jesus upheld the apocalyptic interpretation of history, but related it to his own person. He is the anticipated end, and not the middle of history.

Promise/Fulfillment and the New Testament

The verb *epaggellesthai* and the corresponding noun have become in the Greek Bible specific terms designating divine revelation in connection with salvation history. The word *epaggelia* expresses not merely the promise but also the fulfillment of what is promised. One of the meanings of *epaggellesthai* in classical Greek literature is "to offer to do something, to promise, to vow." It is sometimes said that he who has been given a promise would like to see it fulfilled. "The surprising thing is that throughout the Hellenistic East the word does not merely signify a promise to pay money but is also used as a technical term for a voluntary payment or donation or subscription" (J. Schniewind 578). *Epaggeliai*, "promised gifts," were frequently offered to temples—often to obtain an office—a practice which gradually lifted the term out of the sphere of the secular and gave it a sacral significance. We find in the pagan world several examples of man's promise to a god, but the expression *epaggeliai Theou*, "promises of God," is conspicuously absent. However, in the *Delic Sarapis Aretalogy* it is written that "the god promised me in a dream that we would win."

Paul tended to consider the Old Testament from the standpoint of *epaggelia*, but the term hardly occurs with this meaning in the

Septuagint. But even before Paul "Abraham, promise and law" were interrelated in some Jewish writings, as in the (Syrian) Apocalypse of Baruch (Ba 57:2; 59:2). There, however, the attainment of the promises is made dependent on the keeping of the law (cf. Ba 46:6). Usually in later Judaism the object of the promise is the future world. Luke has given some prominence to the promise in his writings. The infancy narratives of Luke reflect the memory of the promises to the patriarchs, especially in Zechariah's canticle (Lk 1:68-74). According to Acts, the Exodus took place when "the time of the promise drew near, which God had granted to Abraham" (Ac 7:17). Paul himself says in Acts that he stands on trial "for hope in the promise made by God to our fathers" (Ac 26:6). Elsewhere he states: "We bring you the good news that what God promised to the fathers, this he has fulfilled to us their children by raising Jesus" (Ac 13:32f). Christians live in the time of fulfillment. The promise has become a reality in the remission of sins and the gift of the Holy Spirit: "For the promise is to you and to your children and to all that are far off," therefore also to pagans (Ac 2:39).

Paul has particularly developed the relation of the law to the promise. Like the Rabbis he is sure that God does what he has promised (Rm 4:17-21). The promise is a gracious gift; it cannot be made dependent on human action. "The promise to Abraham and his descendants . . . did not come through the law but through the righteousness of faith" (Rm 4:13). Even more sharply he writes elsewhere: "The law, which came four hundred and thirty years afterward, does not annul a *diathēkē*, "covenant/testament," previously ratified by God, so as to make the *epaggelia*, "promise," void (Gal 3:17). It is explained that God would have contradicted himself had he replaced a scheme of salvation based on a spontaneous promise (compared to a will in v. 15) with one based on a bilateral contract (v. 20). He could not have made the fulfillment of the promise depend on the observance of a law, as this would have annulled the promise as a free gift (*see Jerusalem Bible, in locum*). The purpose of the law is clarified in Gal 3:19, 24. The true inheritors of the promise are the spiritual descendants of Abraham, those who believe in Christ (Gal 3:16, 22). In this way are the Gentiles "fellow heirs . . . and partakers of the promise in Christ

Jesus through the gospel" (Ep 3:6).

We have already indicated the importance of the theme "promise" in the Epistle to the Hebrews, where it occurs side by side with covenant (Heb 8:6-7). The promises were received by the patriarchs, by Sarah (11:11), the judges, David, the prophets (11:32f), and the Jewish people (4:1). "All the promises of God converge on the great Messianic salvation whose final consummation is still to come. Abraham dwelt in the land promised to him. But he knew the incompleteness of the fulfillment. Thus he did not settle down there permanently. He lived as a stranger on earth. He awaited the final fulfillment of the city of God which he saw contained in the promise given to him, Heb 11:7f." (Schniewind 584). Only from afar did the fathers of faith see the fulfillment of the promise and as pilgrims they hail their home city (Heb 11:13). God's will to accomplish his promises is unalterable, since it has been sanctioned by an oath (Heb 6:13-18). The true believers run no risk of being disappointed, but unbelief can shut them off from being heirs to the promise, as the example of Israel shows (Heb 4:1-2).

The Fulfillment of Hope

A theology of hope has developed in recent years from the fundamental need to produce an interpretation of Christianity in harmony with the general trend towards optimism reflected in the secular world. The theologians of hope have been especially influenced by the philosophy of Ernst Bloch, an East German Marxist, author of a monumental work, *Das Princip Hoffnung*, in which, from "the principle of hope," he develops a general view of man and the world. For him, religions and hope are strictly bound together: "Where there is religion, there is hope." In his well known work, *The Theology of Hope*, J. Moltmann examines carefully the complex relationship between faith and hope, and explains it as follows: "Faith binds man to Christ. Hope sets this faith open to the comprehensive future of Christ . . . Thus in the Christian life faith has the priority, but hope the primacy. Without faith's knowledge of Christ, hope becomes a Utopia and remains hanging in the air. But

without hope, faith falls to pieces, becomes fainthearted and ultimately a dead faith. It is through faith that man finds the path of true
life, but it is only hope that keeps him on that path. Thus it is that
faith in Christ gives hope its assurance. Thus it is that hope gives
faith in Christ its breadth and leads it into life" (p. 20).

In *The Experiment Hope*, Moltmann has proposed reflections
that are even closer to our subject; he takes a departure from Ex
3:14, where he reads that God told Moses: "I will be who I will be."
He goes on to write (p. 48): "Ernst Bloch is right, therefore, when he
speaks of a 'God who has the future as the mode of his being' (*Das
Princip Hoffnung* II, p. 1458)." And Moltmann makes his own
application: "Whoever follows his promise and mission will experience God's nearness and faithfulness as one who travels with him
going ahead of him. Israel thus left Egypt trusting in the one 'who
will be there,' wherever they went. With this expectation they experienced the miracle of the Sea of Reeds as a demonstration of his
faithfulness to his promise. He who had promised that he would 'be
there' was there, and thereafter in Israel whoever was supposed to
tell his children who was the God of the fathers and the God of the
Exodus had to tell his story of promise, faithfulness, and fulfillment.
In Israel there were no images and no abstract concepts of God.
Here God was understood through remembered history and remembered history led to hope for the coming history" (p. 48).

Also Moltmann insists on the partial fulfillment as an earnest of
even greater hopes, and the pledge of an even greater future: the
promise keeps an open end, looking to the future. "What is the
source of placing this *surplus value of hope* above all historical
experiences, even above the experience of historical fulfillment? It
appears to me that in all the individual hopes there was an anticipation, not just of the land, of security, and of an inheritance, but of
God's future itself. Therefore, the finite promises point beyond
themselves to the eschatological final arrival of *God himself*. For
ultimately, the *author* and the *content* of the promise are one, and
the different fulfillments in history which attest to the promises are
all manifested forms of this one final future in which God himself
dwells with all people" (*Experiment* 50).

Conclusion

In Pannenberg's view, "the connection between the Old and New Testaments is made understandable only by the consciousness of the one history which binds together the eschatological community of Jesus Christ and ancient Israel by means of the bracket of promise and fulfillment. Jesus is the revelation of God only in light of the Old Testament promises" (p. 323). He then quotes approvingly these words of A.A. Van Ruler: "Speaking from a Christian point of view, everything stands and falls with the Messiahship of Jesus. And one can decide about this Messiahship only when the question is raised and answered whether Jesus really does the works of God. But one can know what the works of God are only on the basis of the Old Testament" (*Die christliche Kirche und das Alte Testament*, Munich 1955, p. 70). Van Ruler has correctly stated that the Old Testament must not be simply interpreted in terms of the Gospel of Jesus Christ, but in its own terms. He exaggerates, however, where he states that the Old Testament is the original, essential and canonical Word of God, the New Testament being only its interpretative glossary. For Baker, Jesus Christ is the final act from the OT point of view, but from the point of view of the New Testament he has become the center of history (p. 135). The last words obviously refer to O. Cullmann's well known position, also expressed in his later writings, like *Salvation in History* (London 1967). Christ, we can suppose, is the center of history without having to be the middle of history, since in the apocalyptic view, endorsed by Jesus, the essential eschatological event takes place at the end.

c) The People of God

It is not difficult to justify the inclusion in this chapter of a section on the "people of God." The people of God was the beneficiary of the promise and the other partner of the covenant: "And I will walk among you, and will be your God, and you shall be my people" (Lv 26:12). Furthermore, as Gelin has remarked (p. 131), the Old

Testament is less a text than a people on the march and a developing tradition, until the day when the Jews, reading the old book, realize with God's light that Christ is its total explanation (cf. 2 Cor 3:14-17). Van Iersel expresses the same opinion when he writes that it is not possible to understand Scripture except by starting with the reality of the people of God, that is, with the ecclesial traditions which have assured the growth of the Canon. The Bible, he adds, cannot fully accomplish its task unless the people of God is today conscious in faith of being in continuity with the people of the Old Testament and of the primitive Church (pp. 35-37).

The "Laos" of God in the Old Testament

The term *laos*, "people," occurs over 2000 times in the Greek Old Testament, and its specific sense became normative in the usage of the early Church. The word *laos*, which is difficult to explain etymologically, could be of Aegean origin, borrowed, that is, by the Indo-Germanic Greeks from a non Indo-Germanic language spoken by the earlier inhabitants of Greece. It is characteristic of the Septuagint usage that there *laos* becomes a specific term for a specific people, namely Israel, and it serves to emphasize the special and privileged religious position of this people as the people of God (see *TDNT* 4, pp. 30 and 32). Apart from about forty instances, the Hebrew equivalent of *laos* is always *'am*. There is a tendency in the Septuagint to use *ethnos* when *'am* does not refer to Israel. *Laos* means a united people, as Gn 34:22 shows: "Only on this condition will the men agree to dwell with us, to become one people." Every city has one *laos*, for *laos* is the union of the people. But what counts is less the word *laos* as such, than the continual recurrences of the phrase *laos Theou*, "people of God." "The selection of an archaically poetical and solemn word like *laos* thus expresses a sense of distinction from all other peoples on the basis of religion, an awareness that Israel stands in a special relation to Yahweh, who is incomparably superior to all the gods of the nations" (*TDNT* 4, p. 35).

Because Yahweh has *separated* Israel to himself from among

the nations, the Israelites are a holy people by divine distinction (Ex 19:5f; Dt 7:6). God chose Israel as his people not because of any merit on their part, but only because of his sovereign will and free love, particularly for the Fathers (Dt 4:37), and also because of his fidelity to the promise (7:8). Because Israel's conduct did not respond to her call and obligations, the people will be dispersed and threatened with extinction (4:27). But Yahweh will not totally reject his people, a *Remnant* will survive, a theme well represented throughout the Old Testament, especially in the books prophetically inspired (For ex. Am 3:12; Is 4:3; Ezk 6:8; Ezr 1:4; Neh 1:2). See Jr 24:4-7, where God says he will bring back the exiles, and change their heart: "I will give them a heart to know that I am the Lord; and they shall be my people and I will be their God, for they shall return to me with their whole heart." The notion of the "Remnant," in the words of Pidoux, answered a theological necessity that aimed at assuring the transition between the inevitable misfortune and the final reestablishment (*Le Dieu qui vient* 41).

Even before the exile, voices had been heard that transcended the horizon of nationalistic expectation. The expression of the eschatological prophetic universalism reached a climax, however, after the fall of the monarchy. As may be seen in the following passage: "Sing and rejoice, O daughter of Zion; for lo, I come, and I will dwell in the midst of you, says the Lord. And many nations (*ethnē*) shall join themselves to the Lord in that day, and shall become my people (*laos*); and they will dwell in your midst" (Zc 2:10f., Greek). We shall mention again in connection with the New Testament the particular type of universalism found in early prophecies: Israel does not go to the nations, but the nations are expected to come to Jerusalem (Is 2:2f; Mi 4:1-4).

The new extension given to the term *laos* shows that what it represented had ceased to be a present possession granted by the freely electing love of God, and had passed to the sphere of faith in God's fidelity to his promise. As compared with the prophetic attitude, the tendency of later writings to speak self-evidently of Israel as the *hagioi*, "the saints" (Ezr 8:28), as "holy people and blameless race" (Ws 10:15), or the saints of the Most High (Dn 7:27) "represents a certain regression which forms a transition to Pharisaic Judaism with its stubborn insistence on a position of privilege granted once and for all to the people. This is a transition to the spiritual outlook and conduct against which the protest of John the Baptist was directed" (*TDNT* 4, p. 37). The words of John can be recalled here: "Do not presume to say to yourselves, 'We have Abraham as our father;' for I tell you, God is able from these stones to raise up children to Abraham" (Mt 3:9). There is probably a word-play here on the similarity of the Aramaic terms, presumably used by the Baptist: *banayya*, "children," and *'abnayya*, "stones." But a reference to Is 51:1f is also possible. Paul will say explicitly that men can be children of Abraham spiritually only through Christ (Gal 3:16, 29).

We cannot examine here in detail what Rabbinic literature has to say about "people and peoples" (*see* Meyer 39-50), but we will note that in Palestine in the days of Jesus a universalistic stream ran side by side with the particularistic. It is against this background that Jesus' remark about the proselytizing of the scribes and Pharisees (Mt 23:15) has to be collocated. Only later (66-135 A.D.) did the utterly nationalistic particularism flourish when again Israel was regarded as the privileged nation awaiting a judgment of God to become the dominant world power of the days of the Messiah.

The People of God in the New Testament

More than half of the occurrences (140) of the word *laos* in the New Testament are found in Luke/Acts. In the gospel, it appears in the special Lukan material (Lk 1:10, 21; 7:1, 29), while elsewhere it is usually introduced into passages otherwise borrowed from Mark or other sources. (*See*, for example, Lk 6:17; 8:47; 9:13; 18:43; 19:47; 20:9; 19:26; 21:38; 23:35.) This shows that *laos* is a favorite word of Luke's. Kodell has demonstrated that in describing scenes of division between the hostile leaders and the friendly people at large, Luke consistently employs the term *laos*. "By this technique, Luke preserves the concept of a people guilty, yes, but ignorant and almost unwilling to share in their leaders' crime. *Laos*, both as the Jewish people and as a traditional biblical term, thus emerges untarnished from the Passion. Luke will have further need of *laos* in the sequel to his Gospel. The word is preserved for positive use as a respectable theological concept to designate the New Testament People of God in Acts, composed of both Jew and Gentile" (p. 340). In five incidents of division between people and leaders over the new religion (Ac 4:1-4; 17:21; 5:13-17, 26) the term *laos* is always used to denote the "people." The Jews who continue to respond to the call of God (now the messianic message of Christ) will still be his *laos*. But in Christ God has also called a group of Gentiles to share Israel's status as People of God. *Laos* can now be used for both Jew and Gentile; it figures among the terms which express the historical continuity between Israel and the Church.

In contrast with Luke, Matthew has called *laos* the people as a whole, who demanded Jesus' death (27:25), with the apparent intent of underlining the collective responsibility of the Jewish nation as such. "The failure of the Jews to recognize and accept Christ costs them their special privilege as the Chosen People. They have lost their birthright and even their name, so significant in Hebrew thought, for Matthew will not call them *ho laos Theou* any longer, but *Ioudaioi* (28:15), one race among the others" (Kodell, p. 335). Introducing his theme "the Church of the nations," Trilling notes that the guilt of Israel, for which she forfeited her standing as the chosen people, is the main problem which Matthew has to face, since he does not distinguish "Israel according to the flesh" and "Israel according to the Spirit." Following her refusal of Jesus, Israel no longer exists as the people of the promise. Not Jews-become-Christians nor ex-Gentiles compose the Church, but "all the nations" (Mt 28:19). The judgment of Israel had been anticipated by Jesus in the following words, introduced by Matthew in the conclusion of the parable of the wicked tenants: "Therefore I tell you, the kingdom of God will be taken away from you and given to a nation producing the fruits of it" (Mt 21:43). The term *ethnos*, which Matthew uses in the singular only here and in 24:7 (Mk 13:8), does not mean "the pagans" (the plural would be used) or a specific nation, but another people of God (cf. 1 P 2:9), a religious congregation in whom, in the place of Israel, the reign of God establishes itself. *Ethnos* then has a religious significance and is to be referred to the new messianic community, that is, to the Church. Also in Dillon's view the *ethnos* to which the vine will now be entrusted is the *ethnos hagion* of 1 P 2:9, and not the Gentiles in contrast with the Jews.

The technical use of *laos* for Israel as God's chosen people finds expression in Zechariah's *Benedictus* (Lk 1:68, 77), in other places in Luke (2:32; 7:16), as also in Paul (Rm 11:1f), and elsewhere in the New Testament, usually in quotations from the Old Testament, for example, in Mt 2:6, Ac 7:34, and Heb 10:3. In the figurative sense *laos* is used by the New Testament writers to designate the Christian community. The main references are perhaps Ac 15:14, Rm 8:25f., Tt 2:14, 1 P 2:9f., Heb 4:9; 13:12, and Rv 18:4, 21:3. Strathmann believes that the "figurative use is not found at all in the Gospels" (*see* Meyer, 54). However, in Mt 1:21 *ho laos autou* seems to refer to the people of Jesus, as also perhaps the same expression in Lk 1:17. In Lk 1:77 the reference is quite certainly to the *new* people of God. This is clearly the case in Ac 18:10, where in a vision the Lord speaks of the Christian community in Corinth as "my people." In the same sense the Epistle to Titus says of Christ that he cleansed for himself "a people of his own" (Tt 2:14). Another important text is Ac 15:14 which recalls what Peter had said, "how God first concerned himself with taking from among the Gentiles a people to bear his name." The people of God now includes both the circumcized and the uncircumcized (Ep 2:14). To the latter Peter wrote: "Once you were no people (*laos*), but now you are God's people" (1 P 2:10).

It is probably permissible to read Heb 13:12, as Ehrhardt does (p. 133): "For this reason has Jesus, so that he should sanctify by his own blood *his* people (in Greek only *laos*), suffered outside the gate." Nor does the author of Hebrews believe that "the transfer of the title of Israel to the Christian community needs vindication any more than does the referring of suitable Old Testament quotations to Christ and his work or to the Christian community. These are the concealed and true theme of the Old Testament. Hence, when there is reference to the *laos*, Israel may be meant in the first instance, but the ultimate application is to the Christian community" (*TDNT* 4, p. 55) (*See* Heb 4:9; 8:10; 10:30; 13:12). The unity of the new people of God rests on faith in the one Lord Jesus Christ. The new people of God is kept together by the bond of *koinônia*, "fellowship" among the brethren (Ac 2:42), with the Son (1 Cor 1:9), in the Spirit (2 Cor 13:13), and also with the Father (1 Jn 1:3).

The expression "Israel of God" in Gal 6:16 is referred by some interpreters to the new people of God, the Christian community, but it more probably designates as a collectivity the Israelites who turned to Christ in faith. On the other hand, when Luke speaks of "the desert assembly" in Ac 7:38, he may have seen it as a prefiguration of the Christian community. His use there of *ekklēsia*, "assembly, Church," seems to indicate this intention. In Gal 4:21-31 Paul uses allegory to compare two covenants and two dispensations. The "Jerusalem above" is the community of the New Testament, the people of God of the new covenant, or the Church, considered more as the community of those saved than as institution. The "Jerusalem above" begins to exist here below in the Christian community, which through its destiny, is also eschatological.

Two Particular Texts

In Ep 1:3-4, which is a liturgical eulogy, the expression "people of God" does not occur, but the notion behind it is quite obviously represented. The *election* was the foundation of the Old Testament people of God, as texts like Dt 7:6-8 clearly indicate. We find a *sublimation* of this aspect in Ep 1:3-4, where Paul states that God the Father has chosen us in Christ before the foundation of the world. While the blessings mentioned in Deuteronomy are temporal and earthly (7:13-15), we find in Ep 1:3-4 and elsewhere that to the divine people of the New Testament *spiritual* blessings are granted. The foundation of the new people is certainly part of the "mystery" which was made known by revelation to the holy apostles and the prophets: '. . . the Gentiles are fellow heirs, members of the same body, and partakers of the promise in Christ Jesus through the gospel" (Ep 3:3-6). The Jews and the Gentiles now joined by the cross of Christ form the new eschatological community, as if by the creation of a new man (Ep 2:15-16). As the last Adam (1 Cor 15:47; Rm 5:6), Christ is the patriarch, in a way, of a new human generation, which transcends the frontiers erected by men and gathers them all in one family of mankind (Gal 3:28). The concept of people of God can be used to present the Church as a symbol of unity, of peace, and of human brotherhood.

Another text, often quoted in connection with the people of God and the so-called general priesthood of all the believers in Christ, is found in the First Epistle of Peter: "But you are a chosen race, a royal priesthood, a holy nation, God's own people, that you may declare the wonderful deeds of him who called you out of darkness into his marvelous light. Once you were no people but now you are God's people; once you had not received mercy but now you have received mercy" (1 P 2:9-10). These two verses combine borrowings from different Old Testament texts, namely Ex 19:5f., Is 43:20f., Ho 2:23 (*see* also Rv 1:6; 5:10). In Ex 19:5f. Israel is said to be "a kingdom of priests and a holy nation" because it was set apart as belonging to God, as consecrated to his service (cf. Is 61:6). The text we have quoted from 1 Peter has been prepared in verse 5, which states that on the model of Christ, "the living stone," the believers in him are themselves built into a spiritual house (or "sacred temple"), to be a holy priesthood, to offer spiritual sacrifices acceptable to God through Jesus Christ. Some exegetes have seen here a reference to the Eucharist, but the closest parallel seems to be Rm 12:1, where the Eucharist is not involved, but the persons of the faithful, who are exhorted to offer themselves in "spiritual worship." In 1 P 2:5 also the reference must be to "spiritual sacrifices" that represent the christian life of charity (Lyonnet 375), a life so dedicated to the service of God and of others that it deserves to be called a priestly life, a brotherly ministry. Whereas in Judaism "the priest is aloof from the people, here the whole new people of God form a priestly fellowship . . . What is really meant is a ministry of witness to all humanity along the lines of Is 61:6" (*TDNT* 3, 250f.): "But you shall be called the priests of the Lord, men shall speak of you as the ministers of our God."

Does "faith" constitute a link between the two Testaments? Festorazzi thinks it does, on the ground that the notion of faith is fundamentally identical in both Testaments: it is the total adhesion of man to the revealing and saving God. This conception corresponds perfectly to the historical experience described in the two Testaments. Not without reason Paul could cite Abraham as a model of faith (Rm 4:1-4), and the author of Hebrews proposes the example of the faith of the Fathers (Heb 11). Also collectively Israel believed in God (Ex 14:31). When the people as a whole became in practice unfaithful, the true faith was kept alive among the 'anawim, "the poor," which recent authors have identified as a particular group (see L. Sabourin, The Psalms, pp. 95-98). The two essential moments of faith are the divine initiative as a saving event and man's response; both are well represented in the two Testaments. With regard to the OT we can readily refer to the historical Credo, which epitomized the contents of Israel's faith. The oldest expression of it can be read in Dt 26:5-9, and Schreiner has studied its origin and development. In the NT faith in the saving presence of Christ is explicit; this was implicit in the OT believers, if the whole history of salvation tended from the beginning to its ultimate fulfilment in the redemptive work of Jesus.

Conclusion

Vatican II devoted chapter 2 of the dogmatic constitution on the Church (Lumen Gentium) to "the people of God" and expressly identified "the new Israel" with the Church of Christ (no. 9). Elsewhere, in the "Decree on the Apostolate of the Laity," it stated that "it has pleased God to unite the Christian believers in "the people of God," quoting 1 P 2:5-10 (no. 18), and finally the "Declaration on the Relationship of the Church to non-Christian Religions" declares that "the Church is the new people of God" (no. 4). On the other hand, the Council drew a careful distinction between the common priesthood of the faithful and the ministerial priesthood (Lumen Gentium 10; see Vanhoye). The Council offers in fact no support to those who would propose a new type of ecclesiology, with a sort of popular assembly of the faithful in mind, bound together by little more than a common belief in the saving action of Christ. Both Coppens and Ehrhardt warn against the indiscriminate use of the notion "people of God," when speaking of the Church, as if this was a central teaching of the New Testament. In fact, the NT more often than not mentions "the people of God" with reference to the Old Testament, and this shows that the sacred writers held that it was a notion capable of expressing the unity of the two Testaments and in this we must of course readily agree.

Bibliography for Section A

ANDERSON, B.W. "The New Covenant and the Old," in *Idem*, ed. *The Old Testament and Christian Faith* (New York 1969) 225-42.

BALTZER, K. *The Covenant Formulary in Old Testament, Jewish, and Early Christian Writings* (Philadelphia 1971).

BARR, J. "Some Semantic Notes on the Covenant," in H. Donner, *et al.*, eds. *Beiträge zur Alttestamentlichen Theologie: Festschrift für Walther Zimmerli zum 70. Geburtstag* (Göttingen 1977) 23-38.

BEAUCHAMP, P. "Propositions sur l'Alliance de l'Ancien Testament," RecSR 58 (1970) 161-93.

BEHM, J. *"Diathēkē,"* in *TDNT* 2, pp. 124-34.

BROWN, P.E. "The Basis for Hope: the Principle of the Covenant as a Biblical Basis for a Philosophy of History," *Interpretation* 9 (1955) 35-40.

BRUEGGEMANN, W. "Amos IV 4-13 and Israel's covenant worship," *Vetus Testamentum* 15 (1965) 1-15.

BUCHANAN, G.W. *The Consequences of the Covenant*, Suppl. NT 20 (Leiden 1970); on this book *see* CBQ 1971, pp. 554-7.

CAMPBELL, K.M. "Covenant or Testament? Heb 9:16-17 Reconsidered," *Evangelical Quarterly* 44 (1972) 107-111.

CARMIGNAC, J. "II Corinthiens III. 6,14 et le début de la formation du Nouveau Testament," NSt 24 (1978) 384-6.

CAZELLES, H. "Alliance du Sinai, Alliance de l'Horeb et Renouvellement de l'Alliance," in H. Donner, et al., eds. Beiträge... (see above), 69-79.

CLEMENTS, R.E. Prophecy and Covenant (London 1965).

EICHRODT, W. Theology of the Old Testament in two volumes (London 1961), centered on the Covenant idea.

FENSHAM, F.C. "The Covenant as Giving Expression to the Relationship Between Old and New Testaments," Tyndale Bulletin 22 (1971) 82-94.

GERSTENBERGER, E. "Covenant and Commandment," JBL 84 (1965) 38-51.

GONZÁLEZ, A. NUÑEZ, "El Rito de la Alianza," Estudios Biblicos 24 (1965) 217-38.

GUINAN, M.D. Covenant in the Old Testament (Herald Biblical Booklets, Chicago 1975).

HILLERS, D.RBiblical Idea (Baltimore 1969); on this book see CBQ 1970, pp. 128-30.

JAUBERT, A. La notion d'Alliance dans le Judaisme aux abords de l'ère chrétienne (Paris 1965).

JOCZ, J. The Covenant. A Theology of Human Destiny (Grand Rapids, Mich., 1968).

KUTSCH, E. Verheissung und Gesetz. Untersuchungen zum sogenannten "Bund" im alten Testament, Beih. ZAW 131 (Berlin 1973).

LANG, F. "Abendmahl und Bundesgedanke im Neuen Testament," Evangelische Theologie 35 (1975) 524-38.

LUBSCZYK, H. "Der Bund als Gemeinschaft mit Gott: Erwägungen zur Diskussion über den Begriff 'berit' im Alten Testament," in W. Ernst, et al., eds. Dienst der Vermittlung . . . Erfurter Theol. Stud. 37 (Leipzig 1977) 61-96.

LYONNET, S. "La nature de culte chrétien. Culte eucharistique et prolongation du 'commandement nouveau'," Studia Missionalia 23 (1974) 213-49.

MARTIN-ACHARD, R. "La signification de l'alliance dans l'Ancien Testament," Rev. Th. Ph. 2 (1968) 88-102.

MC CARTHY, D.J. "Covenant in the Old Testament. The Present

State of Inquiry," CBQ 27 (1965) 217-41.

Idem. (quoted in text), *Treaty and Covenant. A Study in Form in the Ancient Oriental Documents and in the Old Testament,* new edition, Analecta Bíblica 21A (Rome 1978).

MENDENHALL, G. *Law and Covenant in Israel and the Ancient Near East* (Pittsburg 1955).

MORAN, G. "De Foederis Mosaici Traditione," *Verbum Domini* 40 (1962) 3-17.

MORIARTY, F.L. "Prophet and Covenant," *Gregorianum* 46 (1965) 817-35.

PAUL, S.M. *Studies in the Book of the Covenant in the light of cuneiform and Biblical law* (Leiden 1970).

PERLITT, L. *Bundestheologie im Alten Testament* (Neukirchen 1969).

PORUBĆAN, S. *Il Patto Nuovo in Is. 40-66,* Anal. Bíblica 8 (Rome 1958).

QUELL, G. *"Diathēkē* (OT)," *TDNT* 2, pp. 106-24 *(berit).*

SELB, W. *"Diathēkē* im Neuen Testament," JewishSt 25 (1974) 183-96.

SMEND, R. *Die Bundesformel* (Zurich 1963).

TESTA, E. "De Foedere Patriarcharum," *Stud. Bibl. Fr. Liber Annuus* 15 (1964-65) 5-73.

THOMPSON, J.A. *The Ancient Near Eastern Treatises and the Old Testament* (London 1964).

TUCKER, G.M. "Covenant Forms as Contract Forms," *Vetus Testamentum* 15 (1965) 487-503.

VANHOYE, A. "La Nuova Alleanza," *Annali dei Sacerdoti Adoratori* 29 (1974) 147-64; 205-14.

VAN UNNIK, W.C. *"Hē kainē diathēkē*—a Problem in the Early History of the Canon," *Studia Patristica* IV, T.U. 79 (Berlin 1961) 212-27.

VON RAD, G. *Old Testament Theology,* vol. 2 (London 1975) 212-16, comparing Jr 31:31-34 and 32:37-41.

WEINFELD, M. "Traces of Assyrian Treaty Formulae in Deuteronomy," *Biblica* 46 (1965) 417-27.

See also G.D. Kilpatrick, *"Diathēkē* in Hebrews,"

ZNTW 68 (1977) 263-65. In his view Heb 9:15-17 should be translated throughout by "covenant"; "testament" is influenced by Gal 3:15-17. "For where there is a covenant, the death of him who made it must occur. For a covenant over dead bodies (i.e. sacrificial victims) must be valid, for it never is in force when the maker is alive."

Bibliography for Section B

BAUMGÄRTEL, F. *Verheissung: zur Frage des evangelischen Verständnisses des Alten Testaments* (Gütersloh 1952).

BEAUCHAMP, P. *L'un et l'autre Testament. Essai de lecture* (Paris 1976).

BLOCH, E. *Das Princip Hoffnung*, published in East Germany from 1954 to 1959, then in West Germany, which resulted in the author's flight to the West.

BRIGHT, J. *Covenant and Promise. The Prophetic Understanding of the Future in Pre-Exilic Israel* (Philadelphia 1976); this is mostly a comparative study of two covenants, the Sinaitic and the Davidic (see BibTB 1978, pp. 132f.).

BRUCE, F.F., ed., *Promise and Fulfillment*, Essays presented to S.H. Hooke (Edinburgh 1963).

BULTMANN, R. "Prophecy and Fulfillment," in C. Westermann, ed., *Essays on Old Testament Hermeneutics* 50-75.

CAQUOT, A. "L'alliance avec Abram (Genèse 15)," *Semitica* 12 (1962) 51-66.

CHILDS, B.S. "Prophecy and Fulfillment," *Interpretation* 12 (1958) 259ff.

FENSHAM, F.C. "Covenant, Promise and Expectation in the Bible," *Theologische Zeitung* 23 (1967) 305-22, where it is explained that to understand the unity of the two Testaments one should consider the relation between them as expressed by the covenant idea in which promise and resultant expectation formed an integral part (*see* NTA 12, p. 365); the title of his other article, quoted in our text, will be found in the General Bibliography.

HOFMANN, J.C.K. VON, *Weissagung und Erfüllung im alten und im neuen Testamente: Ein theologischer Versuch* (Nördlingen 1841-44).

KÜMMEL, W.G. *Promise and Fulfillment. The Eschatological Message of Jesus* (London 1957); half of this book treats of the imminent future of the Kingdom of God.

MOLTMANN, J. *Theology of Hope* (London 1967); *The Experiment Hope* (Philadelphia 1975).

MURPHY, R.E. "The Relationship between the Testaments," CBQ 26 (1964) 349-359.

PANNENBERG, W. "Redemptive Event and History," in C. Westermann, *op. cit.* 314-35.

PREMSAGAR, P.V. "Theology of Promise in the Patriarchal Narratives," *The Indian Journal of Theology* 23 (1974) 112-22.

PROULX, R. "Une forme inédite de la présence de Dieu dans l'Ancien Testament," dans *Après Jésus. Autorité et liberté dans le peuple de Dieu* (Montréal 1977) 198-208.

SCHNIEWIND, J. *"Epaggelia," TDNT* 2, pp. 576-86.

VAN RULER, A.A. *The Christian Church and the Old Testament* (Grand Rapids, Mich. 1966, E.T. from unchanged German edit. of 1955); on his interpretation *see* D.L. Baker, *Two Testaments, One Bible . . .* (Leicester 1977) 97-120.

WESTERMANN, C. "The Way of the Promise through the Old Testament," in B.W. Anderson, ed., *The Old Testament and Christian Faith* (New York 1969) 200-24.

ZIMMERLI, W. "Promise and Fulfillment," in C. Westermann, ed., *op. cit.* 89-122.

Idem. "Sinaibund und Abrahambund. Ein Beitrag zum Verständnis der Priesterschrift," *Theologische Zeitschrift* 16

(1960) 268-80. *See* also on "Promise and Law" E. Kutsch, *Verheissung und Gesetz. Untersuchungen zum sogenannten "Bund"* (Berlin/New York 1973).

Bibliography for Section C

BRUCE, F.F. "The People of God," in *This is That: the New Testament Development of Some Old Testament Themes* (Exeter 1968) 51-67.

CERFAUX, L. "Le royaume de Dieu," "le peuple de Dieu," "la survivance du peuple ancien a la lumiere du Nouveau Testament," in *Populus Dei, Studi Ottaviani*, vol. 2 (Rome 1969) 777-802, 803-64, 919-26.

COPPENS, J. "L'Eglise, peuple de Dieu, dans les écrits du Nouveau Testament," in *Annuaire de l'Institut de Philologie et d'Histoire Orientales et Slaves* 20 (Bruxelles 1973) 165-73.

DAVIES, E.D. "Paul and the People of Israel," NTS 24 (1977) 4-49.

DILLON, R.J. "Toward a Tradition-History of the Parables of the True Israel (Mt 21:33-22:14)," *Biblica* 47 (1966) 1-42.

EHRHARDT, A. "A Biblical View of the People of God," AmEcRev 159 (1968) 126-38.

FESTORAZZI, F. " 'Nous voilà en sureté!' (Jr 7,10). La foi des deux Testaments comme expérience salvifique," *Concilium* 30 (1967) 45-56.

GELIN, A. "Comment le peuple d'Israél lisait l'Ancien Testament," in P. Auvray, éd., *L'Ancien Testament et les chrétiens* (Paris 1951) 117-31.

HRUBY, G., "The Concept and Historical Experience of Peoplehood in Judaism and Christianity," *Encounter Today* 7 (1971) 8-36 (TD 22, 1974, 8-12).

KODELL, J. "Luke's Use of *Laos*, 'People,' Especially in the Jerusalem Narrative (Lk 19, 28-24,53)," CBQ 31

(1969) 327-43.

LYONNET, S. "La nature du culte dans le Nouveau Testament," in *La Liturgie après Vatican II*, Unam Sanctam 66 (Paris 1967) 357-84.

MEYER, R. & STRATHMANN, H. *"Laos," TDNT* 4, pp. 29-57.

MUSSNER, F. "Le Peuple de Dieu selon Ep 1,3-14," *Concilium* 10 (1965) 87-96.

NIXON, R.E. "The Biblical Idea of a Holy Nation," *Churchman* 83 (1969) 9-20.

SCHREINER, J. "Le développement du *'Credo'* israélite," *Concilium* 20 (1966) 31-39.

TRILLING, W. *Das wahre Israel: Studien zur Theologie des (Matthäus-Evangelium* 3rd ed. Munich 1964), pp. 53-96.

VAN IERSEL, B. "Le Livre du Peuple de Dieu," *Concilium* 10 (1965) 27-38.

VANHOYE, A. "Sacerdoce commun et sacerdoce ministériel. Distinction et rapports," NouvRevTh 97 (1975) 193-207; in Vanhoye's view, ministerial priesthood (that of "ordained" ministers) is more specifically but less really sacerdotal than common priesthood, because it is only sacramental, that is, sign of the reality. On the contrary, common priesthood is *real* offering of one's existence to God, in concrete docility (p. 204). References to older authors in TDNT 4, p. 29.

Bibliography on the REMNANT

DREYFUS, F. "La doctrine du reste d'Israél chez le prophète Isaie," RThPh 39 (1955) 361-86.

HASEL, G.F. *The Remnant: the History and Theology of the Remnant Idea from Genesis to Isaiah* (Berrien Springs, Mich. 1972); *see* on this book BibTB 1973, pp. 106-8.

HERNTRICH, V. "The 'Remnant' in the Old Testament," in *TDNT* 4

(1942) 196-209 (about the gr. *Leimma*).

MILLER, W.E. *Die Vorstellung vom Rest im Alten Testament* (1st ed. 1939, new edition Neukirchen 1973).

DE VAUX, R. " 'The Remnant of Israel' According to the Prophets," E.T. in *The Bible and the Ancient Near East* (London 1972) 15-30, from RB 42 (1933) 526-39.

CHAPTER THREE

THE PREFIGURATION OF CHRIST

Commenting on P. Grelot's first major work regarding the unity of the Bible, *Sens chrétien de l'Ancien Testament*, R.E. Murphy has well summarized, it seems to us, some distinctive aspects of this ambitious work, and his remarks can serve to introduce the present chapter. It is true, in particular, that if we wish to see Christ prefigured by the Old Testament as a whole, broad perspectives are necessary. In addition to the more obvious figures of Christ used in the New Testament, Grelot "sees figures structured in the People of God, the kingship, the priesthood and various aspects of cult (sacrifice, temple, and the so-called 'sacraments of the Old Law') and even Israel's geography (Promised Land, inheritance). If these are taken *as a whole* and related to the NT they are seen to have a 'providential function' of prefiguring the mystery of Christ. Israel was involved with Christ by way of anticipation in these figures; he was implicitly an object of faith and principle of justification. Prefigurement means the essential relationship between the elements of the preparatory history (events, institutions, persons) and the eschatological consummation of history" (p. 354, with a reference to p. 297 of Grelot).

Although the Old Testament is a source book of revelation and theology, about God and his work, it is in the first place, as a whole, "a work of history," of a history in which the central figure is God himself (MacKenzie 6-7). It is not of course all the time history in the modern sense of the term, but it is the true history of events interpreted in the light of faith. "As is well known, Israel's contemplation of history is that it was a direct expression of her faith" (Von Rad I, p. 50). It is remarkable that we find in the Old Testament a large scale interpretation of history. Such an undertaking was made possible by the presence in Israel of *prophecy*, which we take here in its broadest sense, to be explained later. But first we must consider briefly another Israelite interpretation of history, that of the Deuteronomist, who exercised a decisive influence on the edition of the OT historical books, from Joshua to the end of Kings.

a) History for the Deuteronomist

In the first volume of his *Old Testament Theology* (our following page references will be to this volume), Gerhard von Rad has masterfully analyzed the Deuteronomist's theology of history (pp. 334-47), summarizing and completing what he had previously written in *Studies in Deuteronomy* (London 1953). It is the Deuteronomist who welded together the stories about the Judges and presented them in the form of one literary work. He was much more interested, however, in the dynasty of David, which became the next great focal point of tradition. "It is in the light of it that the Deuteronomist writes Israel's history after the conquest, and from it the historical line runs down to the great disasters of 722 and 586... The Deuteronomistic history regarded Israel's whole history with Jahweh, as far as its anointed was concerned, as ending in catastrophe" (p. 308).

Decisive for the Dt-history was the prophecy of Nathan, found in the first part of the Succession Document, which runs from 2 S 9 to 20 and then concludes with 1 K 1-2. The question to be answered: How will Jahweh make good his promise "to build a house for David," and "Who is to sit upon the throne of our lord the king and rule after him" (1 K 1:27)? Although the author of the Document refrains from any direct judgment on the persons involved, he shows himself to be a theologian when he introduces the mention of God three times in the completely secular context, in 2 S 11:27, 12:24, and especially in 17:14: "For Jahweh has so ordained it that the good advice of Achitophel might be made in vain, in order to bring evil upon Absalom." This indicates a new way of conceiving God's intervention in history, not intermittently in holy miracles, but by a control over all that happens: "it continuously permeates all departments of life, public and private, religious and secular alike. The special field where this control of history operates is the human heart, whose impulses and resolves Jahweh in sovereign fashion makes subservient to his plan for history" (p. 316).

The Succession Document would be used, with other source material, for writing the Deuteronomistic history, during the Babylonian exile. The author of this Dt-history was greatly influenced by the book of Deuteronomy, which had been known at least since the time of Josiah and was perhaps, in part at least, a product of his reform. The dependence of the Deuteronomist on the book of Dt (*see* 12:1-7) is particularly noticeable by the exclusive allegiance prescribed to the place where Jahweh was present for Israel. "The Deuteronomist brought the whole of the history of the monarchy within the scope of this confessional situation." Further, "since the Deuteronomist wrote in the shadow of the catastrophes of 722 and 587, his work is to be understood as a comprehensive confession of Israel's guilt" (p. 337). But there is more in the Dt-history than there is in Deuteronomy, which knows nothing of any special sacral dignity attaching to the king as the representative of a separate election tradition. "It is only in the Deuteronomistic historical work that the two traditions of election—the Israel-Covenant and the David-Covenant traditions—are finally fused" (p. 338). The place where the fusion of the Mosaic and Davidic traditions can be seen most clearly is the ideal picture which the Deuteronomist drew of King Josiah: "Before him there was no king like him, who turned to the Lord with all his heart and with all his soul and with all his might, according to all the law of Moses; nor did any like him arise after him" (2 K 23:25).

For the Deuteronomist the divine guidance of history is established beyond all doubt. What he especially emphasizes is the conviction that Jahweh directs history *by his word*. In the Deuteronomistic theology of history what is decisive for the life and death of the people of God is the word of God injected into history.

This theology of history "was the first which clearly formulated the phenomenon of saving history, that is, of a course of history which was shaped and led to a fulfillment by a word of judgment and salvation continually injected into it" (p. 344).

The Dt-theology of history did not develop out of nothing. Seeds of it can be found in the previous traditions. For example, the author of the Succession Document also understood history as fulfilling Jahweh's word, since he set the whole complex of royal history in the shadow of the Nathan prophecy (2 S 7). We have seen above indications of his belief in God's continual intervention in the course of history. It must be added here that several chapters of the Book of Kings show how the prophets can "change the gears of history with a word of God" (*see* especially 1 K 20 and 22, as well as 2 K 9-10). The theological theme is already set "which will now in the Deuteronomist be applied in a much more radical way to the whole of the history of the monarchy" (p. 342).

As for the Book of Deuteronomy itself, it was strongly influenced by prophecy. Von Rad admits this and further asserts: "In actual fact, what stands unmistakably in the forefront in Deuteronomy is an interest in prophecy and the problems which it set (*see* 13:1-5). Indeed, the supreme office through which the proper intercourse between Jahweh and Israel is to be carried out is that of the prophet, who will never cease in Israel (Dt 18:18). Thus, according to Deuteronomy, Israel as properly constituted stands explicitly under charismatic leadership" (p. 99). It can be argued from Dt 18:15, "The Lord your God will raise up for you a prophet *like me* from among you," that Moses was regarded as "the fountainhead of prophecy and the prototype of the true prophet" (*Oxford Annotated Bible*), and the prophetical supremacy of Moses is actually affirmed at the end of the book: "And there has not arisen a prophet since in Israel like Moses, whom the Lord knew face to face" (34:10).

b) History and Prophecy

Only from the 19th century did biblical scholarship begin to realize that prophecy was an autonomous phenomenon in religion, and only then did the message of Israelite prophecy begin to be studied independently from the "law," which until then had been thought to antedate it. Julius Wellhausen was among the first who discovered this truth, as he himself explains in the first pages of his *Prolegomena to the History of Ancient Israel*, the main part of which was first published in German in 1878. Von Rad makes this point clear, "The moment that source criticism found a deposit of the prophetic teaching in Deuteronomy and the Priestly Document, thus doing away with the need to understand the prophets in the light of the Pentateuchal tradition, a new approach to the prophets was open" (Von Rad, vol. II, p. 4). On the other hand, as Von Rad explains, "the prophets were never as original, or as individualistic, or in such direct communion with God and no one else, as they were then believed to be" (*Ibid.*) It is now seen better that also the prophets were to a certain degree conditioned by old traditions which they reinterpreted and applied to their own times.

The importance of prophecy in Israel can be seen from the fact that the Hebrew Bible is divided into three parts, the Law, the Prophets, and the Writings, and this threefold division is already mentioned in the Preface to the second century B.C. book of Ecclesiasticus. This may indicate that the early editors understood the Bible as prophetical as a whole. It is also possible that they listed the "historical" books, from Joshua to Kings, among "the Former Prophets" because these books were found to contain many narratives involving prophets, or else because of a tradition that these books were composed largely by prophets (*see* 1 Ch 29:29; 2 Ch 9:29; 12:15; 13:22; 20:34; 26:22; 32:32).

1) The Origin and Meaning of Prophecy

Because of a better knowledge of Egyptian and Mesopotamian literature, it has become increasingly apparent that the phenomenon of prophecy was not limited to Israel, although it became prominent there with distinctive characteristics. We will, therefore, begin our sketch on Israelite prophecy with a look on prophecy outside Israel.

L. Ramlot has investigated the phenomenon of Prophecy in a huge article in the *Suppl*ément au Dictionnaire de la Bible. The first part deals with "Prophetism and politics in the Near East," which includes developments on Egypt (cc. 812-68), Mesopotamia (869-96), Canaan (896-904), the oracles of Balaam (904-908). The second part examines "Biblical Prophecy" (cc. 909-1222), while "Prophetism in the New Testament" is studied by Ed. Cothenet (cc. 1222-1337). From these studies and countless others a few more important aspects can be brought out with the purpose of showing how the Old Testament testifies to a forward movement of history perceived and even directed by prophecy, while the New Testament records and interprets the fulfillment of the Christward movement which it discovers in the events and in the texts that report them.

Prophecy in Ancient Egypt

Egyptian prophetism is poorly represented in the extant texts and monuments, as compared to the rich yield they offer on wisdom. The activity of the Egyptian prophets, if such existed, shows a close affinity with that of the magicians, whose function it was to dispel threatening misfortunes, rather than revealing of divine secrets. What "prophecies" are found in Egyptian literature are poor in content and have no doctrinal or historical consistency. As yet no true prophetic ecstasy has been documented for Egypt of the kind found in Canaan and Israel (cf. 1 S 10:6; 19:23f). Besides, in Egypt oracles were uttered at the request of particular persons, like the king, the priests, or complaining individuals: prophecy there is essentially "situational" in scope and lacking the extension and the continuity needed, for example, in a revelation of salvation history. Nor is Egyptian prophecy disinterested, as was Egyptian wisdom in its highest mystical manifestation. More often than not the Egyptian seer uttered utilitarian oracles for the benefit of his patrons.

The prophetical texts of ancient Egypt do reflect the knowledge of an apocalyptic pattern of development, involving mainly the following motifs: denunciation of social injustice in connection with physical or cosmic disasters, a link between the anger of the gods and social disorders, historical and literary alternation of good and bad fortune, often connected with the accession of a good or bad king. Some of these motifs appear in Israelite prophecy, but with a different trajectory. Egyptian prophecy saw the good reign as leading to personal immortality, while Israelite prophecy took its departure from a collective eschatology in a salvation history framework that would include non-Jewish nations. Whereas some Egyptian wise men were tempted by a certain type of monotheism, the priests and the magician-prophets favored the plurality of gods and of sanctuaries. In contrast, the Hebrew prophets founded their theology, their moral doctrine, and their cult, with a unique sanctuary in view, on strict monotheism.

In prophecy, as in psalmography, the Egyptians had in common with the Israelites the purpose of glorifying the divinity. But this is true also of all the old pagan worship, from Mesopotamia to Rome: the idolatrous cults ultimately reveal the human desire to render homage to the deities on whose benevolence so much depends on earth. Finally, there is one area of easily comparable material between Egyptian and Israelite prophecy: in both Egypt and Israel royal courts entertained so-called "peace-prophets," always willing to predict prosperity and success in battle to the reigning monarchs (*see* 1 K 22). Ezk 13:10 provides a good example: "Because, yea, because they have misled my people, saying, 'Peace,' when there is no peace; and because, when the people build a wall, these prophets daub it with whitewash." The false prophets' message (cf. Jr chs. 28-29) was like whitewash on a mud-brick wall (12:5) which provided no protection against the storm (*Oxf. Ann. B.*).

Prophetism in Mesopotamia

While in Egypt the phenomenon of divination and prophecy was very limited in scope, the same extended in Mesopotamia to a variety of areas, including political life, and in this it offers a field of comparison with Israelite prophecy. Mesopotamian prophetism lay in the hands of a specialized group closely related to sanctuaries, especially that of the moon-god. Not surprisingly a large number of presages were based on moon eclipses. Outside the realm of folklore, writes A.L. Oppenheim, the Mesopotamian diviner is not a priest, but an expert technician, and first of all, a scholar. The diviner derives information on ominous happenings or features from large compendia, the centennial accumulations of divinatory experiences, which he studies, interprets, and comments upon with the help of such philological textbooks as are at his disposal (in *La divination en Mésopotamie ancienne et dans les régions voisines*, XIVe Rencontre Assyriologique Internationale, Paris 1966, p. 40). When used properly the term *divination* designates rather a technique for interpreting omens, while in prophecy oracles are delivered in the name of the divinity. In Mesopotamia the *baru*-priests or "seers" interpreted signs and omens, observed the new moon and the planets, indicated the lucky and unlucky days, explained the intricacies of the calendar. Their activities are frequently mentioned in the state correspondence of the Assyrian kings. Sennacherib always consulted his seers before beginning his various campaigns against Syria and Palestine. These "seers" can be compared to the clairvoyants or diviners of Israel's early history, called *hôzim* (cf. 1 S 9:9-11). With the *baru*-priests are often mentioned the *sa'ilu*-priests, whose primary function was the interpretation of dreams (*see* L. Oppenheim, *The Interpretation of Dreams in the Ancient Near East*, Philadelphia 1956). Oppenheim also writes: "The training of priests specializing in divination techniques of all kinds was considered of vital importance for the well-being and the security of the country" (in V. Ferm, ed., *Forgotten Religions*, New York 1950, p. 76). It belonged particularly to the priest to practice divination by means of special sacrificial rites. Any one can see how far we are in these techniques from Israelite prophecy, which claimed to receive its oracles directly by divine revelation.

Interesting points of comparison have been found between Israelite prophecy and a sort of prophecy in use at Mari, the brilliant Mesopotamian city of the third millennium before Christ. They regard especially the oracles addressed to the king, threatening him with punishment or suggesting what his conduct should be (*see* Ramlot 884-96). But in Mari, as elsewhere outside Israel, prophecy was an episodic phenomenon, in contrast with the Israelite prophetical tradition. Hepatoscopy (ritual inspection of the liver), figured in Mari among the favorite divination techniques and accurate clay models of animal livers have been found (*see Biblical Archeol.* 11, 1948, p. 18). The Hittites also practiced liver haruspicy, already known in Assyro-Babylonia and later developed by the Etruscans. These clay models were used for the training of the haruspices and bore, for that purpose, inscriptions stating the meaning of the various shapes of different parts of the liver. In Hatti, as elsewhere, signs in heaven were also important and it was the function of the astrologers (priests, very often), to discover their meaning and to suggest, if necessary, the proper ways of appeasing the gods.

Canaanite Prophetism

The religious beliefs and practices of Canaan, including Ugarit and Phoenicia, have no doubt influenced in some way the development of Israelite prophecy, although the Israelite prophets, Elijah in particular, strongly reacted to the danger (1 K 18), and tried later to eradicate the Canaanite practices with royal help. "But Baalism was too deeply rooted in tradition and custom to be so easily destroyed. The Canaanizing elements which had entered into official Yahwistic cult with Solomon and Jeroboam were only the public recognition of an increasing tendency to adapt Baalistic practices to the local cult of Yahweh in open-air shrines and at rustic altars throughout the country" (W.F. Albright 309f). The danger for Israel of being contaminated by Baalism appears greater when one bears in mind that the cultic terminology of Ugarit is very similar to the Israelite, as recent studies have shown (*see* L. Sabourin, *Priesthood. A Comparative Study*, Brill, Leiden 1973, p. 70).

Since the work of G. Hölscher was published (esp. pp. 129-43) it is often repeated that the prophetic movement originated in group-ecstaticism, obtained through prolonged physical movement leading to a sort of hypnotic state and mystical experience which can generate in some persons a prophetical consciousness. The "Report of Wen-amun," from the early 11th cent. B.C., describes a case of ecstatic trance at Byblus in Phoenicia, but it may have been a pathological condition, and not one derived from group activity. However, the available documentation, mainly from the Old Testament (see 1 K 18), indicates that ecstatic prophecy existed in Canaan at a time when prophecy was about also to develop in Israel. From about 805 B.C. we have the Aramaic stele of Zakir, according to which this 8th century king of Hamath (now in Syria) obtained a favorable oracle as he had to face a formidable coalition against him. The king is reported to have said: "I lifted my hands towards Baal-Shamain"—using a formula represented in Ps 63:5—"and the god spoke to me through seers and diviners." "Diviners" is here a conjectural translation of an hapax Aramaic term, with the consonants ain followed by two daleths and a nun, this being the plural ending. The same root is used in 2 Ch 15:1 and 8, in the phrase "son of Oded," and (probably) the gloss "Oded the Prophet," while 28:9 speaks of "a nabi (prophet) of the Lord by the name of Oded." It seems, writes Ramlot (c. 902), that at an early stage of Hebrew there was a connection between the term 'oded and prophetism. The root is represented in other West Semitic dialects, notably in Ugaritic, with the noun 'dd meaning "herald." The Zakir stele would testify to the existence of two categories of "prophets:" the seers (hâziyin) and the 'adidin, which can be rendered "revealers," those who repeated the words of the god.

The Oracles of Balaam

According to Numbers 22 the Moabite king Balak invited a Mesopotamian diviner, called Balaam, to put a curse on the Israelites who, he feared, would invade his country, as they journeyed along its frontiers on their way from the wilderness to the promised land. Then, of course, a remarkable thing happened: Balaam was unable to curse the Israelites, instead he pronounced oracles of blessings over them (Nb 23-24). Also remarkable is the fact that he alone, a foreigner, declares (23:21) that God "has discovered no iniquity in Jacob, and has seen no mischief in Israel" (*NEB*). If this is the correct reading of the text—*RSV* understands it differently—the statement can partially be explained from the fact that the oracles of Balaam figure, with the Song of Miriam in Ex 15, among the earliest compositions of the Bible (13th to 12th cent., according to Albright, p. 14). Another surprising feature of the event: a Mesopotamian is reported by the Bible to have been graced with true revelations from the God of Israel. That Balaam had no control over what he said reflects the oriental belief in the *ex opere operato* efficacy of God's word (cf. Is 55:11).

Several features of the story represent Balaam as a Mesopotamian diviner. According to Nb 22:5 Balaam lived at Pethor, "near the River, in the land of Amaw." Several recent scholars, including Albright (*Yahweh and the Gods of Canaan*, London 1968, p. 13, n. 38), identify this Pethor with Pitru, in Mesopotamian Syria. Also Nb 23:1-6 point to Balaam as Mesopotamian, since Babylonian diviners resorted to this kind of sacrificial ceremony to obtain an omen, so that Balaam could have been a Babylonian *bârû (see* S. Daiches). R. Largement has found in Assyro-Babylonian divination analogies for the speaking ass (Nb 22:28-30). As we have noted above, the Mesopotamian *baru* were also astrologists, and this can be related with the nature of one of Balaam's oracles: "I see him, but not now; I behold him, but not nigh: a star shall come forth out of Jacob, and a scepter shall rise out of Israel" (Nb 24:17). It should besides be observed that the Bible does not give to Balaam the title of *nabi'*, "prophet," or *hôzeh,* "seer," but "the fees of divination (*qesem*)" were offered to him. In Jos 13:22 Balaam is identified as "the son of Beor, the soothsayer (*haqqôsem*)."

The Jewish tractate *Pirke Abot* sets in contrast the disciples of Balaam, "the impious one," with the disciples of "our father Abraham" (V, 19). According to an early Jewish tradition, God brought forth Moses for Israel and Balaam for the idolaters. This negative judgment is reflected in the late Jewish-Christian Second Epistle of Peter, where the wrongdoers are described as those who "follow the way of Balaam" (2:15). On the other hand, a non-Jewish current of interpretation praised Balaam, with the purpose of reducing the disparity between the prophetical gifts bestowed on Israel and those conceded to the nations. It appears quite probable to this writer that Matthew's midrashic composition of the Wise Men from the East was influenced by the oracles of Balaam, even if Nb 24:17, quoted above, is not strictly a messianic prophecy (*see* my commentary on Matthew, ch. 2).

Israelite Prophecy

Concluding his study of the so-called prophecies reported from Mari, which do offer some interesting parallels with biblical prophecy, F.L. Moriarty has this comment: "The Mari texts speak of particular dangers to be avoided, of political maneuvers to be performed, of this or that sacrifice to be offered in a temple, usually to placate an offended god. One can hardly avoid the impression that the Mari revelations concern what is trivial, ephemeral, a tactic to be followed here and now. Missing are the great biblical themes of judgment and redemption, sin and guilt, the burden of the past and the hope of the future—all of which characterize Israelite prophecy. There is no similarity in the context of prophecy. The prophetic experience of Israel can be understood only against a covenant background, entirely missing in Mari. The prophet works from the covenant as a basis; his role is that of representative of the divine Suzerain who speaks to His vassal people through the prophetic word. The psychology of the prophets, ecstasy included, merits study on a comparative scale but not at the expense of overlooking what Israel did in applying that experience to a new and higher involvement of certain men in the divine plan for the world. No prophet at Mari can stand comparison with an Isaiah or a Jeremiah. The light shed on biblical prophecy by the new discoveries is welcome; but it must be said again that this new material only confirms the uniqueness of prophecy in Israel" (p. 277). With these words Moriarty has not only pinpointed the superiority of Israelite prophecy, he has also brought out some of its distinctive aspects.

It is not our purpose to present a complete overview of Israelite prophecy, as, for example, Ramlot has done in the *Supplement*.

Our interest lies in the meaning of OT prophecy as pointing forward to Christ, as even orienting history towards the messianic fulfillment. This Christward inclination we shall examine in the following sections. We wish beforehand to make some observations on the phenomenon itself of prophecy in Israel, a subject which, surprisingly enough, is not often examined. Given the interest we have mentioned, it should be clear that we have in mind the prophets who exercised the function of interpreting or foretelling history, and not the bands of ecstatics who roamed the country in the earliest periods of Israelite history (1 S 10:5.; 19:20-24). Elijah was certainly a man of enormous powers, who held religious syncretism in horror and undertook to purify the faith of the people. As champion of the true religion he played a leading role in his own time and was instrumental to a certain degree in shaping salvation history. However, his action was limited, and he left no writing containing large scale revelation on the mystery of divine rule in the world, as some classical prophets have done. The same is true—even more so—of Elisha, who succeeded him and was, according to extant reports, more a miracle worker than anything else.

Whereas it was still fashionable a few decades ago to oppose priest and prophet, biblical scholars, like A.R. Johnson and A. Haldar, have begun to have a more balanced view on the subject and have unhesitatingly written about "cult prophets." "In the earliest period in Israel the priest was not originally in the first instance sacrificer but, as with the old Arabs, custodian of the sanctuary, oracle priest, 'seer' and holder of the effectual future-creating and future-interpreting word of power, the blessing and the curse" (S. Mowinckel, *The Psalms in Israel's Worship*, II, p. 53). At a certain period at least the priest was a giver of Oracles (see L. Sabourin, *The Psalms* 46). To admit the prophetic role of the priest is to question the supposed fundamental rivalry between prophecy and priesthood. The Chronicler writes of the psalmists that they "prophesy" (1 Ch 25:1; 2 Ch 20:14). He also mentions Asaph "the seer" (2 Ch 29:30). This almost certainly means that the Asaphite guild was originally a group of cultic prophets in Jerusalem who were later relegated to the position of Temple singers. The existence of cult prophets would show that prophecy at a certain period became, at least partly, institutionalized, that is, attached to a function rather than dependent on ecstatic experience or sudden revelations. It is known that Judaism ascribed prophetic inspiration to the high priest (cf. Jn 11:51).

Several functions are ascribed to the prophetic office, as can be known from the activity and teaching of the Israelite prophets. They can be catalogued as follows (cf. Ramlot 1036): (1) Prophetic involvement in the national life of the people, especially in periods of crisis, for the reformation and even the resurrection of the nation; (2) Prophetic intervention in the demythization of royalty elsewhere, in anointing Israelite rulers and in admonishing them (Nathan, for example), in preaching the Holy War (cf. Zp 1:14-16), and in announcing the future coming of the Messianic King (cf. The Immanuel Prophecies in Is 6-12); (3) Prophetic revelation of forthcoming divine judgments on the nations (a large part of Is 1 to 39); (4) Prophetic denunciation of social injustice and moral evil (cf. Scharbert), and prophetic preaching of universal peace; (5) Prophetic mission in salvation history. More often than not the prophets had to accomplish singlehanded these enormous tasks, and were often opposed by both the ruling powers and the people. A man like Jeremiah felt overburdened by his mission and pleaded to be released from it, but the Lord told him: "Do not say, 'I am only a youth;' for to all to whom I send you you shall go, and whatever I command you you shall speak. Be not afraid of them, for I am with you to deliver you" (Jr 1:7f). Their calling is the key to the superhuman work done by the prophets. Precisely, the more common word used for "prophet" in the OT is nabi'—almost always translated in Greek by prophētēs—and by its etymology nabi' means "to be called," since it derives from the accadian nabû, meaning "to call:" "This interpretation of the word suits its meaning exactly; the prophet was a man who felt himself called by God for a special mission, in which his will was subordinated to the will of God, which was communicated to him by direct inspiration. The prophet was thus a charismatic spiritual leader, directly commissioned by Yahweh to warn the people of the perils of sin and to preach reform and revival of true religion and morality" (Albright 303).

Explaining to Moses that he has designated Aaron as his aide and spokesman, God told him: "He shall speak for you to the people; and he shall be a mouth for you, and you shall be to him as God" (Ex 4:16). It seems suggested here that the relation between God and his prophetic spokesman is analogous to the relation between Moses and Aaron. This meaning suits well the etymology of the Greek *prophētēs*. In relation to the (pagan) Greek oracle, we are told, the word group formed by *prophēteuô, prophētēs*, etc., "denotes appointed men and women and their work, which is to declare something whose content is not derived from themselves but from the god who reveals his will at the particular site" (*TDNT* 6, p. 791). However, the oracle prophets and prophetesses of Greece were chosen for their ministry by men and not by the god. Not so, as we have seen, the Israelite prophets, who received from God their calling (cf. Is 6) in a variety of ways (*see* Von Rad II, 50-69). With this calling they received the word of God to proclaim, a force within they could not resist, similar to "a burning fire" (Jr 20:9). It could be a source of great inner agony for the prophet, as he confronted the unheeding godlessness of those he was sent to admonish (20:14-18). According to Nb 12:6f., the Lord would communicate with prophets indirectly through dreams or visions (cf. Dt 13:1). This obviously reflects the popular notion of prophecy, not one that applies to the true biblical prophets. In contrast with what took place in Egypt, "in Israel's prophetic literature we have no case of a command issued in a dream and then reported by the prophet" (Moriarty 262). In connection with the prophetic calling, Am 7:14 has always been a source of difficulty, where Amos tells Amaziah, the priest of Bethel: "I am no prophet, nor a prophet's son; but I am a herdsman . . ." It can be explained thus: these words are meant to explain the strange fact that Amos began suddenly to speak by inspiration, like a *nabi'*, though as a peasant he was not entitled to do so; it was an exceptional calling (*see* Von Rad II, p. 131).

In the following sections it will be seen that prophecy has to do with the interpretation of history, with the making of history, especially of salvation history. But prophecy is also "prediction." J.D. Smart has explained quite well in what sense: "Prediction in the Old Testament belongs in the context of promise and fulfillment. The prophet's knowledge of the future is not a mystic penetration of future events but a penetration by faith into the secret counsel of God by which future events are determined. 'The Lord God does nothing without revealing his secret to his servants the prophets' (Am 3:7). The prophet knows what God will do because he knows who God is. God's future action is therefore not a fixed and determined event that nothing can change, but depends in some measure upon the response of Israel to him. Even though disaster has been predicted as judgment upon sin, the repentance of the nation may yet make possible an escape from death into life. A fixed scheme of prediction and fulfillment belongs together with a static conception of history in which from the beginning God has determined all events, a conception totally alien to the dynamic character of the prophetic faith in which history consists of a succession of situations in which the nation is called to choose between the way of life and the way of death" (p. 104). One purpose of the "prophetic" book of Jonah consists precisely in showing that prophecies of doom, even unconditional, may not be fulfilled if the reason that prompted them, the spread of sin, has been annulled by the conversion of the people.

2) Yahweh and His Word in History

It would be difficult to find a text better adapted than the following to introduce the present section. It comes from second-Isaiah and it concerns the infallible efficacy of God's word: "For just as from the heavens the rain and snow come down and do not return there till they have watered the earth, making it fertile and fruitful, giving seed to him who sows and bread to him who eats, so shall my word be that goes forth from my mouth; it shall not return to me void, but shall do my will, achieving the end for which I sent it" (55:10f). Isaiah himself had proclaimed the special efficacy of the word in shaping the history of Israel: "The Lord has sent a word against Jacob, and it will light upon Israel" (9:8). Also for Jeremiah, God's living word has the power to burn like fire (5:14) and to devastate like "a whirling tempest" (23:19). We have spoken above of the word of God in connection with the deuteronomist view of history. We shall present the prophetic view in this coming section.

Salvation in History and Prophecy

The approach to OT biblical theology has changed significantly since 1960. In his survey article, "The New Diachronic Biblical Theology of the Old Testament (1960-1970)," J. Harvey has documented and evaluated this change (BibTB 1971, 5-29). He has especially drawn attention to the importance and meaning of G. von Rad's work, to which we often refer in our own study. Von Rad has particularly developed the concept of salvation history.

Not convinced that a synthesis of OT theology is possible—on the "center" of biblical theology, see our ch. IV—von Rad looked rather for a continuity and unity in the divine plan for history, in this sense that Yahweh's interventions form a series opened to the future in a course of events teleologically oriented towards an eschatology of fulfillment. Having been unable to discover in the OT an axis of theological development, he contents himself with narrating what the OT says about its own contents (*nacherzählen*). This amounts in practice to making OT biblical theology *the history of Israel's faith lived and proclaimed.* Von Rad knows that the fundamental question has to be faced: what exists? a true, objective, salvation history, or only a religious reading of common historical events? He claims that for him the biblical texts are related to history inasmuch as they deal with the continuous action of God in time, which is the history of Yahweh-with-Israel. The only events that count, for the biblical authors, are those in which they see God at work and constituting through dialogue a community. For von Rad, besides, not only a distinction should be made between history as event and history as kerygma, but *a choice*, and this choice should be made in favor of the sole kerygmatic history.

Some critics disagree with von Rad because he does not seem to require any historically objective reality, any history as event, on which to establish his study of the kerygma and its evolution. However, it would not be correct to imagine that von Rad is a kerygmatician as resolute as Bultmann, who has abandoned in practice salvation history and founded the NT kerygma exclusively on eschatology. It is evident that for von Rad there is no duality between factual history and interpretation: both together constitute the real history. Were there no specific faith to sustain and proclaim the reading of events, rooted in belief, there would be no unity of the twelve tribes as we know it through history, the monarchy would not be the specific davidic monarchy, a concrete Jerusalem would not be, nor a concrete temple, the return from exile would not be what it has been historically. There is no doubt, on the other hand, that the successive readings in faith, dependent on changing historical and cultural situations, reach beyond the event and overload it with meanings. Think of the successive readings on the crossing of the Red Sea, by the Yahwist, the Elohist, second-Isaiah, the priestly tradition and the later sapienial writings, including some Psalms. The evidence gathered from an improved archeology allows one to ascertain, on the other hand, that the essential nucleus of the event has not been created by faith. The etiological narratives deserve special consideration (see BibTB 1972, 199-205).

It is today generally recognized that the oldest form of the history of the patriarchs—and therefore of recorded salvation history—which has come down to us, is found in the opening sentence of the old Credo in Dt 26:5, in the laconic mention of the "wandering Aramean who went down into Egypt and there became a great nation." This Aramean is of course Jacob. It is Yahweh who controls all that happens in the history of the patriarchs, although this formulation is an anachronism from the historical standpoint, since prior to Moses the ancestors of Israel are not supposed to have worshipped God under the name of Yahweh, but as "the God of the ancestors." "The basic strata of OT literature in the Pentateuch, in the historical books, and in the prophets bear witness to an acting and speaking of Israel's God, which is throughout directed to Israel in the midst of the nations of the world. This thoroughgoing nature of the witness of faith which is strictly related to history finds, quite apart from all parallels in detail, no explanation in terms of the literary types of the surrounding world, for which the mixture of god-myths and cultic legends on the one hand, and royal annals and similar historical documents on the other, is characteristic" (H.W. Wolff, "The Hermeneutics . . ." 167). As we have seen, the Promise was gradually amplified to incorporate larger areas of Israelite history. This is how von Rad puts it: "Thus, compared with the area in which they were originally current, the old traditions were given an enormously wider reference, for now it is the whole of Israel which relates these far-off happenings to herself and recognizes in them what is her very own. These stories of the patriarchs are not retold in that exclusively historical sense whose sole concern is merely to reproduce exactly what happened at the time: instead, experiences and insights of succeeding ages also found expression in them. The narrators often digest in but a single story of only a few verses the yield of a divine history which in fact stretches from the event spoken of down into their own time" (vol. 1, p. 167).

Other authors also have stressed the difference between the religious history found in the OT and that recorded in the Mesopotamian myths. K.A. Keller calls theology of history "an overall view of the destinies of man in his relations with God" (p. 124). These relations culminate in Jesus Christ, but Keller examines them in the OT as connected with divine providence and the personal involvement of God in the course of history. Biblical man is found to be a valid partner of God, his collaborator, and a qualified interlocutor. Whereas in Mesopotamian myth the gods were terrified by the Flood they had unleashed, for the biblical writer Yahweh remains in control of the situation and thus appears as the Master of history. At the other end of the OT salvation history, Daniel concentrates his attention on the political world, against the background of the eschatological advent of God's reign.

S. Amsler recognizes that in the OT there is no history except that known through faith and confessed by faith (p. 239), but he finds faults in the systematization which von Rad proposes. Why is the Sinai covenant never mentioned in the historical *Credos*? Besides, they belong to different literary forms. Whereas in Dt 6 and 26 we find the "we" of the confessing community, it is the "I" of divine interpellation that is found in the historical recapitulation of Jos 24:2-13. Amsler, with others, proposes to examine the historical *Credos* against the background of the ancient treaty formularies, which we have mentioned in the beginning of ch. 2. Few critics would go as far as F. Hesse in his rejection of "Salvation History" (*Abschied von der Heilsgeschichte*, Zurich 1971). Bultmann borrows something from salvation history in line with his other theories. Israel's covenant history, he argues, proves to be a history of failure (*Scheitern*); only from the standpoint of Christian revelation can this "abortive history" be understood as "promise," in this sense: it shows in retrospect the impossibility of gaining access to God in history and points beyond failure to God's action in Christ, which "deworldizes" (*entweltlicht*) man and transposes him into an eschatological existence: "Faith requires the backward glance into OT history as a history of failure, and so of promise, in order to know that the situation of the justified man arises only on the basis of this miscarriage" (p. 75).

But all is not negative in the OT salvation history. "On the one hand, F.C. Fensham explains, there were the religious traditionalists who believed that the promises of the Lord to David would stay in effect in spite of anything that happened; and on the other hand there were the prophets who emphasized the fact that unfaithfulness had broken the covenant and eliminated the promises; all that was left was imminent doom" (p. 89). However, in between the prophecies of doom there appear prophecies of hope, of Messianic hope. Sometime in the future a new David would appear who would rule his people in righteousness. It is clear that the prophets, especially a prophet like Jeremiah, had no confidence in the living kings of Judah; their hope was placed on a future king, the Messianic king.

God Rules History

In contrast to what happened in polytheism, the basis of the Israelite sacred literature was not nature, because "the God of Israel was first of all the Lord of history who used nature to accomplish his purposes in history" (Wright, 28). God's intervention is remarkable also by its manner. He does not work at certain moments in men and at other times in history. "But at the very moment when he works in men he works in history, *he molds history*" (Lys 89). For E. Jacob the Israelite prophets, for the first time in recorded history, have envisaged a universal history: not only is the God of the prophets the God of history, but faith in this God, now considered the ruler of universal history, has priority over faith in God the Creator (*Théologie de l'Ancien Testament*, 2nd ed., Neuchatel, 1968, pp. 148-86).

Also H.W. Wolff has underlined the prophetic concept that Yahweh who rules history is present in history. He in person, for example, will confront Israel in the invading Assyrian troops, will be "a lion to Ephraim" (Ho 5:14). In the prophetic word future history is unveiled, also because the Hebrew *dabar* means both "word" and "event:" thus we have both "narrated" history and "eventuated" history. History is entrusted to the prophet *in the word*. Thus is history "dialogue" between God and Israel, and the historical future is usually involved, not the end of history, because history is meant to bring conversion, especially for Jeremiah. But Yahweh is God of both future and past, and in this identity resides the unity of history; *for the past supplies a pattern for the present and the future.* It belongs especially to prophecy to find this pattern of God's action and to interpret it. In this sense prophecy can also be prediction, because if God's pattern of action is known, the trajectory of the future can be detected from what happens at the present. The course of salvation history will not depend on arbitrary divine interventions, it will follow guidelines, those of an inviolable covenant. *Prophetic history* is therefore oriented, typologically oriented, because it is the same Yahweh who takes up again his own work, according to predetermined patterns. This is especially noticeable in the later sections of Isaiah (chs. 40 to 66).

G. von Rad has particularly examined "the prophets' conception of the Word of God" (*OT Theology* II, 80-98). We can recall here the texts quoted in the beginning of this section and the importance the Deuteronomist assigns to the word. In the early cultures the power of the word was first expressed in terms of magic and dynamism, later it was connected with the rituals of exorcism and with blessing and cursing. One distinctive character of Israelite prophecy consists in the fact that its contents are communicated directly to the prophet and by him to the people. The expression *dabar Yhwh* occurs more than 240 times in the OT, mostly in connection with prophetic oracles, and in the form "the word of

Yahweh came to so and so," which indicates that the perception of the divine word was understood as an event, setting the recipient "in a new historical situation" (Von Rad 87).

The prophets had also recourse to "symbolic actions" to express the content of the divine message, thus making it also easier for the people to understand it, as it were, visually (on these symbolic actions see Ramlot 969-73). The dialogue with Israel in judgment often followed what is called "rib-pattern" (see Harvey) an accusation formulated in legal terminology (rib means to contend or to plead a cause). Is 1:2-5, Jr 2:4-13, and especially Mi 6:1-8 provide good examples of rib-speech. It can be lengthy and formulated in psalmic form, as the Canticle of Moses, introduced towards the end of Deuteronomy (ch. 32), after its later composition under the influence of prophetical speech. J. Hempel believes that in fact the Israelite idea of history is that of a judgment of God on the sin of man (p. 5). He also finds that in the prophetical writings a time of salvation always succeeds the times of misfortune. There exists a constant personal confrontation between Yahweh and Israel: change is possible on God's part, since divine judgment, being educative in scope, remains subordinated to the will to save. The ultimate judgment of history will have to guarantee the only absolute, the honor of God, but not the manner in which history will achieve this, by way of judgment or of salvation (pp. 41f).

The Prophets and History

It is not difficult to document from the Bible the concrete involvement of the prophets in the political life of Israel, and consequently their contribution in making history. More than once Nathan intervened in the life of David on behalf of God (2 S 7 and 12); Ahijah the Shilonite prompted Jeroboam to the revolt which brought the division of the kingdom (1 K 11); Elisha instigated Jehu's revolution that took him to the throne with the slaughter of Ahab's descendants (2 K 9-10); Amaziah, the official priest of the royal sanctuary at Bethel, denounced Amos for allegedly conspiring against the house of Jeroboam II (Am 7:10-17); Isaiah intervened constantly in the political life of his time in the course of the Syro-Ephraimite war (734-33 B.C.). King Ahaz of Judah disregarded the prophet's advice (Is 7-8), as his embassy to the Assyrian king shows (2 K 16). We know from 2 Ch 28:16-21 and from newly found inscriptions that the Assyrian campaign was also directed against the Philistines (cf. Ramlot 1118). Sedekiah could have saved Jerusalem and the temple from destruction, had he followed Jeremiah's advice to capitulate before the king of Babylon (2 K 25; Jr 38).

H. Donner has attempted to define the attitudes of the prophets. For Isaiah, it is God who directs world politics; not political neutrality is demanded, but confidence in Yahweh and his word. This is in reaction to the fact that Israel has abandoned the grace of the election. Hosea finds his ideal in the past: since the danger of pagan contamination remains, Israel must not forget her origin and past commitment. It must be added to this that the prophets are the interpreters of history, which for them is in the hands of the nations, but God remains in control, he who directs the course of history. What for the Yahwist author of some sections of the Pentateuch was an epic, showing how the people of God was gathered into a nation, becomes in the prophets a tragedy, because they knew what calamities would be visited on this people for its unfaithfulness to God and the covenant. From the eighth century onwards the attention of the prophets was centered on the destiny of Israel in the midst of the empires. Their interpretation of history is religious—the relation of Yahweh with Israel is the deepest theme of prophecy—and nationalistic (the destiny of Israel occupies the foreground), but at the same time its range is universal because the God of Israel reveals himself to them as the God of universal history (Procksch 4-5). As E. Jacob explains, history in the OT is done under the sign of the election: God is always he who was and who calls. There is nothing more certain than the election. The privileges of the election will disappear only when Yahweh's sovereignty is universally recognized ("L'Ancien . . ."). Then Israel will be blessed together with the nations (Is 19:24f). We will conclude this development with an observation that attempts to formulate the essential role of Israelite prophecy: "The final mission of prophecy was to liberate the eternal truths of religion from their temporary national embodiment and disclose their true foundation in the immutable character of God and essential nature of man" (Skinner 14).

Revelation as History

The years 1960 to 1970 saw the appearance of a particular school of thought around the theme "revelation as history." Its first publications appeared in supplements to the periodical *Kerygma and Dogma* (1961). We have already mentioned about Promise/Fulfillment (ch. 2) the name of W. Pannenberg, the theologian from the University of Mainz, who headed the group, which included also at first Rolf Rendtorff (OT), U. Wilckens (NT), and others. For Pannenberg God's revelation comes to men not immediately (as Barth and Bultmann hold) nor through a special redemptive history (as Cullmann proposes), but mediately and indirectly, mirrored in the events of history. "Since history becomes the locus of revelation, revelation is verifiable by the methods of historical scholarship. And if revelatory history is knowable by reason, then faith does not produce, but rather presupposes rational knowledge. Faith does not give us the inner meaning of events of past history, but is trust-oriented to the future, to the final end of universal history anticipated in the Christ-event" (*Jerome Biblical Commentary* 41:58). For G.G. O'Collins, however much Pannenberg's theology of revelation can be welcomed as a reaction to the excesses of existentialist "Word-theology," it is an exaggerated reaction. It seems impossible to explain God's self-revelation merely as indirect, through his mighty deeds in history. The Fourth Gospel, for example, presents us with words which reveal God directly not merely in Pannenberg's sense of direct, i.e., having God himself as their immediate content, but also in the sense of being communicated directly from God in the person of his Son. "The word is not merely about God, but from God" (p. 406).

Reactions to the positions taken by other members of the "school" have also been heard. W. Zimmerli (in Ev. T.) has accused Rendtorff of "absolutizing" history as the means through which all the peoples can come to know Yahweh. This approach would belittle the role of the word as compared to the event, and put in the shadow a theme as important as the divine name (*see* Ramlot 1115f). Besides, if history as a whole is revelation, how can it teach us anything definite before it comes to an end? It is not in a deeper understanding of history that Israel has believed in its continuity, but because of the certainty that God is faithful to his promises. Rendtorff recognizes that in the earlier stages the word comes before the event, as in the history of the patriarchs and in the narrative about the succession to the throne of David. Then the fulfillment of the oracles could easily be verified. Also the classical (writing) prophets presuppose that Yahweh rules history, but in this they offer no new revelation, they only open the eyes of their fellowmen. Henceforth it will be the role of history to demonstrate the validity of the word, whose potentiality can be unlimited, up to the far ends of eschatology.

In *Old and New in Interpretation: a Study of the two Testaments*, J. Barr has expressed some views on the debate we are discussing. He points out various OT areas which fail to support the idea that revelation through history is the center of Hebrew thought. "The most obvious relevant area is of course Wisdom literature. In this literature, while it is known that God may and does act in human affairs, there is no impression that any particular series of historical acts are the sole or even the central foundation for all knowledge of him. On the contrary, it seems rather that God is knowable or known without appeal to such a source of revelation. Something analogous can be said of many materials which have a cultic setting, mainly in the Psalms" (p. 72f). Besides God's intervention cannot be considered independently of his word: the acts of God are meaningful because they are set within the frame of verbal communication in which God tells what he is doing or what he intends to do (p. 77). Even the Exodus narratives do not properly constitute revelation in history. They are rather interpretation of or meditation on the events. Revelation is certainly not the organizing principle of these narratives. On the other hand, Barr also recognizes that the Bible is *Heilsgeschichte*, a series of events through which God has in a particular way revealed himself. Revelation through history is a central theme of the Bible, but other aspects are equally important, as for example direct verbal communication of God with a particular individual, to entrust him with a special mission or make with him a covenant (see *Interpretation* 17, 1963, pp. 200-203).

Also, according to B. Albrektson, history can have religious significance only through the divine word, which in the Near East understanding, he says, does not come directly, but through oracles. He recognizes, however, eleven explicit mentions of the divine plan, ten of which are found in the prophets, and one in the psalms, namely Is 5:19; 14:24-26; 25:1; 46:10; Jr 23:20 (30:24); 29:11; 49:20 (50:45); 51:19; 51:29; Mi 4:12; and Ps 33:10f. What is essential and specific for Israel, Albrektson asserts, is the revelation of God through the word. Not all Albrektson's views have gone unchallenged, especially those he expressed on pagan beliefs. As W.G. Lambert has observed, the Mesopotamian deities were very much part of the physical universe, and no overall control of the course of history was ascribed to them as was the case in Israelite prophecy with regard to Yahweh (p. 171f).

3) Prophecy, Apocalyptic, and Eschatology

J. Carmignac has warned against the dangers of an indiscriminate use of the term "eschatology," which apparently for the first time G. Bretschneider employed in 1804. Etymologically the word of course refers to the knowledge or science of the *eschata*, "the last things." In a study of the prophetic writings it means specifically what the prophet taught on the future of the world and of humanity, on the teleological orientation of salvation history. In Carmignac's view the concept of the reign and kingdom of God should be substituted for "eschatology" as being more biblical and accurate. It seems to us, however, that "eschatology" is preferable in a study of a general nature like ours, especially where history is concerned, because eschatology refers to the end of history, and history is specified by the aim and the end of its course.

Forms of Eschatology

Apart from the traditions centered on the royal Messiah or the prophet of end-time, a well represented current of OT prophecy concerns "eschatology without a Messiah," the coming of God himself to establish his rule and ensure the effective recognition of his royalty. Reflecting a prophetic theme, especially second-Isaiah, the author of one of the eschatological psalms of Yahweh's kingship, invites the heavens, the earth and its inhabitants to exult "before the Lord, for he comes; for he comes to rule the earth. He shall rule the world with justice and the peoples with his truth" (Ps 96). According to G. Pidoux, "the fact that *God will come* is the only permanent element in OT eschatology; all the colorings that describe his return are but secondary and impermanent elements" (*Le Dieu qui vient, esperance d'Israel*, Neuchatel 1942, p. 53). Joel prophesied the day on which God would personally enter into judgment with the nations assembled in the valley of Jehoshaphat (4:2).

It is not possible to discuss here in any detail the different theories regarding eschatology. We will note, however, that Mowinckel agrees with Sellin on the existence of a link between the eschatological hopes and the future establishment of God's reign. This is an important point, which can serve as a common denominator between the eschatology of the Psalms and that of apocalyptic. We wish to summarize also, with Ramlot (c. 1187), the ideas which Procksch proposed in the article *Eschatologie* in *Die Religion in Geschichte und Gegenwart* (2nd edit. 1929). While he notes with his predecessors a correspondence between protology (*Urzeit*) and eschatology (*Endzeit*), he also considers that the external borrowings concern above all the imagery of the creation, while eschatology would be proper to Israel. If in the latter area there has been a borrowing, it has been entirely assimilated. For Procksch, eschatology begins with David and the figure of a future king, a Judean representation. However, earlier still would be the promises of a land. The glorious future of the tribes in a blessed land had been revealed to the Fathers, as several texts show: Gn 28:28f; 48:21f; 29:22f; Dt 33:13f. These representations of the future, preserved in the North, figure in Ho 2:16-23. From this it appears that biblical eschatology does not begin with the oracles of doom.

Ramlot concludes with the following words his survey of the theories on eschatology: "We have therefore found maintained the antiquity of a hope in a 'God Who Comes,' a hope closely allied with the old historical traditions, the election, and the representations of a transcendent God, who is absolute master of history, therefore of the future, as he is the Lord of the past and of the present" (c. 1193).

Was there a pre-exilic eschatology? The answer to this question depends on the manner one understands eschatology. If it is simply a doctrine of the end of the world, then it is possible to find it before the Exile. If, on the other hand, eschatology means the conclusion of history, the introduction of a new, trans-historical world, as we find in apocalyptic, no such eschatology can be found among the pre-exilic prophets, for they speak of events within history and not outside history. The main Israelite expectation was political and crystallized in royal messianism, a current well represented in the Prophets and in the Psalms. Also an intercessor was expected, the Suffering Servant, in whose figure many hopes and ideals have coalesced (Is 53). At other times, and in other books the hope centered on the eschatological prophet (Dt 18:15-18) or the anointed prophet (Is 61:11). Jeremiah expected "a new covenant" (31:31-35), while Ezekiel (16:60), and the second-Isaiah (55:3) had in mind "an everlasting covenant" (cf. Ezk 37:26; Is 61:8). The future universal Reign of God is celebrated in a number of Psalms (47, 93 and 96-99). As for the apocalyptic expectation, we shall deal with that later on.

The Day of Yahweh, the Remnant, and Reinterpretations

The essence of eschatology, as a turning point in Israelite prophecy, resides in a *qualitative change*, in the perception of a passage from one world to another: not the end of the world but the end of a world is the core of the message. Zephaniah first describes the day of Yahweh, which will put an end to the present world

(1:16-18), and then the appearance of the new world (3:8-20). Perhaps the division between the two worlds found its original formulation in the beginning of the Book of Consolation (Is 40:1-8), but in Is 43:18f. the expression is even sharper: "Behold, I am doing a new thing." A lot has been written on "the day of Yahweh" (*see* Ramlot 1197f), which became after the exile the *cliche* formulation of God's end-time intervention. The way the expression appears suddenly in Amos (5:18) makes one suppose it was already known in his time. Mowinckel links the day of Yahweh with the feast of Yahweh's Enthronement (*The Psalms in Israel's Worship*, vol. 1, p. 116), but he had little following in this. More acceptable is von Rad's interpretation that connects "the day of Yahweh" with the holy war ideology (vol. 2, 119-25), a theory expanded by Langevin. M. Weiss does not welcome this idea, however, and he holds that the concept has its roots "in the ancient motif-complex of the theophany-descriptions." In fact it is obvious that the description of the day of Yahweh has theophanic connotations (*see* Na 1:3-6; Ps 18:8-16). More on these ideas can be read in L. Sabourin, *The Psalms*, 2nd ed., pp. 132-44.

In connection with "the people of God" (ch. 2, c), we have written something about the Remnant. This is a relatively important theme also in the prophets and it has been studied in particular by Dreyfus, Hasel, Herntrich, Miller, and de Vaux (*see* end of ch. 2). As MacKenzie explains, the limiting of salvation to a Remnant was paradoxically a step in the direction of universalism. It detached the religion of ancient Israel from its identification with one ethnic group, substituting the personal requirement of faith and loyalty to Israel's God for the physical qualification of being children of Abraham. "By asserting the doctrine of the *remnant*, both Jeremiah and Ezekiel had affirmed that the relationship between Yahweh and his people was not broken for good. Hosea had foreseen the restoration of the covenant, after infidelity, punishment, and repentance. Jeremiah and Ezekiel prefer to picture it as a new covenant, different in several important respects from the old. To break the fatal downward spiral of human infidelity, Yahweh must work an interior change in the humanity that he allies with himself" (pp. 107f).

This note on the Remnant brings us to consider the tension created by the prophetical tendency towards universalism as against the election of Israel. Only Christianity will fully solve—in a brutal rending—this passage from the election of Israel to the election of the nations (cf. Mt 21:43), but it was foreshadowed in the OT, also in an eschatological perspective, as in Is 2 and 11 (Ramlot 1199). Altmann (ch. 7) has shown that for second-Isaiah the belief in a unique God (43:11) who wishes to create something entirely new regards in the first place salvation for Israel, but also salvation for the whole world. Israel plays the role of Servant (44:1, 21), of messenger (42:19), and of witness (43:10). The nations need the preaching of the one God (42:4). For this reason God has elected Israel from the extremities of the earth (41:8f), a cause of suffering. Mission and suffering combine, as the parabolic figure of the Servant indicates.

In his study of reinterpretation in OT eschatology, P. Grech distinguishes between what he calls "intra-historical eschatology," concerned with a particular situation in history, and "ultra-historical eschatology"—found immediately before or during the Exile— which transcends an historical situation and looks forward to a more universalistic act of God (for ex., Is 9 and 11). Eschatological prophecy detached from definite historical situations and used liturgically becomes *pattern eschatology*. It is rather a philosophy of history, which then can be reapplied to any similar situation. The eschatology of the Psalms and of the cultic prophets Habakkuk, Joel, and Malachi is sometimes of this kind. A prophetic word never dies, it speaks to succeeding generations until it has been fulfilled and this does not happen before it has reached the fullness of its salvific message. Salvation itself is raised to a higher level, from national restoration it becomes eschatological end-time salvation, closely akin to Jesus' "Kingdom of God." The new exodus of second-Isaiah is a good example of this, where the concept of liberation is spiritualized, given a moral, religious sense, applying to the inner life of individuals, as well as to the national messianic salvation (cf. other types of "re-readings" in Gelin's study). Reinterpretation is often done with the help of typology.

Eschatology in Apocalyptic

According to H.D. Preuss it would be impossible to draw a threshhold-line between prophecy and apocalyptic: they are united in their understanding of history as a unity with a goal, a concept to which the Wisdom corpus is entirely alien (p. 217). It is, besides, instructive to note, with G. Fohrer, that in apocalyptic God changes first the world and then through it men, not first men and through them the world, as perhaps in prophecy. Whereas the prophetic message is specifically rooted in the saving history, in definite election traditions, this is not so in apocalyptic: "In the panorama of history given in Daniel's two great night-visions, the picture of the empires and the vision of the four beasts, there is absolutely no mention of Israel's history; here God deals only with the empires, and even the son of man does not come from Israel, but 'with the clouds of heaven' " (Von Rad 2, 303). In apocalyptic, history is minutely patterned in advance; there is no room for the prophets' spontaneous interventions of God, to meet the changing situations. The literatures of both discern a meaning in history, but differently. "For the prophet this is limited to what we ought to be doing today. The apocalypt deals with *universal* history, the unity of history in its totality with emphasis on the remote future, and only ambiguous relevance to the point where we are now standing" (North, 67).

Traditionally prophecy is contrasted with apocalyptic along the following line, to show their incompatibility:

	PROPHECY	APOCALYPTIC
Eschatology	Native, monistic	Foreign (Iranian)
Object of Hope	Fulfilment of creation	Dissolution of creation by a different type of world
Judgment	Coming event announced to the unrepentant, but is not irrevocable	Unalterable final event with firmly fixed date

P.D. Hanson, however, questions this position, and claims, to the contrary, that the rise of apocalyptic eschatology is neither sudden nor anomalous, but follows the pattern of an unbroken development from pre-exilic and exilic prophecy. Outside influences (e.g. Persian dualism and Hellenism) upon this apocalyptic eschatology appear to be late, coming only after its essential character was fully developed. They are thereby limited in their influence to peripheral embellishments (pp. 7-8).

Under the rubric "philosophy of history" can be classified all the attempts made to understand or reconstruct the past with the avowed intention of giving a meaning to it. These attempts can be reduced to two main lines of development (*see* Harvey). The first, which is sometimes labeled "positivist," finds a basis in the general laws of history, from which it claims to develop futurology, the science of the future. Other philosophies of history are not positivistic, but idealistic, in the sense that they consider history as intelligible, not as resulting from deterministic laws, but as following projecting patterns. If these are seen to depend on human efforts only, we have *secular* minded philosophies. If they are related to faith, then we have *theologies of history* in which what counts is the development of God's project in the shaping of history. To this current belong both biblical prophecy and Jewish-Christian apocalyptic, with similarities and differences.

Jewish-Christian apocalyptic, the beginning of which ran parallel to the later OT prophecy, founded a part of its creed on acquisitions of OT faith: the certainty that God rules the world, the unity of creation and history, the existence of a divine project, the role of the Messiah in the gift of salvation. Other elements are new, but some were inferable by theological reflection from the preceding data: the resurrection of the dead, the reality of a future aeon, the existence of spiritual beings (angels or devils) that influence the course of history. A third group of apocalyptic beliefs are entirely new: the notion of a preestablished and unchangeable divine plan, the division of history in fixed periods, the idea of a progressive aging of the world, of its approaching end, and of its total destruction when this comes. It can be sustained that in the periods of crisis the classical orientations of the non-positivistic views tended to withdraw from history and become self-centered, unless themes related to the future intervened to preserve or revitalize the idealistic perspective of history. One concrete example of such self-centered development can be found in the Maccabean period. It consisted in regenerating hope after the disaster by turning to the past, to a strict observance of divine law—a tendency already partly operative since Ezra, the father of Judaism—in the framework of a renewed but narrower nationalism.

A careful evaluation of apocalyptic would first view positively what it has in common with the traditional faith of Israel and authentic prophecy. Another positive contribution is the affirmation of two aeons, which enriches the interpretation faith proposes of history by asserting the existence of a future world on which hope is based. Much of the rest regarding the future consists of unverifiable projections that can have a negative impact on the conduct of the present. That should be preserved from apocalyptic which is necessary or useful to live in the present according to the sure guidelines of rationality and authentic revelations.

Prophecy in the New Testament

Half a century after the Book of Daniel, the author of 1 Maccabees deplored the disappearance of the prophetic gift (9:27), but he foresaw the coming of a prophet who would decide what ought to be done with the stones which composed the altar of the holocaust (4:46). Probably during the Babylonian exile a psalmist had also lamented the absence of prophecy intended to make known God's saving will (Ps 74:9), and the author of Lamentations declares that the prophets have received no vision from the Lord (2:9). Ezekiel had foreseen that in the forthcoming disaster "prophetic vision shall fade, instruction shall be lacking to the priest, and counsel to the elders" (7:26). The *Community Rule* exhorts the members of the Qumran sect to hold fast to the Law "until there shall come the Prophet and the Messiahs of Aaron and Israel" (IX, 11). Carmignac observes that a clear distinction should be made between the ordinary intervention of God in the life of the community and his decisive end-time intervention: the War of Liberation, he thinks, will be a spectacular divine intervention, a judgment of God in the manner foreseen by Ezekiel, which will mark the beginning of an era of human prosperity and fidelity on earth. It is in no way the equivalent of the last judgment in Christian theology.

. Many Jewish doctors believed that the Holy Spirit or the Spirit of prophecy was one of the five things which the second temple did not enjoy, in contrast to the prerogatives of Solomon's temple, the others being the heavenly altar-fire, the ark, the Urim and Thummim, and the anointing oil (*Taanit* 2.1). Another rabbinic tradition extends the age of prophecy to cover also the earlier part of the post-exilic era, after which the *Bat Qol* will be used to communicate the divine will (*see* Meyer 817). The voice from heaven at the baptism of Jesus has some external similarity with the rabbinic *Bat Qol*. Jn 12:28 is much closer to that conception: "Then a voice came from heaven, 'I have glorified it, and I will glorify it again.'" As C.K. Barrett notes, about this verse, whereas in the rabbinic literature these voices are looked upon as a sort of inferior substitute for prophecy, the New Testament community represents them as the directly heard voice of God (*The Gospel According to St. John*). The *Bat Qol*, litt. "daughter of the Voice," was really only an echo of the divine voice. Another Jewish tradition attributed the gift of prophecy to the high priest. According to Josephus God deemed John Hyrcanus (134-104 av. J.C.) "worthy of three privileges, the government of the people, the function of high priest, the gift of prophecy" (*Antiq.* 13,299). The Fourth Gospel alludes to this belief, where it says of Caiaphas: "Being high priest that year he prophesied that Jesus would die for the nation" (11:51). On the expectation of the eschatological prophet see the last section of this chapter.

Out of 144 occurrences of the term *prophetes* in the NT, 123 refer to the OT personages, and only 21 apply to Christian inspired persons. On the other hand, the proportion changes in the use of *propheteuo*, "to prophesy" (21 Christian out of 28) and of *propheteia*, "prophecy" (16 Christian out of 19). To appreciate correctly the word statistics, a distinction must be kept in mind between the title itself "prophet," relatively rare in the primitive church, and the prophetic function, understood in a broader sense and occasionally fulfilled in the Christian community by him who imparts the blessing or exhorts the brethren. The massive NT use of the term *prophētēs* to designate God's spokesmen of the past is very significant: it shows that although conscious of possessing the eschatological gifts, the Christians did not cut themselves off from the Israelite past, but interpreted their own experience in the light of the word of God. This suggests also the presumption that there is no need to seek extrabiblical analogies but that Christian prophecy has its place within the tradition of the people of God. Aware of this the OT Greek translators kept *prophētēs* to render *nabi'* and used *mantis* when referring to the pagan diviners. The *Corpus Hermeticum* would perhaps offer certain parallels to NT prophetism, but its contents are not earlier than the 2nd century and are not therefore directly useful for the NT period (cf. Cothenet 1223, who also refers to E. Fascher, *Prophētēs*, Giessen 1927). Although gnosticism or pregnosticism could be in theory more relevant, it is methodologically erroneous to base any study of Christian prophetism on the vague and nebulous gnostic manifestations.

For the NT writers the OT prophets proclaimed in advance what was later fulfilled in Christ (*see* Ac 2:31; 3:18; Rm 1:2; 2 P 3:2). In particular the "Fulfillment quotations" in the first gospel are all attributed to prophets, because for Matthew only prophecy can account for true prediction and fulfillment. This is so true that the Law itself played a prophetic role (*see* 11:13 and my article). In his Emmaus account Luke relates of Jesus: "And beginning with Moses and all the prophets, he interpreted to them in all the scriptures the things concerning himself" (24:27). In addition, for the New Testament the OT prophets did not simply proclaim future events. They are also authorities that can be quoted to support the truth of what is done in the new economy. Jesus appealed to the sayings of the prophets to justify his action in the temple (Mk 11:17) and he uses Is 54:13 to back up his own statement that God will teach any man (Jn 6:45). It is proved from the words of the prophets that Israel has been guilty of idolatry (7:42) and that God does not dwell in the temple (7:48). All the prophets, it is claimed, have proclaimed the forgiveness of sins through the name of Christ for all who believe (Ac 10:43), and James appealed to the authority of the prophets to justify the receiving of Gentiles into the community (15:15). Many more examples could be quoted to show that the words of the prophets are adduced to confirm important points of preaching and to lend emphasis to proclamation.

According to G. Friedrich, "primitive Christian prophecy is the inspired speech of charismatic preachers through whom God's plan of salvation for the world and the community and His will for the life of individual Christians are made known" (p. 848). The NT prophet knows something of the divine mysteries, particularly God's saving will for the Gentiles (Ep 3:5f). According to Rv 22:6f. one of his chief concerns is to declare imminent eschatological events. But primitive Christian prophecy does not only consist in the disclosure of future events (cf. Ac 11:28; 21:10f.), or in keeping expectation of the *parousia* alive in the community, it also speaks out, as OT prophecy, on contemporary issues (1 Cor 14:3) and sets forth God's will for the world and for individual believers. The prophet does not disclose what he has taken from revelation, but what has been revealed to him. Prophecy is very closely related to revelation (1 P 1:10-12).

Under the viewpoint of authority the Book of Revelation has the closest affinity with OT prophecy. In Rv also there can be no question of testing the correctness of the seer's sayings since they are declared to be reliable and true by the supreme authority, God himself. The seer's authority can be compared with that of the apostles. His proclamation is the Word of God and testimony of Jesus Christ (1:9; 19:9) and it has decisive significance for the conduct of one's life (1:3). After the last book of the Scripture canon, no new revelation is expected, although the wealth of the given revelation will become better known and its latent meanings explored and uncovered. The rapid decline of prophecy attests in a way that the hour of laying the foundations has passed. The time has come to build upon these foundations. Sustained by the Spirit, the Church prophesies in the vast arena of the world, proclaiming the victory of the Lamb and his future return (Cothenet 1336).

c) The Christward Inclination of Salvation History

Introducing his study of "the actualization of the Old Testament in the New," G. von Rad states: "All these writings of ancient Israel, both those which were concerned with her past relationship to God and those which dealt with her future one, were seen by Jesus Christ, and certainly by the Apostles and the early Church, as a collection of predictions which pointed to him, the savior of Israel and of the world" (vol. 2, p. 319). True, nowhere is Jesus Christ explicitly mentioned in the OT, but he was announced by Old Testament figures. What is more, the whole salvation history was oriented Christwards, and Christ fulfilled the hope to which the OT pointed, or at least with his advent the eschatological age dawned, the age in which the Kingdom of God will finally erupt.

Such an inclination of salvation history is possible because for the Bible history does not follow a cyclic pattern but a linear course running from an absolute beginning to a final conclusion. The concept of God who acts "forms the basis for Israel's understanding of reality as a linear history moving toward a goal" (Pannenberg 317). Bultmann refers to J.C.K. Hofmann, *Weissagung und Erfüllung*, as having written that since Christ is the goal of history, history is prophecy of Christ. "Hofmann's way of speaking about prophecy and fulfillment is manifestly a philosophy of history which is influenced by Hegel, and gains its Christian character only because for him Christ is the goal of history" (p. 57). Then Bultmann proposes what seems to be his own view: "According to the New Testament, Christ is the end of salvation history not in the sense that he signifies the goal of historical development, but because he is its eschatological end" (p. 58). This shows once more that Bultmann is more interested in kerygma and existential meaning than in salvation history. As G.E. Wright explains, for Bultmann what should be sought "is not an objective understanding of what *once* happened in history, but a personal concern for how the past events illumine my self-understanding at this moment of time" (p. 180). Whether Bultmann admits it or not, it remains true that salvation history was oriented Christwards and that it has in this way exercised also an influence on general history, at least in the geographical area connected in some way with Israel.

1) The Christward Significance of Israel's Religious Experience

In the biblical view, taken over by Christian theology, nothing in human history, from creation to the final judgment, stands outside the divine plan, which fulfills itself in sacred history. None of the components of history, however obscure and enigmatic, remains therefore without meaning. On the other hand, when we speak of *the meaning of things* in the Bible, we do so under a limited viewpoint, that of supernatural revelation. Since that revelation takes place jointly through the word of those divinely inspired to speak and write, and through significant realities, all the things that belong to the life of God's people have a meaning in relation to the unique object of revelation: the mystery of God manifested in the mystery of Christ. Biblical symbolism does not therefore rest on the data of common religious experience, as in other religious systems, but *on a specific experience* bound up with the actualization in history of the salvific design. History *is involved* in biblical symbolism, since God's revelation takes place through the mediation of the events in which his people, illumined by the Word, recognize his sovereign intervention in view of the salvation of humanity. As the Savior through whom this design is carried out, Christ is the key to its understanding, and all is preordained in function of him (*see* Grelot, 231-309).

Did the historical religious experience of Israel carry a manifestation or a revelation of the divine plan of salvation? If revelation is simply a proclamation of the message of grace, and faith an existential acceptance of it, as the Bultmannian school suggests, then, of course, sacred history could be considered irrelevant, and the growth of Israel's religious beliefs, as well as the language used to express them, could be attributed to a natural process subject to the same laws as other religious phenomena. Those who hold this view understandably claim that the sacred writers have transformed history into myth. It can be admitted that in several cases, for example, in the deliverance from Egypt and the conquest of Canaan, the facts have been interpreted theologically, with an emphasis on God's miraculous intervention in favor of his people. However, this handling of history can hardly be called "mythologizing." It expressed in dramatic representations the conviction that God was revealing and carrying out through Israel's history his plan of salvation. Although the course of Israel's history was subject to the natural rules of development, operative in other peoples, through it God's design was gradually realized, and his Word was there to disclose the true meaning of the events, polarized on Christ and his salvation. The author of Hebrews wrote that the OT true believers "all died in faith, not having received what was promised, but having seen it and greeted it from afar" (11:13).

The distinctive role of the OT prophets consisted precisely in pointing out the *signs* of God who acts in the course of history, in the formation of institutions, in the appearance and work of representative religious figures. They are not the product of fate or of purely natural causes: they are there according to a designful disposition of God who directs history towards its *eschaton*. Also characteristic of prophetical preaching is the notion that salvation is the graceful gift of God who acts, and that his design will be carried out in spite of the malevolence of men. Because of its infidelity Israel will fall under God's judgment, but a Remnant will be saved, and this again through God's mercy. However, the significance of the religious experience of Israel came to full light only later, with the advent of the Christ, in whom Simeon saw the salvation prepared in the presence of all peoples (Lk 2:31).

Application to Christ's Saving Mystery

In the life of Christ, in the mystery of his death and resurrection, was effected the passage from the old world to the new, from the condition of suffering and death, proper to sinful humanity, to that of immortality and blessedness. In the sacrificial transformation of Christ human temporality virtually passed to that state to which it is called in God's salvific design (Ph 3:20f). According to Matthew's infancy narrative the child Jesus in a way relived Israel's exodus experience. This is seen again in the temptation of Jesus in the desert: where Israel failed, Jesus was faithful. Later episodes of the public ministry, like the miracle of the loaves, recalled decisive events of Israel's sacred history, and prefigured the future messianic gathering of the redeemed through the eschatological prophet.

Particular suffering figures of the OT traced a red trail of poured blood of the just from Abel to the Maccabees. The death of the OT martyrs can be considered as anticipated sharing in the mystery of the Cross. Jesus himself referred to the righteous and the prophets slain for their testimony of faith (Mt 23:29-37), and the author of Hebrews mentioned several types of torture endured by them (11:36-38). Although Isaac was not actually immolated, the fact that he was bound (the *Aqedah*) and put on the altar like a lamb was considered as a sacrifice in the Jewish tradition. Several NT passages see in him a figure of Christ, who like Isaac was not spared by a loving Father (Rm 8:32). And of course several verses of Ps 22 on the suffering just are alluded to or quoted in the passion narratives. This is also true of the texts on the Suffering Servant (*see* Lk 22:37) whose figure is behind several NT statements on Jesus' redeeming death (cf. 1 P 2:21-25). If a collective interpretation of the original fourth Servant Song is admitted, it becomes easier to state that Jesus has relived Israel's experience also in his sufferings.

Several intimations of the resurrection of Jesus can be read in the OT, like those indicated in Ac 2:27. Although it concerns directly the national restoration of Israel after the Exile, Ezekiel's vision of chapter 37 may also indirectly point to the eschatological salvation of God's people, as does a later text attributed to Isaiah: "Thy dead shall live, their bodies shall rise, O dwellers in the dust, awake and sing for joy" (26:19). Also Ho 6:2, as understood by the Targums, may have been instrumental in the formulation of Jesus' resurrection "after three days" (*see* de Surgy 38f). However, only in the late book of Daniel do we find an explicit formulation of an eschatological existence of the Remnant of Israel. It is expressed in the corporate personality attributed to the Son of man, more or less identified with "the saints of the Most High" (7:13f., 18). In any case, Christ is the true Israel of God, and in his mysteries he is the Event towards which the whole saving history was oriented and in which it now finds its achievement.

To conclude, there are many ways in which we can speak of a Christward figurative significance of the historical experience of Israel. The few indications we have given could be multiplied in the light of additional NT texts, which would include several sections of the Epistle to the Hebrews, since it describes how the people of God are on their way to their resting place under their leader and pioneer, Jesus, the Son of God (*see* especially chaps. 3-4). St. Irenaeus says that through the patriarchs and the prophets Christ trained his people into the divine economies and signified in advance what would happen (*Adv. Haer.* IV, 21, cf. Camelot 162). It can also be said that the historical and spiritual experience of Israel has contributed to the fashioning of Jesus' personality, of his aspirations, and of his deepest religious attitudes. In him, again, two testaments meet and the old dispensation elapsed, replaced by the definitive economy of grace and salvation.

Although we do not wish to expose this point here (*see* Grelot 278-81), Israel has also a Christward significance in its cultic life. In fact the language of the prophets is often colored by the cult, and the liturgical feasts took on more and more eschatological and messianic meanings. Apart from explicit references found in the Epistle to the Hebrews, others, also connected with Jesus' sacrifice, could be mentioned (*see* 1 Cor 5:7; 1 P 1:19). In Rv 5:9-10 we find a confluence of expressions that show how the Old and New Testaments meet in the cultic formulation of the sacrifice through which Christ has redeemed the Remnant from many nations.

2) A Time of Preparation and Fulfillment

The advent of Jesus Christ was both prefigured and prepared in the OT revelation and in the divine dispensation which governed the people of God through the election and the economy of the covenants. Salvation history went through different stages marked from time to time by new beginnings. The time of Christ came as the decisive turning point in this history.

The Time of Christ

Christ's place with regard to time constitutes a relevant issue in any discussion on the unity of the two Testaments. For the time of the earthly Jesus stands between both as the hinge that joins them. This time has its strong moments. In his incarnation Christ, who preexisted as Logos, entered into the terrestrial time, and by assuming human historicity transformed its meaning radically. Sent as Son, he appeared as the temporal epiphany of the invisible Father. His divine origin and his mission were made manifest with the beginning of the public ministry marked by the baptism and the first proclamation. The message of the Gospel is both the Kingdom of God and the Proclaimer himself: "That which was from the beginning, which we have heard, which we have seen with our eyes, which we have looked upon and touched with our hands, concerning the word of life" (1 Jn 1:1).

The presence of God's glory in Christ, the Son and the expression of the Father (Jn 1:14, 18), was given external manifestation at the transfiguration (2 P 1:17), in several miracles, and generally in the visible *exousia*, "authority," of Jesus in word and deed. The third and strongest moment of Jesus' time occurred at the end of his earthly life. Christ's assumption of man's temporality and mortality—in the likeness of sinful flesh (Rm 8:3)—was brought to its ultimate consequence in the passion and death on the cross. Jesus' sacrifice was the crucible in which humanity died to sin, to be reborn to God in the resurrection (Rm 4:25; 6:10f). Through his sacrificial passage to God, Jesus attained his own *teleiôsis*, "perfection" or "fulfillment," and as high priest led redeemed humanity to salvation (Heb 5:8-10). This makes it clear that both as the incarnated Son, and as the redeeming Savior, Jesus is the Sacrament of mankind. The old sacrificial institution, represented by the desert tabernacle (Heb 9:1-10) was unable to purify truly from sin, but through "the greater and more perfect tent"—Christ's sacrifice described as a liturgy—every believer, like Jesus himself, secures an eternal redemption (Heb 9:11f). Christ has expressed in the following terms his own involvement in the world: "I came from the Father and have come into the world; again, I am leaving the world and going to the Father" (Jn 16:28). The time of Christ meaningful to us embraces his whole lifetime although, as we have explained, there were in its moments of particular and even definitive significance.

According to a central teaching of the Johannine Christ, the eternal destiny of every man henceforth depends on his acceptance or rejection of Christ as the life-giving Son of God (Jn 3:16-21; 5:25-29). The truly existential faith experience would have no meaning if it were not based on a mystery rooted ontologically in the being of Christ and in his redeeming power. Such a significance of Christ for the individual represents for religious humanity a radical change, since it involves a new understanding of salvation, one in which God making himself man entered visibly into history to reveal its meaning and accomplish the mystery which lies at the center of all. The religious history of the world as seen by the Bible in its Christian interpretation develops in three stages, all centered on Christ and expressible as follows:

1) The economy of preparation, leading to Christ.
2) The center of time: the Son becomes man and redeems humanity.
3) The sacramentary economy: Christ's salvation perpetuated in the Church.

The first of these stages is not immediately clear; it requires an explanation. It is a Christian interpretation, but we regard it as founded on objective data, not on preconceived speculation or prejudiced reading of the texts.

The Preparation of Christ

It has become customary to divide the time of preparation into three periods. The first is that of the *origins*, in which the permanent traits of humankind are described in etiologies, which ascribe them to religious causes (*see* BibTB 1972, pp. 199-205). Because sin entered the world from the beginning, through the instigation of the devil (*see* Ws 2:23f), humanity has been very early divided into just and wicked, and this state of things will remain until the end (Mt 13:49f). Paul will develop the Adam typology, showing the universal range of Christ's redemption (Rm 5:12-21; 1 Cor 15:45). Medieval theology designated the second period as the *primitive economy*, in which man could know God through his works (Rm 1:19-21) and accomplish his will by following the dictates of his own conscience aided by divine inspirations. Gn 4-11, which embody popular traditions in anecdotal form, contain illustrations of permanent truths on which rests man's pursuit of eternal salvation. To this economy of the natural law (Rm 2:14f), succeeded with the vocation of Abraham the *ancient economy proper*, the Old Testament, explicitly oriented towards the salvation revealed and fulfilled in Christ (Grelot 251f).

The Christward orientation regards directly *sacred history*, humanity's relationship with God. But for the believer secular history is also involved, since in God's design all history tends to an end which can be no other than himself. Sacred history received in Jesus' first advent a fulfillment, and it awaits in all confidence its consummation with the second coming, the parousia. Secular history follows its course in the ambiguity of several allegiances. Only at the end will its overall orientation, meaning and positive values be fully revealed in the final establishment of the Kingdom of God. By orientation we mean the inclination of history towards the whole reality of Christ: his appearance in the world, his redeeming work, and his continuing salvific presence in and through the Church, until the end of time.

In other words, the sacred history that preceded the Incarnation tended towards the new and definitive economy of salvation, inaugurated when the time was ripe (Mk 1:15). Jesus came, Paul explained to the Ephesians, to accomplish God's "plan for the fullness of time" (1:10) and it is only when "the fullness of time" had come that he sent his own son to be born of a woman (Gal 4:4).

Implicit expectation of the Christian salvation may be read in the great religions of the world, which contributed indirectly, but providentially to the economy of preparation. But this groping in the dark of man's religious instinct remained without an explicit revelation on God and his will. This was provided in the Old Testament, but incompletely. In fact only in the New Testament do we find a clear interpretation of God's ways in salvation history. This explains the choice of most of the references in the following exposition.

Adam, Abraham, David

The *historical* preparation of Christ *himself* can be traced as far back as Adam, as Luke's geneology seems to indicate (3:23-38). What Christ took over was humanity's temporality, the concrete existential condition, a combination on the one hand of the innate divinely inscribed Godward desire to live and love in happiness, and on the other hand, the struggle, calamity and death resulting from sin. Christ has espoused this human lot as son of Adam, born from a woman (Gal 4:24). He himself was without sin (2 Cor 5:21), but he came "in the likeness of sinful flesh" (R 8:3), accepting its consequences, mainly suffering and mortality (Lyonnet 248-53). Thus, in a way, humanity's past history prepared Christ's coming, conditioned his historical advent, binding him to human temporality. Thus could Christ call men his brethren (Heb 2:11) and redeem humanity from the inside, by transforming it. As a consequence of sin, suffering and death entered the world, and the avenues of salvation appeared closed. A dialectic of division, opposing good and evil, happiness and despair, has characterized the condition of humanity ever since. This could be remedied only through the God-man Mediator and Savior.

Christ's historical preparation is in second place, and more specifically, linked with Abraham and David, as Matthew has indicated in the beginning of his gospel: "Book of the history of the origin of Jesus Christ, the son of David, the son of Abraham" (1:1). Christ's descent from the ancestor of Israel, and from David, its first king, links him firmly to a particular nation and to the Messianic lineage. In the Christian interpretation, founded also on OT texts, the call of Abraham was the first of a series of divine choices and initiatives, which polarized the salvific design, restricting its immediate and direct bearing to a limited circle, the Remnant of Israel. To the common conditioning inherited from the origins was now added the polarization from the *eschaton*, from the future economy of grace, centered on Christ. He would be the Messiah, a descendant of David. This shows how the preparation of the historical Jesus commanded a series of providential interventions that shaped the history of Israel and influenced the course of events even outside this restricted sphere. Matthew has shown in his well structured geneology how Jesus has recapitulated in his person the history of Israel, both as the true Remnant and as the promised King-Messiah. It was God's will that Christ would experience human temporality in that form and save the world in circumstances determined in great part by the conditions prevailing in Palestine at a given period.

The Center of Salvation History

If what has been said is true, it is not difficult to see how the Old Testament is necessary to a complete understanding of Christ: it reveals to us, not only traits of his human personality and of his historical situation, but also important aspects of God's salvific design, which it was Jesus' task to realize. Christ's entry into history marked the fullness of time (Gal 4:4), firstly because with him the *eschaton* invaded in its very center human temporality, secondly because in Christ both man's history (Luke's genealogy) and Israelite history (Matthew's genealogy) were in a sense recapitulated for a new beginning.

In Cullmann's view, "the entire redemptive history unfolds in two movements: the one proceeds from the many to the One; this is the Old Covenant. The other proceeds from the One to the many; this is the New Covenant. At the very midpoint stands the expiatory deed of the death and resurrection of Christ" (p. 117). This concept of salvation history has raised several issues, including the following: (1) Can we rightly speak of salvation-history as the central concept of the Bible, when the Bible contains many theologies and historical perspectives? (2) Were Israel's faith and concept of history really unique in the ancient world? (3) Is there a legitimate distinction between "lived history" (*Geschichte*) and history such as can be recorded and evaluated by all scientific historians (*Historie*)? (4) Is salvation-history existentially relevant for both the individual and the community of faith today? Leaving others to debate these issues (Baker III, 7), we will restate in conclusion that Christ lies at the center of the religious history of the world and in him the two Testaments meet and illumine each other. There is no doubt that Christ is the centre of the New Testament. An interesting question is: what is the center of OT revelation or of OT theology? *See* below, ch. 4 a.

d) The Figures Unified in Christ

Prefigurement, the subject we wish to discuss now, has close connections with typology, especially with the first three components of typology: persons, institutions, events. *Prefigurement* differs from typology as much as figures differ from types. But are not figures also "types?" They can be, yes, and Grelot (p. 266) speaks of "figures" where he obviously means "types." But in French "types" does not have a uniform meaning in current language, and is rather difficult to use as a technical term. We would say that typology is a kind of prefigurement, which is a more comprehensive category. Adam, Isaac, and David appear in the OT as historical figures and should be considered as "types" of Christ. On the other hand, the titles we will examine here, Messiah, Son of God, Son of Man, Servant, Prophet are figures rather than types, having been concepts rather than persons before they became realities in Christ. Only a few prefigurations will be studied here, and in a limited way, in the perspective of the unity of the two Testaments. By emphasizing the fulfillment of the figures in Christ the NT authors have implicitly and even explicitly affirmed the

Christwards inclination of the OT and its contribution to the preparation of Christ and to the understanding of him.

It is not possible to discuss fully the new trends in christology. From a scriptural viewpoint the works of Bruce, France, Higgins, Longenecker, and Marshall are particularly reliable and instructive, as they do not adopt radical views but occasionally criticize them. Here is a summary of the critical assessment H. Boers made of some prominent christologies. "The fundamental problem posed by W. Bousset's *Kyrios Christos* was that the view of Jesus found in the Christology of the NT was not historically true of Jesus himself. This undercut the basic assumption on which NT Christology depends, namely that it is an expression of the truth about the historical Jesus. With his existential interpretation R. Bultmann was in effect resolving NT Christology in an anthropology, a process which was completed by H. Braun. By assuming that the foundation of NT Christology was Jesus' activity, O. Cullmann interprets the primitive Christian formulations of faith as merely the articulation of an already underlying Christology and does not even appear to recognize the problem of Jesus' relationship to the various activities of the Christ. F. Hahn tends to blur the distinct characteristics of Jewish and Hellenistic thought, limits himself to the Synoptics and tacitly assumes that the task is to show the unbroken development from Jesus to the Christology of the New Testament. This tacit assumption becomes the explicit intention in R. Fuller's work" (NTA 15, p. 266). Refusing to admit Kasemann's contention that apocalyptic has been the mother of Christian theology, W.G. Rollins observes that early Christian theology with its focus on Jesus, its positive attitude toward the world, and its choice of preaching rather than scribal activity as its basic mode of expression differs radically from Jewish apocalypticism. Criticism of approaches to particular titles will follow.

Christ the Messiah

The title *ho Christos* has a broader extension than Son of David. Jesus as the Christ is Son of David, but he is more than this, since *ho Christos*, as "The Anointed One," is equivalent to Messiah, and this term received in the course of time more than one acceptation. Even the connection of messiahship with the Davidic line has not been uniform. The messianic expectation, first based on the prophecy of Nathan to David, was also connected by the writer-prophets with the Davidic lineage, although quite early a new David line came to be envisaged instead of the old historical one.

Even though Jesus was probably influenced by the current Jewish messianic concept, he certainly did not claim to be that Messiah who was popularly expected. No Gospel text can be produced to show that Jesus had political ambitions or that he favoured a zealot-type interpretation of messiahship. When faced with a question which was meant to force him to take sides on the political problem, he simply recalled in general terms to his listeners the duty to pay their tribute to the state from which they receive benefits, as long as this seemed reconcilable with their higher duties towards God (Mt 22:17-22 par.). Jesus does not reject the messianic claims made by others on his behalf, but his activity shows that he is not the type of Messiah whom John and the Jews expected (cf. Mt 11:2f). Similar remarks could be made about other texts, including Peter's at Caesarea. There Jesus did not say he was not the Christ; he enjoined the disciples not to say that he was (Mt 16:20), for the probable reason that neither they nor the people could as yet understand what type of Messiah he was (cf. 16:22).

"It is indisputable," Hahn writes, "that Jesus was condemned and crucified as a messianic rebel, and that the concept of the kingly Messiah played a decisive role in the trial of Jesus" (p. 159). The accusation that he was "a messianic pretender" was basically false, since he did not wish, like other "messiahs," to overthrow by force of arms or by a political revolution the established order. It was not, however, without some foundation, since his sayings and his activity revealed his exceptional vocation. He could not completely prevent the people from acclaiming him as the expected King (Mk 11:10) nor refrain from certain actions, like the cleansing of the Temple, which could provide his enemies with a basis for denouncing him to the authorities as a political offender (Lk 23:2). That the messianic claim, diversely understood, was the official reason of Jesus' condemnation on the part of the Romans appears in the *titulus crucis* imposed by them: "the King of the Jews," which implied that the condemned had sought political independence for his people. But for the Jews the claim was different: he had pretended to be "the Christ, the King of Israel," a religious title (Mk 15:32). In our view Jesus was not sentenced to death by the Jews for claiming to be the Messiah (*pace* Hahn), but for pretending to be equal to God ("Sitting at the right hand of God *in heaven*," Mk 14:62), or more precisely for making *himself* God though in the eyes of the Jews he was but a man (Jn 10:33).

According to Ac 2:36 Peter on the day of Pentecost told his listeners: "Let all the house of Israel therefore know assuredly that God has made him both Lord and Christ, this Jesus whom you crucified." Basing their argumentation on this and on other texts, like Mk 12:35-37, some modern critics claim that the concept of Messiah only gradually came to be applied to Jesus, in the context of his exaltation. Ps 110:1, "Sit at my right hand," originally addressed to the earthly Davidic King, was transferred to Jesus now believed to be the exalted Lord. Besides, the already acquired description of Jesus as the apocalyptic Son of Man helped to detach the notion of Messiah from its original form and to make it applicable to Jesus, mainly in his ultimate and transcendent mission. The equation of the Messiah with the Son of Man would appear clearly in Mk 14:61f. This text would represent the oldest form of the primitive concept of Jesus as the *future* Messiah.

There is some truth in the reconstruction just presented in a simplified form. Only after his resurrection was Jesus fully recognized as the Messiah by his followers and became what he was from the beginning by right or by vocation. But to state that the title of Messiah was only secondarily applied to Jesus is an exaggeration. The truth is rather that Jesus was first proclaimed Messiah in the primitive Jewish community and only afterwards Lord, mainly in the Gentile mission. The Christian conviction that Jesus was the Messiah arose from a larger number of factors than several critics would admit. In addition to texts often quoted, like Mt 11:2, not necessarily a product of the community, we should mention: (1) Jesus' own declaration of his special mission, at Nazareth (Lk

4:16-21); (2) the confession of Peter at Caesarea Philippi (Mk 8:29); (3) the qualified acceptance of the title by Jesus on certain occasions (Mt 16:17; Mk 14:61f); (4) explicit messianic identifications in the post-resurrection ministry (Lk 24:26, 46), and, preeminently, (5) the resurrection of Jesus from the dead, according to Ac 13:33f., quoting Ps 2 (*see* Longenecker 80f).

The Son of God

The belief that Jesus was the Messiah, confirmed by his resurrection, seems to have been the basic datum which led the disciples to the understanding of their Master. For Jesus himself, however, it is the consciousness that he was, uniquely Son of God, the Father, that gave him insight into his own mission and guided him to fulfill it (cf. Jn 10:18).

The origin of the title Son of God in the primitive Christian tradition seems to be connected with royal messianism (cf. Ps 2:7; Heb 1:5), in the context of which there are probably early pre-Christian attestations of the titular use of "Son of the Blessed" (cf. Mk 14:61). "The little messianic hymn," perhaps of Jewish origin, preserved in Lk 1:32-34, seems to confirm this interpretation: "He will be great, and will be called the Son of the Most High; and the Lord God will give him the throne of his father David" (v. 32). It should be noted that the Messiah and Son of Man conceptions appear together in Mk 14:61f., where Ps 110 is associated with Dn 7:13. In addition Hahn (p. 286) points to 1 Th 1:9-10 as a significant text in that connection: there to the Son are attributed functions which elsewhere belong to the Son of Man, as he who comes from heaven. This would indicate that the title Son of God was early associated with the eschatological work of Jesus. But the exaltation of Jesus soon became more prominent in Christian belief than the expectation of the parousia.

For some critics the title "Son of God" of the early tradition was applied *to the earthly Jesus* on Hellenistic soil, where the transfer was made easier by the *theios anēr*—"divine man," conceptions prevalent there. In contrast to this it must be said that the parallels produced do not prove that Greek religious speculation or pagan beliefs have influenced the course of the early Christian belief or even its formulation (*see* Hengel). Even W. Bousset wonders how "the basic ideas and attitudes of Hellenistic Oriental piety could have come to Paul, the rabbinically minded Jew" (p. 21). The fact that the titles "Messiah" and "Son of God" are brought together in a number of passages (cf. Mt 16:16; 26:63; Lk 4:41; Ac 9:20-22; Jn 11:27; 20:31) only shows that the NT writers "were aware of their distinct connotations and considered Son of God as the logical implication of Messiah" (Longenecker 94). E. Pinto could conclude as follows his examination of "the testimony of the Gospels:" "Consequently, the title Son of God was no alien import and cannot be interpreted simply in terms of popular religious notions circulating in the Hellenistic world. It is Matthew among the Synoptics who gives increased prominence to the Sonship of Jesus, and John who makes this theme the cornerstone of his christology. Mark and Luke unquestionably believe Jesus to be the Son of God, but only repeat traditional wording" (p. 90). It is useful to examine the literary *Vorlage* of the title, and the possible stages of its use in the NT, but the self-awareness and the revelations of Jesus himself should not be left out of the picture: since Jesus obviously spoke of God as being uniquely his Father, it is difficult not to conclude that he considered himself to be his Son in a unique way, so that the Gospel texts can be believed when they report self-revelations of himself in terms of sonship.

In a well documented study A. Descamps has examined the possible influence of the concept "Son of Man" on that of "Son of God," and the connection between "Son of God" and Messiah (pp. 557-70). E.D. Freed believes, on his part, that the title Son of Man in the Fourth Gospel is only a variation for Son of God and Son. So that it is useless to look for a Son-of-Man christology in John. That contamination took place between "Son of God" and "Son of Man" is a distinct possibility and can perhaps be documented. Outside the gospels the title "Son of God," understood transcendently, replaced that of "Son of Man," which very soon became obsolete (*see* A. Gelin, "Messianisme," *S.D.B.,* vol. 5, c. 1209). According to M. de Jonge the title "Son of God" was actually used to correct

Jewish misunderstanding of the title "Messiah."

A traditio-historical investigation of the type Hahn proposes (278-346) can uncover strata in the NT application of the title "Son of God" to Christ, that is sometimes illuminating. In connection with the baptism and the transfiguration, Hahn himself confesses that "it is, however, by no means a simple matter to distinguish in detail earlier and later parts, earlier and later meanings of the statements. It is not accidental that the proposals of a traditio-historical analysis deviate widely from one another and are occasionally withdrawn by their authors" (p. 334). This is quite instructive, coming from Hahn, who is himself an investigator of the traditio-historical school.

The Son of Man

Several books and scores of articles have been devoted in recent years to the discussion of the Gospel usage of the expression "Son of Man." This is not the place to review the whole debate. It is, however, necessary to adopt a position on a few key issues, like the authenticity of the sayings where "Son of Man" occurs. I agree with those who claim that at least some "Son of Man" sayings go back to Jesus himself, while it remains possible, even probable, that in some cases the evangelists have introduced the title in other sayings on the basis of Jesus' thought expressed elsewhere.

According to J. Jeremias "Son of Man" is the only title used by Jesus of himself whose authenticity is to be taken seriously (even "Son of God," "Messiah," "Son of David" would not stand the test of authenticity as self-designations used by Jesus himself). Of the 51 Son of Man sayings in the gospels 37 have parallels where the term "Son of Man" is replaced by *ego* or other designations. These parallels probably represent the earlier traditions. Other occurrences can be eliminated as mistranslations of a generic or indefinite Aramaic expression *bar 'enaša* (=simply "man"), for example, in Mk 2:10; 3:28f; Mt 8:20; 11:19 and par. Despite this, a solid core of Son of Man sayings remains, in which *ho huios tou anthrôpou* was intended as a title from the beginning: Mk 13:26

par.; 14:62 par.; Mt 24:27; 37b-39 par.; Lk 17:24, 26; Mt 10:23; 25:31; Lk 17:22, 30; 18:8; 21:36; Jn 1:51. Of these only Jn 1:51 does not concern the future, but even this text may have referred originally to the future epiphany of the Son of Man (*see* Jeremias 257-76).

Another important investigator in the matter, Carsten Colpe, recognizes as authentically from Jesus himself eight future-apocalyptic Son of Man sayings, which, "seem to stand up to critical analysis." If I am not mistaken, they are Mt 10:23; 24:27, 30, 37; Lk 17:30; 18:8; 21:36; 22:69. As can be seen, five of these sayings are represented directly in Jeremias' list of references where "Son of Man" was certainly a title from the beginning; the others coincide indirectly as parallels (*see* Colpe 430-61). Only as an authentic dominical saying can Mt 10:23 have survived the tendency to ascribe to Jesus a work among the Gentiles (p. 437). In the case of Lk 21:36 "if one accepts the principle that inauthenticity has to be proved rather than authenticity, this saying will have to be attributed to Jesus" (pp. 434f). According to Colpe "the apocalyptic Son of Man is a symbol of Jesus' assurance of 'perfecting' (through the resurrection). With a shift from the assurance to the one who has it, the whole process may be interpreted as a dynamic and functional equating of Jesus and the coming Son of Man with the future perfecting of Jesus in view. On this basis, the primitive community then made a static personal identification accomplished already in the present Jesus" (p. 441).

Do those Son of Man sayings retained as coming from the primary Gospel sources originate with Jesus or the primitive community? According to Jeremias it can at least be shown that the application of the title Son of Man to Christ is *early Palestinian tradition*. Several arguments could be presented showing that the Son of Man sayings have pre-Easter origin. The apocalyptic Son of Man sayings which belonged to the earliest stratum of the Gospel tradition must in essentials go back to Jesus himself. Otherwise we cannot understand why the community at a very early stage avoided the title, not using it once in a confessional formula, and yet handed it down in the sayings of Jesus. This does not mean that Jesus created the title "Son of Man" himself. It had been used in the

Jewish apocalyptic, first collectively in Dn 7:13f, and later in the Similitudes of Ethiopian Enoch, IV Ezra, and elsewhere, to designate a superhuman figure with transcendent features who would achieve a victory over the pagan rulers by supernatural means and be set by the Lord of the Spirits on the throne of glory. In the earliest Son of Man *logia* found in the gospels "Son of Man" is also a term of glory. There is much to suggest that the revelation of the Son of Man was first imagined in the form of an assumption to God. For Jesus the epiphany of the Son of Man expressed a supra-national hope destined to comfort and strengthen the disciples in the face of hardships springing from the eschatological persecutions and tribulations.

Even though Jesus always speaks of the Son of Man in the third person, it does not follow (against Wellhausen, Bultmann, and others) that Jesus thought the Son of Man as a saving figure distinct from himself, whose coming he awaited and that it was the community which identified the Son of Man with Jesus. Lk 12:8f, where Jesus clearly distinguished between the Son of Man and himself, should be read in the light of the parallel Mt 10:32 which has *ego* instead of "Son of Man." It is impossible to suppose that Jesus visualized himself as a mere forerunner or prophet of the Son of Man, since he clearly claimed to be the fulfillment of the messianic hope. The explanation of the textual anomalies, writes Jeremias, is that *when Jesus speaks in the third person he does not distinguish between two different figures, but between his present and his future state of exaltation: he is not yet the Son of Man, but when he has been exalted, he will become the Son of Man* (p. 276). By fulfilling his mission as the Suffering Servant of God Jesus expected to pass from the humble state of his earthly life to the future glory.

Other scholars have of course defended diverging views. The work of H.E. Tödt has exercised a wide influence in recent research. He deserves praise for his thorough investigation of the Synoptic tradition, but his basis for interpreting the data has been questioned on several important points. In particular the stages of development he has identified do not seem to stand the test of unprejudiced countercheck, especially where it is claimed that the early church identified the risen Jesus with the coming Son of Man and then proceeded to read back the title into the earthly ministry of Jesus as a means of expressing his authority on earth (cf. Mk 2:10). The community may have done so in a few passages, but a general statement on the matter can only be misleading and is unfounded, as I.H. Marshall has shown (NTS 12, 1965f, 327-51).

In "Son of Man' Imagery . . ." Longenecker has expressed the acceptable view that the title "Son of Man" should be understood in terms of Jesus' redemptive identification with humanity and his sufferings for humanity as the way by which he entered into his glory. A.J.B. Higgins has particularly investigated the OT roots of the christological titles. We cannot here mention all his suggestive comments. He discovers the intrusion of the Son of Man into the Son of God concept where the author of Hebrews marshalls a series of OT quotations in the first two chapters, including Psalm 8. The verses following Heb 2:5-8 make it clear, he thinks, that the author in quoting Ps 8 "has in mind a Son of Man christology, for the promise of sovereignty held out to man has been fulfilled in Jesus as the Son of Man" (p. 136). Later, in Heb 5, we have a quotation of Ps 2:7 followed by the words: "You are a priest forever according to the order of Melchizedek." The result is, writes Higgins, "the intrusion of the Son of Man into the Son of God concept, and, on the other hand, the association of the idea of the Son of God with that of the High-Priest. The importance of this association for our present purpose lies in the close affinities between the ideas of the Son of Man and the High-Priest, and the possible source of the application to Jesus of Ps 4" (Ibid.). Also Walker suggests that Ps 8 forms the most probable link between the primitive Christian use of Ps 110:1 and Dn 7:13.

The title "Son of Man" as used by Jesus is particularly associated with the idea of judgment (Mt 16:27; Jn 5:27). This is not surprising, considering that Jesus, foreseeing the impending coming of the Kingdom, calls the people to repentance. This invitation takes a particular sense of urgency precisely in these texts where the Son of Man appears in the function of judge (cf. Mt 25:31f). At least two authors, Cortes and Leivestad, have suggested that "*the* Son of *the* Man" is equivalent to "the Son of Adam," or in Pauline terms "the second Adam" (cf. 1 Cor 15:45). A connection may have been seen by Jesus himself, since as we have said above he has used the title also to express his solidarity with the humanity he had come to save, a consideration brought out with insistence in Heb 2:15-18. Finally, we have to reckon with the possibility M. Black believes, that behind the use of Ps 118:22 at Mk 12:10 (the "rejected stone" text which concludes the parable of the wicked husbandmen), there lies the Hebrew word-play between *eben*, "stone," and *ben*, "son." In this perspective Lk 20:18 seems to refer to Dn 2:34. It is conceivable that already in Daniel the Stone concealed the word for Son, a cryptogram there for Israel, corresponding to the Son of Man of Dn 7.

According to R. Schnackenburg, all thirteen texts in John which speak of the Son of Man form a consistent and well-knit whole. The Son of Man is the Johannine Messiah, the giver of life and the judge. "He alone can and does exercise these functions in his actual activity, because he is the Son of Man who has come down from heaven and ascended there again" (p. 532). Other texts possibly refer to the title in a somewhat different sense. One of these could be the "*ecce homo*" (Jn 19:5). The trial of Jesus in John undoubtedly has overtones. To the theologically minded evangelist it probably represented another and greater "trial" on a cosmic scale. "At most, one could find in the '*ecce homo*' an indirect allusion to the 'Son of Man,' insofar as this title also designates the Messiah in the Johannine sense (cf. 12:34). But there is not the least suggestion that Jesus is the archetypal 'Man' in the sense of any '*Anthropos*' myth. According to the context, however, the primary meaning of the scene is again different. Pilate dismisses 'this man' contemptuously; immediately afterwards, the Jews themselves accuse him of 'claiming to be Son of God' (19:7)—and this, in truth, is what he is!" (pp. 532f).

The Servant of God

In Second Isaiah four lyric enclaves depict a perfect disciple of Yahweh sent to preach the true faith to nations and destined to be handed over as an expiating sacrificial victim with the hope of a mysterious rehabilitation. The poems do not follow a very definite plan and the same themes are taken up repeatedly. In the *first* song (Is 42:1-9) Yahweh himself speaks, introducing his Servant, his chosen one, to whom he grants his spirit to accomplish the mission entrusted. The *second* song (49:1-6) returns to the same ideas and completes them, now with the Servant speaking, now with Yahweh. In the *third* song (50:4-11) the Servant describes the mistreatment that the fulfillment of his mission draws down on him. Yet he renews his trust in Yahweh, in the one who exhorts believers to listen to the voice of his messengers. The *fourth* song, a sort of prophetic liturgy or elegy, describes the Servant's sacrifice in its various aspects: expiatory suffering, intercession, personal rehabilitation, and justification of the many. It must be noted here that some authors, like Coppens, do not consider Is 50:4-11 as a Servant poem, but describe vv. 4-9 as an "autophony" of the hagiograph (p. 110). In addition, Is 42:5-9 is not generally accepted as being part of the first poem, but only vv. 1-4.

Servant research has progressed in recent years, without, however, reaching a consensus on all important matters. In *Le Messianisme* Joseph Coppens has presented his own views and a masterful survey of all the relevant debate, both for the OT (41-113) and for the NT (195-241). According to the Catholic exegete N. Fuglister, the Servant was seen by the OT as *an individual*, as a prophetic figure *of the future*, as the definitive mediator to come, with a mission for both Israel and the nations, a mission to be accomplished in two phases, one preceding, the other following his sacrificial death. For Fuglister there exists in the Servant Poems an implicit ascription of priestly and royal traits to the saving figure, especially in the vocabulary used. For some scholars, in the fourth poem the man of sorrows could represent the exiled generation, "taken away," "cut off from the land of the living (=the Holy Land)" buried "among the wicked" in Babylon (Is 53:8f). It atoned for the sins of the "many" (the past generation) so that the "many" (the future generations) might live and prosper (53:10).

According to Coppens, Is 53:2-10a appears as a psalm of individual lament, but expresses the sentiments of a group of penitent Jews, or more generally of Israel purified by the Exile, and now composed in a later prophet's view of the just only (60:21; 61:9). On the other hand, Is 53:11 would be the voice of those who although never unfaithful suffered exile just the same and so by their vicarious suffering obtained divine pardon for all (p. 112). Thus would Coppens answer the objection to the collective interpretation: the prophets considered the punishment of Israel as deserved while the Servant appears as an innocent victim. Hahn notes (p. 55) that Is 53 is "the earliest evidence for the idea of a vicarious expiatory death," especially one extended to all. Is 53 has independently carried further what was obviously an older motif. As E. Lohse has shown, the conception of death for one's own sins and as a vicarious atonement received a large diffusion in late Palestinian Judaism. Surprisingly, the whole of later Judaism consistently avoids reference to Is 53 in its statements about expiation (Lohse 107).

Some verses of Is 53 constitute a compendium of the Suffering Servant theology and are remarkably although freely reflected in 2 Cor 5:21. The primary thought-pattern of this Pauline verse can be described as follows (Hoad): "Christ (a) who had done no wrong, (b) was made an offering for our sins, (c) that we might come into a right relationship with God through him." The same precisely is said of the Suffering Servant in Is 53:

v. 9: Though he has done no wrong . . .

v. 10: Truly he gave his life as a sin-offering (*'asham*) . . .

v. 11: Through his suffering, my servant shall justify many . . .

The Servant's sacrifice is described as an expiatory sin-offering of the *'asham* type (*see* Lv 7:1-10), which in the Septuagint is rendered by *peri hamartias*, offering the possibility of reading Rm 8:3 as follows: "God sent his Son in the likeness of sinful flesh *as a sin offering*, thereby condemning sin in the flesh." There is also one clear case at least in which *hamartia* is used alone to translate *'asham* (making the reference to Is 53:10 in 2 Cor 5:21 more obvious): among the oblations in which the priests have a right to share, Nb 18:9 includes *ulekôl 'ashamam*, which the Septuagint translates literally: *kai apo pasôn tôn hamartiôn*, "and from all the (sacrifices for) sins."

Apart from such direct connections of the Suffering Servant theme with the sin-offering interpretation of 2 Cor 5:21 and Rm 8:3, other texts suggest the same conclusion, those namely which describe the suffering mission of Jesus as being "according to the Scriptures" (1 Cor 15:3), thereby alluding primarily to the mission of the Suffering Servant (*see* Ac 4:24, 28; 8:26-40). This association reflects the teaching of Jesus himself: "This is my blood of the covenant, which is poured out for many" (*huper pollôn*; Mk 14:24); "For this is my blood of the covenant, which is poured out for many (*peri pollôn*) for the forgiveness of sins" (Mt 26:28); "The Son of Man came not to *be served* but *to serve*, and to *give his life* as a ransom *for many*" (*lutron anti pollôn*; Mk 10:45). It is quite certain that the term *polloi* of these texts corresponds to the Hebrew *rabbim* (LXX: *polloi*), used five times in the fourth Servant Song. Hahn, who tends to minimize the presence of the Servant motif in the Gospels, admits that "a direct allusion to the prophetic text must be assumed for the Markan-Matthaean form of the word over the cup" (p. 59). On the Servant for Jesus, *see* France.

Apart from the verbal references, certain *actions* performed by Jesus in the last days of his life recall also the fourth Servant Song. The *silence* he observes before the Sanhedrin (Mk 14:61), before Pilate (15:5), before Herod (Lk 23:9), corresponds to the Suffering Servant's attitude (Is 53:7). Like the Servant too, Jesus intercedes for sinners (Lk 23:54), although he has been ranked with scoundrels (Lk 22:37; Is 53:12). In addition, the anointing at Bethany suggests (cf. Mk 14:8) that in normal circumstances the Crucified would have received only a dishonorable burial as did the Servant who "was assigned a grave among the wicked and a burial place with evildoers" (Is 53:9). Even if a collective interpretation of the Isaian poems is retained, such applications remain relevant. Does not Jesus personify in a way the Remnant of Israel, and is not the true Messianic people represented by him?

Is 42:1-4 is quoted in Mt 12:18-21 in a secondary application of the text to Jesus' ministry as being carried out without ostentation and with a will to avoid conflicts. By quoting Is 53:4 in his gospel (8:17), Matthew wishes to prove also that Jesus' therapeutic activity fulfills Scripture, and therefore God's will there manifested.

Matthew's application of the text to a rather different situation can be justified from the fact that Jesus, the Servant, could relieve men from their temporal ills precisely because he took upon himself the expiation of sin, the ultimate source of all evils.

The Eschatological Prophet

According to the Fourth Gospel the delegates of the Pharisees asked John: "Why are you baptizing, if you are neither the Christ, nor Elijah, nor the prophet?" (1:25). As this question shows, three figures filled the horizon of popular expectation: the Messiah, Elijah *redivivus*, and the prophet, that is, the eschatological prophet. Other Gospel texts are connected with similar motifs, and we shall try to see more clearly what traditions or beliefs they reflect. Since it was felt that prophecy had disappeared, at least for a time, and insecurity for the future became an increasing worry for the Israelite nation, the expectation of a prophet who would bring divine guidance and indicate the ways of salvation naturally became more and more intense as the years passed without a sign from heaven (Ps 74:9). But the expectation of *the eschatological prophet* took two quite different forms: one was connected with Moses, on the basis of Dt. 18:15-18; the other, with the person of Elijah, on the basis of Ml 3:1, 23f.

Although no indication is found in the NT that John himself felt or claimed to be the eschatological prophet, he was understandably believed to be such by those who knew him. The angel of the annunciation to Zechariah uses the words of Ml 4:6 to describe the boy's future role, as to go before the Lord "in the Spirit and power of Elijah" (Lk 1:6f), while Zechariah himself in the *Benedictus* calls the future Baptist "the prophet of the Most High" (1:76). According to vv. 76-79 of this canticle on the birth of John, however, this prophet is not the forerunner of God, but of the Messiah Jesus. The earliest Gospel evidence for the equating of the Baptist to Elijah within the Christian tradition is found in Mt 11:14, and must be the work of the evangelist, not of the common source Q. While in Mk 9:11-13 the same equation is indicated in the suggested analogy

between the suffering of the Baptist and that of Jesus; the identification of John with Elijah is explicit in the same context of the
Transfiguration in a remark of Matthew himself (17:13), showing
that also in 11:14 it should be ascribed to the evangelist.

In the Fourth Gospel John the Baptist is quoted as denying
explicitly to be Elijah (1:21). This probably reflects the historical
truth. Synoptic texts also show that the identification was not taken
for granted by others (Mk 6:14f; 8:28). But, as R.E. Brown notes,
"early Christian theology saw in the role of Elijah the best way to
interpret the relation of John the Baptist to Jesus, namely John the
Baptist was to the coming of Jesus what Elijah was to have been to
the coming of the Lord" (*The Gospel According to John* 48f).

Dt 18:15-18 did not refer originally to the eschatological
prophet, but it was given this sense later. The Old Testament
supplies no clear evidence of the hope for an *eschatological*
prophet like Moses, but this may have been associated with the
'ebed Yhwh, "Servant of God," who was regarded as a prophetic
figure. The difficulty with the identification of the eschatological
prophet stems from the fact that there have been "successive
re-readings on the prophet of the future" (*see* on this Coppens, *Le
Messianisme* . . . 114-44). The Qumran Essenes expected an
eschatological prophet recalling Dt 18:15-18 (*Community Rule*
9:11 and 4Q *Testimonia*). In Ac 3:22 Jesus is identified in Peter's
sermon precisely with the prophet of Dt 18. Jesus himself, however, referred in Nazareth to another anointed prophet, that of Is
61:1f (Lk 4:17-19). To this figure can be referred also the bestowal
of the Spirit to Jesus at his baptism (*see* also Ac 10:37f).

The Gospel texts on the Baptist's preaching (Mt 3:11f par.)
constitute an ideal *locus* for the study of *the theology of Q*, since it
is possible to compare here, better than elsewhere, the Marcan
tradition and the Q tradition. Only in Mt/Lk do we find the impending
judgment as a motivation for the immediate conversion. Behind *Q*
recent scholars discover self-styled groups or communities of end-
time whose leaders took seriously the apocalyptic expectation of
an imminent end (*Naherwartung*) through a sudden and decisive
intervention of God. More precisely, the tradition represented by *Q*,
of prophetical type, proclaimed the proximity of the Kingdom, rec-

ognized in Jesus a prophet of end-time and identified him with the Son of Man, the eschatological Judge (*see* P. Hoffmann, *Studien zur Theologie der Logienquelle*, Muenster 1972, 15-33). Possibly, the essence of the Baptist's preaching consisted of the following message: "I baptize you with water, the coming one will baptize you with fire." It is quite certain that the *Q* version is closer to the historical John than the watered down message preserved in Mk. *Q*-preachers could join the Baptist's message to their collection of Jesus' sayings, because for them Jesus the Son of Man was this eschatological Judge whom John had not fully identified.

We have not, of course, offered an exhaustive study of the prefigurement of Christ in the Old Testament. Bruce has devoted all chapter 8 of his book *This is That* to the title "Shepherd King," showing especially how Zc 9-14 present a pattern of revelation and response which the Evangelists recognize as recurring in the story of Jesus. Matthew's gospel reflects a special interest in Jesus as the *Shepherd of Israel* (*see* Martin). Already in 2:6 he is referred to as "a leader who will shepherd my people Israel" (cf. Mi 5:1). Later Jesus himself declares: "I was sent only to the lost sheep of the house of Israel" (15:24). The connection of this thought with the healing ministry is suggested by the wording of the summaries in 4:23 and 9:35f, which seem related to Ezk 34, where we read that God himself will become the shepherd of Israel, leading the flock to good pasturage, and taking a special care of the weak and wounded sheep (v. 16), until, in the Messianic times, a faithful Shepherd is raised, the new David, who will be prince among the people. Particularly interesting in this respect is the great judgment scene where the Son of Man as the Shepherd King separates sheep from goats (25:31f), fulfilling the end-time separation pre-announced in the parables of ch. 13 (vv. 30, 49).

All the figures we have examined, and others that could only be mentioned, have been fulfilled and unified in Christ, who is thus the center of convergence of the whole Bible. In addition, his saving work has brought to fulfillment vast promises and latent hopes that prophecy had proclaimed in terms that only the reality would completely unveil (2 Cor 3:12-18). Bruce has summarized in the following lines the achievement of Jesus with regard to the Old Testament expectation. "In Jesus the promise is confirmed, the covenant is renewed, the prophecies are fulfilled, the law is vindicated, salvation is brought near, sacred history has reached its climax, the perfect sacrifice has been offered and accepted, the great priest over the household of God has taken his seat at God's right hand, the Prophet like Moses has been raised up, the Son of David reigns, the kingdom of God has been inaugurated, the Son of Man has received dominion from the Ancient of Days, the Servant of the Lord, having been smitten to death for his people's transgression and borne the sin of many, has accomplished the divine purpose, has seen light after the travail of his soul and is now exalted and extolled and made very high" (*This is That* 21).

Bibliography for Sections A and B

ALBREKTSON, B. *History and the Gods. An Essay on the Idea of Historical Events as Divine Manifestations in the Ancient Near East and in Israel*, Conjectanea Biblica, OT Ser. 1 (Lund 1967).

ALBRIGHT, W.F. *From the Stone Age to Christianity* (2nd ed., New York 1957).

AMSLER, S. "Les deux sources de la théologie de l'histoire dans l'Ancien Testament," R.Th.Ph., 3e série, t. 19 (1969) 235-46.

BARR, J. *Old and New in Interpretation: A Study of the Two Testaments* (London 1966).

BEAUCHAMP, P. *L'un et l'autre Testament. Essai de lecture* (Paris 1976) 74-105.

BERTEN, I. *Histoire, révélation et foi. Dialogue avec Wolfhart Pannenberg* (Bruxelles 1969).

BLANK, S.H. *Prophetic Thought: Essays and Addresses* (Cincinnati 1977). See the list of essays the book contains in CBQ 1978, p. 648.

BRUCE, F.F. *This is That: the New Testament Development of Some Old Testament Themes* (Exeter 1968).

BULTMANN, R. "Prophecy and Fulfillment," in C. Westermann, ed.. *Essays on Old Testament Hermeneutics* (50-75).

CLEMENTS, R.E. *Prophecy and Covenant* (London 1965).

COTHENET, E. "Prophétisme dans le Nouveau Testament," *Supplé*-ment au Dictionnaire de la Bible, vol. 8 (1971) cc. 1222-37.

CULLMANN, O. *Christ and Time* (London 1962).

Idem, "The Connection of Primal Events and End Events with the New Testament Redemptive History," in B.W. Anderson, ed., *The Old Testament and Christian Faith* (New York 1969) 115-23.

DAICHES, S. "Balaam, a Babylonian *'Baru.'* The Episode of Nb 22, 2-24 and some Babylonian Parallels," in *Hilprecht Anniversary Volume* (London 1909) 60-70, also re-printed *Bible Studies* (London 1950), 110-119.

DANIÉLOU, J. *Essai sur le mystère de l'histoire* (Paris 1953).

DONNER, H. *Israel unter den Volkern*, Suppl. VT 11 (Leiden 1964).

EICHRODT, W. "Is Typological Exegesis an Appropriate Method?" in C. Westermann, ed., *Essays . . .* 224-44.

ELLERMEIER, F. *Prophetie in Mari und in Israel* (Herzberger 1968).

FENSHAM, F.C. "The Covenant as Giving Expression to the Relationship between Old and New Testament," *Tyndale Bulletin* 22 (1971) 82-94.

FREEDMAN, D.N. "The Biblical Idea of History," *Interpretation* 21 (1967) 32-49.

FRIEDRICH, G. "Prophets and Prophecies in the New Testament," *TDNT* 6 (1968) 828-61.

GEFFRÉ, C. "La théologie de l'histoire comme problème herméneutique: W. Pannenberg," *Etudes théol. et relig.* 46 (1971) 13-28.

GRELOT, P. *Sens chrétien de L'Ancien Testament. Esquisse d'un traité dogmatique* (Tournai 1962).

GUILLAUME, A. *Prophecy and Divination* (London 1938); according to Albrektson 302, G. has exaggerated the similarity between the Hebrew seer and the Mesopotamian diviner.

GUNNEWEG, A.H.J. *Mündliche und schriftliche Tradition der vorex-ilischen Prophetenbucher als Problem der neueren*

HALDAR, W. *Associations of Cult Prophets among the Ancient Semites* (Upsala 1945).

HARRINGTON, W. "A Biblical View of History," *Irish Theol. Quart.* 39 (1962) 206-222.

HARVEY, J. *Le "Rib-Pattern," réquisitoire prophétique sur la rupture de l'Alliance. Etude d'une formule littéraire de l'Ancien Testament,* coll. *Studia* 22 (Montreal-Paris 1967), in shorter form in *Biblica* 1962, pp. 172-196.

HEMPEL, J. *Die Mehrdeutigkeit der Geschichte als Problem der prophetischen Theologie* (Göttingen 1936).

HESCHEL, A. *The Prophets* (New York 1962).

HÖLSCHER, G. *Die Profeten* (Leipzig 1914).

JACOB, E. "Les prophètes et la philosophie de l'histoire," *Et. Th. Rel.* 1946, pp. 135-156.

Idem, L'Ancien Testament et la vision de l'histoire," *R.Th.Ph.* 3rd ser. 7 (1957) 254-65.

JEPSEN, A. "The Scientific Study of the Old Testament," in C. Westermann, ed., *Essays* . . . 246-84.

JEREMIAS, JORG. *Kultprophetie und Gerichtsverkündigung in der späten Königszeit Israels* (Neukirchen 1970); on this book see CBQ 1971, 589f.

JOHNSON, A.R. *The Cultic Prophet in Ancient Israel* (Cardiff 1944).

KELLER, K.A. "L'Ancien Testament et la theologie de l'histoire," *R. Th. Ph.,* 3rd ser. 13 (1963) 124-51.

LAMBERT, W.G. "History and the Gods: a review article," *Orientalia* 39 (1970) 170-77.

LARGEMENT, R. "Les oracles de Bileam et la mantique suméro-akkadienne," in *Mémorial du Cinquantenaire de l'Ecole des Langues Orientales anciennes de l'Istitut Catholique de Paris* (Paris 1967) 37-50.

LIMBURG, J. "The Prophets in Recent Study: 1967-1977," *Interpretation* 32 (1978) 56-68.

LINDBLOM, J. *Prophecy in Ancient Israel* (Oxford 1962).

LYS, D. *The Meaning of the Old Testament* (New York 1967).

MAC KENZIE, R.A.F. *Faith and History in the Old Testament* (Minneapolis 1963).

MALEVEZ, L. "La vision chrétienne de l'histoire," NRT 71 (1949) 113-34; 244-64 (faith in K. Barth).

MARROU, H.-I. *Théologie de l'histoire* (Paris 1968).

MORAN, W.L. "New Evidence from Mari in the History of Prophecy," *Biblica* 50 (1969) 15-56.

MORIARTY, F.L. "Prophet and Covenant," *Gregorianum* 46 (1965) 817-33.

Idem.,"Antecedents of Israelite Prophecy in the Ancient Near East," *Studia Missionalia* 22 (1973) 255-77.

MOWINCKEL, S. *Prophecy and Tradition* . . . (Oslo 1946).

MUILENBURG, J. "The Office of the Prophet in Ancient Israel," in J. Ph. Hyatt, ed., *The Bible in Modern Scholarship* (London 1965) 74-97.

MURPHY, R.E. "The Relationship between the Testaments," CBQ 26 (1964) 349-59.

NEHER, A. *L'essence du prophétisme* (Paris 1955).

NIEBUHR, R. *Faith and History* (New York 1949).

NORTH, R. "Pannenberg's Historicizing Exegesis," *Heythrop Journal* 12 (1971) 377-400 (summary in NTA 16, p. 142).

O'COLLINS, G.G. "Revelation as History," *Heythrop Journal* 7 (1966) 394-406.

PANNENBERG, W. "Redemptive Event and History," in C. Westermann, *Essays* . . . 314-35.

PROCKSCH, O. *Geschichtsbetrachtung und geschichtliche Ueberlieferung bei den vorexilischen Propheten* (Leipzig 1902).

RAMLOT, L. "Prophétisme," *Supplément au Dictionnaire de la Bible* 8 (1971) cc. 811-1222.

RENDTORFF, R. "Erwägungen zur Frühgeschichte des Prophetentums in Israel," ZThK 59 (1962) 145-67.

Idem., "Geschichte und Wort im Alten Testament," *Evangelische Theologie* 22 (1962) 621-49.

ROBINSON, T.H. *Prophecy and the Prophets in Ancient Israel* (London 1923).

ROSS, J.F. "Prophecy in Hamath, Israel, and Mari," HarvThRev 63 (1970) 1-28.

SCHARBERT, J. "Die prophetische Literatur. Der Stand der

Forschung," in H. Cazelles, ed., *De Mari à Qumran* (Göttingen 1969) 58-118.

SKINNER, J. *Prophecy and Religion* (Cambridge 1936).

SMART, J.D. *The Interpretation of Scripture* (Philadelphia 1961).

VAWTER, F.B. "Etudes récentes sur les prophètes," *Concilium* 10 (1965) 99-110.

VERMEYLEN, J. "Les prophètes de la conversion face aux traditions sacrales de l'Israël ancien," RevThLouv 9 (1978) 5-32.

VON RAD, G. *Old Testament Theology* vols. I and II (Study edition, London 1975), esp. vol. II, pp. 6-125.

WENHAM, G.J. "History and the Old Testament," in G. Brown, ed., *History, Criticism & Faith: Four Exploratory Studies* (Downers Grove, IL 1976).

WESTERMANN, C. *Forms of Prophetic Speech* (Philadelphia 1967).

Idem., "The Way of the Promise through the Old Testament," in B.W. Anderson, ed., *The Old Testament and Christian Faith* 200-24.

WOLFF, H.W. "The Hermeneutics of the Old Testament," in C. Westermann, ed., *Essays* . . . 160-99.

Idem., "The Understanding of History in the Prophets," *ibid.*, 336-56.

WRIGHT, G.E. *The Old Testament against its Environment* (London 1950).

ZIMMERLI, W. "Offenbarung im Alten Testament," *Evangelische Theologie* 22 (1962) 15-31.

Idem., "Der 'Prophet' im Pentateuch," in G. Braulik, ed., *Studien zum Pentateuch: Walter Kornfeld zum 60. Geburtstag* (Herder 1977) 197-211.

Bibliography for Prophecy, Apocalyptic, and Eschatology

ALTMANN, P. *Erwählungstheologie und Universalismus im Alten Testament* (Berlin 1964).

BOWMAN, J. "Prophets and Prophecy in Talmud and Midrash," *The Evangelical Quarterly* 22 (1950), three art.

CARMIGNAC, J. "Les dangers de l'eschatologie," NTS 17 (1971)

365-90.

Idem, "La future intervention de Dieu selon la pensee de Qumran," in M. Delcor, ed., *Qumran. Sa piete, sa theologie et son milieu*, BiblETL 46 (1978) 219-29.

COTHENET, E. "Prophétisme dans le Nouveau Testament," *Supplément au Dictionnaire de la Bible* 8 (1971) 1222-1337.

DELCOR, M. *et al.*, *Apocalypses et théologie de l'espérance: Congres de Toulouse, 1975* (Paris 1977); list of essays in CBQ 1978, p. 656.

DODD, C.H. "The Prophecy of Caiaphas (John XI, 47-53)," in *Neotestamentica et Patristica* . . . (Leiden 1962) 133-43.

DÜRR, L. *Ursprung und Ausbau der israelitisch-judischen Heilserwartung* (Berlin 1925).

FOHRER, G. "Die Struktur der alttestamentlichen Eschatologie," *Th.Lit.Z* 85 (1960) 401-20.

FRIEDRICH, G. "Prophets and Prophecies in the New Testament," TDNT 6 (1968) 828-61.

GALOT, J. "Eschatologie Biblique," *Dictionnaire de Spiritualité 28 (1960) 1021-42.*

GRECH, P. "Interprophetic Reinterpretation and Old Testament Eschatology," Augustinianum 8 (1969) 235-65, summarized in *Theology Digest* 18 (1970) 154-63.

GRELOT, P. *Sens chrétien de l'Ancien Testament* (Paris 1962) 329-403.

GRESSMANN, H. *Ursprung der israelitisch-jüdischen Eschatologie* (Göttingen 1905).

GRONBACH, J.H. "Zur Frage der Eschatologie in der Verkündigung der Gerichtspropheten," *Svensk Exegetisk Arsbok* 24 (1959) 5-10.

GUNKEL, H. *Schöpfung und Chaos in Urzeit und Endzeit* (Göttingen 1895).

HANSON, P.D. *The Dawn of Apocalyptic* (Philadelphia 1975); on this book *see* BibTB 1976, 303-6.

HARVEY, J. "Philosophie de l'histoire et apocalyptique," ScEcc 25 (1973) 5-15.

LANGEVIN, P.-E. "Sur l'origine du 'Jour de Yahvé'," ScEcc 18 (1966)

359-70.

MAC KENZIE, R.A.F. *Faith and History in the Old Testament* (Minneapolis 1963).

MEYER, B.F. "Jesus and the Remnant of Israel," JBL 84 (1965) 123-30.

MEYER, R. "Prophecy and Prophets in the Judaism of the Hellenistic-Roman Period," *TDNT* 6 (1968) 812-28.

MOWINCKEL, S. *He That Cometh* (Oxford 1959).

MULLER, H.-P. *Ursprunge und Struckturen alttestamentlicher Eschatologie* (Berlin 1969).

MUÑOZ IGLESIAS, S. "Los Profetas del Nuevo Testamento," *Est. Bibl.* 6 (1947) 303-37.

NORTH, R. "Prophecy to Apocalyptic via Zechariah," *Suppl. to VT* 22 (1972) 47-71.

PREUSS, H.D. *Jahweglaube und Zukunftserwartung* (Stuttgart 1968).

RAMLOT, L. "Prophétisme," *Supplément au Dictionnaire de la Bible* 8 (1971) cc. 811-1222.

ROHLAND, E. *Die Bedeutung der Erwählungstraditionen Israels für die Eschatologie der alttestamentlichen Propheten* (Munich 1956).

ROWLEY, H.H. *The Relevance of Apocalyptic* (London 1947).

SABOURIN, L. "Matthieu 5,17-20 et le role prophétique de la Loi (cf. Mt 11, 13)," ScEcc 30 (1978) 303-11.

SELLIN, E. "Alter, Wesen und Ursprung der alttestamentlichen Eschatologie," in *Der alttestamentliche Prophetismus* (Leipzig 1912) 103-94.

VAN DER PLOEG, J.P.M. "Eschatology in the Old Testament," OTS 17 (1972) 89-99.

VAN LEEUWEN, B. "La participation universelle à la fonction prophétique du Christ," in *L'Eglise de Vatican II*, Unam Sanctam 51b (Paris 1966) 425-55.

VAWTER, F.B. "Apocalyptic: Its Relation to Prophecy," CBQ 22 (1960) 33-46.

VON RAD, G. "Israel's Ideas about Time and History, and the Prophetic Eschatology" *Old Testament Theology*, vol. 2 (Study Edition, London 1975) 99-125.

VRIEZEN, T.C. "Prophecy and Eschatology," Congress Volume, Suppl. V.T. 1 (Leiden 1953) 199-229.

WEISS, M. "The Origin of the 'Day of the Lord'—Reconsidered," *Hebrew Union College Annual* 37 (1966) 29-60.

Bibliography for Sections C and D

BERGER, K. "Zum traditionsgeschichtlichen Hintergrund christologischer Hoheitstitel," NTS 17 (1970-71) 391-425.

BLACK, M. "The Christological Use of the Old Testament in the New Testament," NTS 18 (1971-72) 1-14.

BOERS, H. "Jesus and the Christian Faith: New Testament Christology since Bousset's *Kyrios Christos*," JBL 89 (1970) 450-56.

BOUSSET, W. *Kyrios Christos. A History of the Belief in Christ from the Beginning of Christianity to Irenaeus* (E.T. from the 1964 edition of a book first published in German in 1913, Nashville 1970); on this book *see* BibTB 1972, 89-92.

BRAUN, H. "The Meaning of New Testament Christology," JThChurch 5 (1968) 89-127 (from art. in German of 1957).

BRUCE, F.F. "Promise and Fulfillment in Paul's Presentation of Jesus," in *idem*, ed., *Promise and Fulfillment*, Fs. S.H. Hooke (Edinburgh 1963) 36-50.

Idem., This is That: The New Testament Development of Some Old Testament Themes (Exeter 1968).

BURGER, C. *Jesus als Davidssohn. Eine traditionsgeschichtliche Untersuchung*, FRLANT 98 (Göttingen 1970); he has not proved his thesis: that Jesus did not see himself as a descendant of David (*see* NTA 17, p. 202).

COLPE, C. *"Ho Huios tou Anthrôpou,"* TDNT 8 (1972) 400-77.

Idem, "New Testament and Gnostic Christology," in J. Neusner, ed., *Religions in Antiquity. Essays in Memory of E.R. Goodenough* (Leiden 1968) 227-43.

COPPENS, J. "Le prophète eschatologique. L'annonce de sa venue.

Les relectures," ETL 49 (1973) 5-35.

Idem., *Le messianisme et sa relève prophétique. Les anticipations vétéro testamentaires. Leur accomplissement en Jésus,* BiblETL 38 (Gembloux 1974).

Idem., *De Mensenzoon-Logia in het Markus-Evangelie* (Brussel 1973), exposé et bibliographie.

CORTES, J.B. and atti, f.m. "The Son of Man or the Son of Adam," *Biblica* 49 (1968) 457-502.

CULLMANN, O. *The Christology of the New Testament* (Philadelphia 1959).

DUPONT, J. ed., *Jésus aux origines de la christologie,* BiblETL 40 (Gembloux 1975).

DESCAMPS, A. "Pour une histoire du titre 'Fils de Dieu.' Les antécédents par rapport a Marc," in M. Sabbe, ed., *L'Evangile selon Marc,* BiblETL 34 (Gembloux 1974) 557-70.

FEUILLET, A. *Christologie paulinienne et tradition biblique* (Bruges 1973).

FRANCE, R.T. "The Servant of the Lord in the Teaching of Jesus," *Tyndale Bulletin* 19 (1968) 26-52, shows against Moule, Barrett, Hooker, that Jesus found in Is 53 indications for his vicarious redemptive death.

Idem., *Jesus and the Old Testament: His Application of Old Testament Passages to Himself and His Mission* (London 1971).

Idem., "Old Testament Prophecy and the Future of Israel: A Study of the Teaching of Jesus," *Tyndale Bulletin* 26 (1975) 53-78.

FREED, E.D. "The Son of Man in the Fourth Gospel," JBL 86 (1967) 402-9.

FUGLISTER, N. "Alttestamentliche Grundlagen der neutestamentlichen Christologie," in *Mysterium Salutis* (J. Feiner and M. Lohrer, eds.), vol. III, 1 (Einsiedeln 1970) 105-225.

FULLER, R.H. *The Foundations of New Testament Christology* (New York 1965).

GRELOT, P. *La Bible Parole de Dieu* (Tournai 1965) 231-309.

HAHN, F. *The Titles of Jesus in Christology. Their History in Early Christianity* (London 1969, ET from 1963 German edition).

HENGEL, M. *Der Sohn Gottes: Die Entstehung der Christologie und die jüdisch-hellenistische Religionsgeschichte* (Tübingen 1975): it was not in the speculation of the syncretistic Hellenistic world that a Son of God theology was elaborated, but in Sir, Wis, the intertestamental apocrypha, from Qumran and elsewhere in the Jewish tradition (*see* CBQ 1976, 392f).

HIGGINS, A.J.B. "The Old Testament and Some Aspects of New Testament Christology," In Can.J.Th. 6 (1960) 200-10, published in revised form in F.F. Bruce, ed., *Promise and Fulfillment* 128-41.

HOAD, J. "Some New Testament References to Isaiah 53," ExpT 68 (1957) 254f.

JEREMIAS, J. *New Testament Theology*, vol. 1 (London 1971).

DE JONGE, M. "Jewish Expectations about the 'Messiah' according to the Fourth Gospel," NTS 19 (1973) 246-70.

KÄSEMANN, E. "The Beginnings of Christian Theology," in *New Testament Questions of Today* (Philadelphia 1969).

LAFLAMME, E. ed., *Le Christ, hier, aujourd'hui et demain* (Québec 1976); on this book *see* BibTB 1978, p. 94.

LARCHER, C. *L'Actualité chrétienne de l'Ancien Testament d'après le Nouveau Testament*, Lectio Divina 34 (Paris 1962) 119-98 (on "Servant" and "Son of Man").

LEIVESTAD, R. "Exit the Apocalyptic Son of Man," NTS 18 (1972) 243-67.

LOHSE, E. *Martyrer und Gottesknecht. Untersuchungen zur urchristlichen Verkündigung vom Sühntod Jesu Christi*, FRLANT 46 (Gottingen 1955).

LONGENECKER, R.N. *The Christology of Early Jewish Christianity* (London 1970).

Idem., " 'Son of Man' Imagery: Some Implications for Theology and Discipleship," JEvThSoc 18 (1975) 3-16.

MARSHALL, I.H. "The Synoptic Son of Man Sayings in Recent

Discussion," NTS 12 (1966) 327-51.

Idem., The Origins of New Testament Christology (Downers Grove, Ill., 1976).

MARTIN, F. "The Image of Shepherd in the Gospel of Saint Matthew," ScE 27 (1975) 261-301.

MARXSEN, W. *The Beginnings of Christology: A Study in its Problems* (Philadelphia 1969).

MC ARTHUR, H.K. "From the Historical Jesus to Christology," *Interpretation* 23 (1969) 190-206.

MC CULLOUGH, J.C. "Jesus Christ in the Old Testament," *Biblical Theology* 22 (1972) 36-47.

MEEKS, W. *The Prophet-King. Moses Traditions and the Johannine Christology* (Leiden 1967).

MOLONEY, F.J. *The Johannine Son of Man* (Rome 1976).

MOWINCKEL, S. *He That Cometh* (Oxford 1956).

PINTO, E. "Jesus as the Son of God in the Gospels," BibTB 4 (1974) 75-93.

RAHNER, K.-THÜSING, W. *Christologie—systematisch und exegetisch*, Quaest. Disp. 55 (Herder 1972).

ROLLINS, W.G. "The New Testament and Apocalyptic," NTS 17 (1971) 454-76.

SABOURIN, L. *The Names and Titles of Jesus* (Macmillan, New York 1967).

SCHNACKENBURG, R. "The Son of Man in the Fourth Gospel," in *The Gospel According to St. John* 529-542.

SCHNIDER, F. *Jesus der Prophet* (Freiburg, Sch. 1973).

SYKES, S.W. and clayton, j.p. eds., *Christ, Faith, and History*, Cambridge Studies in Christology (Cambridge 1972).

TEEPLE, H.M. *The Mosaic Eschatological Prophet* (Philadelphia 1957).

TÖDT, H.E. *The Son of Man in the Synoptic Tradition* (London 1965, E.T. from German 1959).

VAN IERSEL, B.M.F. *"Der Sohn" in den synoptischen Jesusworten* (Leiden 1961).

WALKER, JR. W.O. "The Origin of the Son of Man Concept as Applied to Jesus," JBL 91 (1972) 483-90.

CHAPTER FOUR
HOW THE SCRIPTURES ARE READ

Only after the rise of Judaism with Ezra did the Hebrew Scriptures receive definite editions and begin to be considered as normative in a definite sense. This is especially true, of the Torah, the Pentateuch, the only group of writings which the Samaritans accepted as sacred. As J.A. Sanders explains (p. 51), from that period onwards Judaism came to be identified with the Torah. Before that, more stress was given to the authority of the assumed author of the books, like Moses or the prophets, than to the written texts itself. That a Palestinian "canon" of Scriptures ever existed is open to doubt, since it is difficult to see how the Alexandrian Jews, who followed the spiritual leadership of Jerusalem, could have formed a different canon. "In Catholic belief the canonicity of the Bible is determined entirely by the tradition of the Church, which alone is empowered, as the custodian of divine revelation, to determine the sacred books" (McKenzie 118). Almost till the end of the OT period the Scriptures were subject to rereadings and reinterpretations, which often affected the older texts themselves, as when glosses were introduced. It is necessary to comment on this before passing to the New Testament.

a) How Israel reread its Past

The Old Testament rests on the basic assumption that God

personally intervenes continually in history and reveals his will through events. The many divine epiphanies for the Israelite are components of a *dialogue* with the personal God. The value of history springs from its relation with God, who assures its continuity by a direction coming from above. Abraham's election is open to the future and to what is definitive, the future of God himself manifested in history. This conception of a linear development of history, between an absolute beginning and a truly final end rests on two conceptions: tradition and messianism, one looking in the past, the other in the future (*see* Gelin 118-22).

The OT text appears in many places worked over, loaded with corrections, additions, glosses, incorporating "documents" from different sources, and attributing their content to the authors of other texts. These reworkings or rereadings testify to the constant desire of the sacred writers to put into their texts the new data of divine revelation manifested in the ongoing history of salvation. Thus, as a prophet bent towards the future of which he sees the pattern in the past, Second Isaiah proclaims the new exodus, the new covenant, the new conquest (49:8f), the new Jerusalem (chs. 52 to 54), and sings the new canticle (42:10), which recalls the Mosaic song of praise (Ex 15). The grace of the covenant (Is 55:3), now reserved to a chosen portion of Israel, especially Yahweh's poor (49:13; 51:7), the sufferings of the exile sensitized the people and the prophets to understand Moses as being the type of this mysterious Servant who would finally achieve God's design (53:10). History read by a qualified community under the guidance of the prophet, has become the point of departure of a religious progress. A concrete example of text rereading in the light of the events can be found in Zc 6:11, where a scribe substituted the name of Joshua, the high priest, for that of the Davidic Zorobabel, when the high priest had become the head of the community.

We shall later try to define more precisely *typology* in connection with its use in the New Testament. Typology already within the OT itself, was a logical consequence of the understanding that past events in the history of salvation can provide a pattern for the future. Harvey has devoted an article to demonstrating that, in fact, we find in the Hebrew Psalter few typological uses of the exodus. One

exception, an important one, would be Ps 106 with a clear application in v. 47. The limited use of the exodus motif could indicate that
most of the Psalms have a pre-exilic origin, therefore not influenced
by the later use of exodus in prophecy, for example, in Jr 16:14f,
Ezk 20:32-44, Is 43:16-21. The return to paradise motif has been
also quite efficiently reused, especially in Second Isaiah, as will
become apparent from our treatment of typology in a later section
(d). The 3rd/2nd cent. B.C. Greek translation of the Old Testament,
the Septuagint, constitutes a significant link in the chain of development marked by rereadings of former texts. It represents a matura-
tion, an exegesis of the Hebrew text, even the beginning of that
targumization which will be in full swing at the time of Jesus (cf. Le
Déaut). The Targums do often serve as links between the two
Testaments (BibTB 1979, p. 41). (On Septuagint study *see* especially Vaccari, Flashar, Sperber, Jellicoe, Dubarle, and Brock's
bibliography.) The earlier Church Fathers held the Septuagint to be
inspired because the NT authors generally quote from the Greek
Bible. Besides, the Church has accepted as inspired several books
known to us only in their Greek version from an original Hebrew. It is
hardly admissible, however, that the Septuagint as a whole could
be an inspired version, uneven as it is in the rendering of the original
text, with some books not attaining in this respect even mediocrity.
Rather, particular translations that truly convey progress in revelation, to which the NT testifies, should be considered inspired in their
own right, perhaps Gn 3:15; 12:5; 49:10; Nb 24:7, 17; Ps 15:8-11
(16 in Heb.); 109:3 (110 in Heb); and Is 7:14; 25:1-5. Useful research work could probably be done on the way the Septuagint
tends in many places, particularly in the Psalms, to accentuate the
messianic significance of the texts.

Before passing to a new section we would like to point out the
role of biblical theology in the understanding of the Old Testament.
Biblical theology differs from exegesis by an effort at synthesis, with
a view to coordinating the elements dispersed throughout
Scripture. It attempts to do this in formulations taken from Scripture
itself, refusing to impose on the Bible present-day categories (more
on this in Lyonnet, *Sin* . . . introd.). Several biblical theologians have
attempted to determine what is the central conception of the Old

Testament. Only Eichrodt has systematically constructed a complete biblical theology around one concept, that of covenant, defining it as the divine-human relationship embodied in the OT accounts of the covenant at Sinai. According to Spriggs, he has not given sufficient attention to the Abrahamic and Davidic covenants (p. 33). In G.F. Hasel's view, "the task of an OT theology, which takes God as the dynamic unifying center of the OT but refrains from making this center into a static organizing principle, will consist of giving ample room to the word of that God who himself speaks in it and leads to hearing the full kerygma of the OT as the organ of his self-revelation (p. 82). Without being Centers in the strict sense of the Old Testament (see Smend and Zimmerli), some conceptions deserve in a true sense to be called "central" aspects of biblical thought. Certainly "Kingdom or Rule of God" is one of them, which like God's "presence" (Cousineau, de Vaux), has the added advantage of spanning both Testaments. Another is "communion with God" (Grelot), which is more clearly defined in the New Testament as koinônia (see Panikulam). G. Fohrer argues that "rule of God" and "communion between God and man" should constitute the central point of an OT theology, while for Kaiser and Jasper it appears to be the Promise. These varying viewpoints are not in conflict with one another. Rather, they express different aspects of the wealth biblical theology can produce from the Scriptures.

b) The NT Hermeneutics of the Old Testament

In the beginning of this book we have recalled that the NT authors, following the example of Jesus, considered what the Christians call "the Old Testament" as the word of God. Christian theologians are bound to adopt a similar attitude. "A Christian theology which clings to the revelatory character of the Gospel and recognizes Jesus Christ as its Lord cannot but maintain the revelatory character of the Old Testament, not only because He has accepted this Old Testament as revelation of God and because His preaching is inconceivable without the Old Testament message concerning God, but especially because Christ's Messianic office cannot be confessed and maintained without the Old Testament" (Vriezen 19).

Generally speaking hermeneutics is the science of the rules which permit one to discover and explain the true meaning of texts, while exegesis—an art, not a science—applies these rules to the texts (*see* P. Cruveilhier in *SDB* 3, c. 1483). The NT authors did not consciously, of course, follow the rules of modern hermeneutics, but they did adhere to some norms of interpretation, in force in the Jewish tradition, and to others that the leaders of the early Church found necessary under the guidance of the Holy Spirit (cf. Cazelles). It should be noted immediately that the NT authors are first of all witnesses to Christ, not exegetes of the Old Testament. Their whole attention concentrates on the historical events of salvation, to which they bring their testimony (cf. Lk 1:1-4). This can be illustrated from the fact that Matthew introduces his fulfillment quotations *after* the event to which they are appended (cf. 2:23; 4:15f). The resurrection of Jesus, in particular, opened the minds of the disciples to understand the meaning of the Scriptures (Jn 2:22; 12:16). This procedure assured that the argument from Scripture would remain what it should be, a testimony, and would not be used as a "proof" replacing faith in Christ. The return to the historical perspective was a sane one, after a long period in which a religion of the book had prevailed in Judaism. Israel had been the people of history before becoming the people of the Law. The historical perspective of NT hermeneutics appears new when confronted with the legalistic hermeneutics of Judaism. NT hermeneutics nevertheless reflect the most authentic OT tradition, that interprets the history of God's relationship with his people, and through it explains how God is related to all the nations of the earth.

Amsler discovers several stages in the development of NT hermeneutics. It starts, he believes, with the Synoptic *dei* ("must"), connected with the passion: "Everything that is written of the Son of Man by the prophets will be accomplished" (Lk 18:31). The fullest theological formulation is found in Lk 24:44, which mentions the three parts of Scripture, and the necessity of their fulfillment. At a very early stage this general statement was illustrated by the quotation attributed to Jesus of particular texts (Dn 7:13; Ps 22:1; 31:6), which was followed by references found in the apostolic discourses, attesting the advent of the Messiah (Dt 18:15, 18), the meaning of his death (Is 53), and of his resurrection (Pss 2, 16, 110, 118). In one form or another there existed a collection of *testimonia*, mostly messianic texts, which the early Christian preachers could use for their presentation of Christ and his Gospel (*see* Grech). In addition, the apostolic witness and the primitive cultic community expressed their beliefs in the use of christological titles, which contain many implicit allusions to Scripture. Some NT authors have made a more conscious and systematic use of OT texts than others, for example Matthew with his fulfillment quotations and the author of Hebrews, especially in the first chapters.

Several scholars have examined the use Jesus himself made of the OT in his teaching. Both Gerhardsson (p. 327) and Wenham (p. 37) emphatically state that for Christ the written Torah, the holy Scripture was the word of God (*see* also Guillemette and Mirtow). From the manner in which Christ quotes Scripture, writes Marcel, "we find that he recognizes and accepts the Old Testament in its entirety as possessing a normative authority, as the true Word of God, valid for all time. He believes in inspiration by the Holy Spirit since the time of Adam (Mt 19:5), in the infallibility of the oracles . . . (Mt 13:14-15; 15:7-9), in the Davidic authorship of Psalm 110, for example, and in David's full inspiration" (p. 133). T.W. Manson finds that the quotations used by Jesus rest on real parallels between the OT situation and that of his ministry, as, for example, in Mk 7:6f with respect to Is 29:13: "In both places the divine revelation through the prophet or through Christ is frustrated by the rigid adherence of the people to their man-made religious conventions" (p. 331). As Duesberg has recalled, Jesus also made the unheard of claim to be the person of whom several Scripture texts spoke (Lk 4:17-21; 24:44). He also found in some texts, like the Servant Songs, guidance to accomplish his mission (*see* Mk 10:45), and for his daily conduct, as it appears from the temptation story (Mt 4:1-11).

Midrashic, Symbolical, and Liturgical Interpretation

The Qumran covenanters had recourse to *midrash* exegesis to show that the Scriptures were relevant for their own situation. In their *pesher* treatment of the OT (*see* Fitzmyer) they tried to determine the application of prophecies to current events, for example in a writing called *pesher Habbakkuk*. The following is a significant passage: "And God told Habakkuk to write down that which would happen to the final generation, but He did not make known to him when time would come to an end. And as for that which He said, 'That he who reads may read it speedily,' interpreted this concerns the Teacher of Righteousness (*môreh hassedeq*), to whom God made known all the mysteries of the words of His servants the Prophets" (1QpHab VII, 1-5). "In a real sense," writes Longenecker (p. 12), "they understood the passages in question as possessing a *sensus plenior* which could be ascertained only from a revelational standpoint, and that the true message of Scripture was only heard when prophecy and interpretation were brought together."

Also Philo of Alexandria wished to *contemporize* the sacred accounts so as to make them relevant to current situations and experiences. He treated the Old Testament as a corpus of symbols given by God for man's spiritual and moral benefit. He set aside the literal or historical sense of Scripture, and stressed its allegorical meaning. Also in the New Testament we find midrashic treatment of some Scripture themes, particularly in Mt 1-2, as I have indicated in the first *excursus* of my commentary on Matthew (*see also* Daube, Sanders, and Wright). The Christian significance of the Old Testament has been abundantly investigated in recent years. We can recommend for further reading the studies of Anderson, Auvray, Barrett, Benoit, Box, Charlier, Donner, Higgins, Krinetzki, Larcher, Lohfink, Marangon, and Murphy. Achtemeier and Gunneweg have proposed reflections on the possibility of using the OT texts in Christian preaching, while other authors have restated the permanent authority of the Old Testament for the faith of the people of God (Bright, Driver, Kuyper). In more than one way, however, the OT values are superseded by the New (Muñoz Iglesias). For

Huffmon "the Old Testament is God's *indirect word* to us, which becomes direct only when heard in the light of Jesus Christ and measured by the touchstone of the Word made flesh" (p. 72).

The influence of the *liturgy* on the OT texts does not have to be demonstrated. It is evident in the Psalms (cf. Mowinckel), and many of the exodus stories grew from liturgical recitals in the Israelite shrines (cf. Pedersen). Systematic studies of the Israelite *feasts* (Kraus) have shown what an important role they played in the ongoing adaptation of God's revelation to the life of the nation and of the individuals. They also contributed to an appreciable degree to the reinterpretation and the development of the written Scripture. Martin-Achard observes that a better knowledge of the religious solemnities can lead to a just appreciation of the meaning of the OT and its message. The reason is that the feasts bring forward key themes ("certaines idées forces") which can be referred to OT texts and when assembled form a sort of biblical theology (p. 9). In sacred liturgy, which celebrates the mysteries of salvation, "the faithful can express in their lives, and manifest to others, the mystery of Christ and the real nature of the true Church . . . In the liturgy full public worship is performed by the Mystical Body of Jesus Christ, that is by the Head and His members" (Vat. II *Constitution on the Sacred Liturgy*, nn. 2 and 6). In the liturgy "the treasures of the Bible are to be opened up more lavishly, so that richer fare may be provided for the faithful at the table of God's Word" (n. 51). As Alonso-Schökel remarks, one of the principal tasks of the liturgical homily consists in making the language of the Scriptures intelligible to the people (p. 339).

The hymnal corpus of the OT has been taken over by the Christian Church for the praise of God and of her Lord Jesus Christ. The Catholic Church has, besides, her own *sacrificium laudis* (Ps 107:22), her *tôdâh* (Ps 50:14, 23) or thanksgiving sacrifice, which is the Eucharistic celebration, fulfilling according to the early Christian writing *Didachè* (ch. 14) and the Council of Trent the prophecy of Malachi on the future universal sacrifice to be offered among the nations (1:11). Other examples could be produced showing that the liturgy makes it own contribution to the unity of the two Testaments. One outstanding illustration is the passage from Passover to Easter and from the old to the new Pentecost in the formation of the liturgical cycle of feasts.

c) Relevance of the Fuller Sense

Although we cannot here comment on this division at length, the traditional way of classifying the Scripture senses must be kept in mind also when examining the more recent category of the fuller sense (*see* de Lubac). Older authors spoke of one literal sense (I) and of three mystical or spiritual senses (II, III, IV).

> I.   The *literal* sense is that which flows immediately and directly from the words understood according to their current usage.
> II.   The traditional meaning of "*allegory*" should not be confused with "allegorism," which finds or seeks a mystery under every word, as, for example, a reference to the Cross wherever the Old Testament speaks of "wood." In its deeper classical meaning "allegory" discovers everywhere in Scripture the mystery of Christ, or in the words of Hughes of St. Victor (12th cent.): "All Scripture is one book, and this book is Christ." In its authentic sense the purpose of allegory was to put Christ in the center of Scripture.
> III.   The *tropological* sense of Scripture does not consist in moralizing Scripture artificially, but it finds that Scripture has a deeper meaning which is instructive for Christian life as a whole. In this sense the mystery of salvation is seen as interiorized, salvation history has correspondences in the history of each one's spiritual life and guides its movements in a way similar to the liturgy, which conveys to our lives the mysteries of Christ.
> IV.   In its *anagogical* sense Scripture regards the future, especially the future life. It concerns the mystery of the eschatological wandering of the people of God.

The *four senses* just mentioned can be illustrated around the term "Jerusalem." In its literal sense Jerusalem refers to the capital of Judea (very probably also "the holy city" of Mt 27:53). Allegorically it is the Christian Jerusalem, the Church, new spiritual center of the messianic people (cf. Gal 4:26). In the moral or tropological sense Jerusalem has been used for the temple of the soul, while anagogically it is the heavenly Jerusalem of the book of Revelation. With de Lubac it can be said that with the four Scripture senses the mystery of Christ is prefigured in the Old Testament, is made present in the NT events, is interiorized for the believer and fulfilled in the Kingdom of Heaven. In other words, the letter teaches the facts, allegory what to believe, tropology what to do, and anagogy where we are going. As Gribomont explains, Thomas Aquinas saw the senses of Scripture as resulting from the unity of the two Testaments. For him the non-literal senses are variations of the "spiritual" sense of Scripture. "That first meaning whereby the words signify things belongs to the sense first mentioned, namely the historical or literal. That meaning, however, whereby the things signified by the words in their turn also signify other things is called the spiritual sense; it is based on and presupposes the literal sense" (*Summa* I, 1, 10). The term "spiritual" can be confusing, however, since it does apply to everything Scriptural because the Holy Spirit inspired the whole Bible, also in its literal sense. (On the "spiritual" sense(s) in particular *see* Kerrigan for the usage in St. Cyril of Alexandria and Mailhiot for what regards Thomas Aquinas.)

The Need for a Sensus Plenior

No authentic Scriptural sense can contradict what the human author meant to say. It is disputed whether or not such a sense is limited to what was the explicit intention of the author. Literary criticism alone is unable to decide, since it understands the text as it is found in its immediate context, taking into account the historical and cultural conditions of its redaction. Theology, on the other hand, is not bound by these limitations. For theology the Bible is *one book*, having internal unity, and one global object: the revelation of the redemption of men in Christ, and the revelation of God in this mystery. Each author in this Book contributed to the global revelation with his particular message, but he may have only a limited knowledge of the total scope to which it was ordained. This is particularly true of the OT authors who before the actual advent of Christ, could formulate only inadequately the mystery of which they had at best more or less clear intimations. Yet, if one follows the traditional belief that the Holy Spirit is the principal author of Scripture as a whole, he is bound to admit the possibility that a text may possess a meaning broader and deeper than that which the human author explicitly and knowingly intended. This meaning is generally referred to as "the fuller sense." This *sensus plenior* need not be "another sense:" it is the *textual* (or literal) sense at a deeper level (for our exposition we have found useful developments in Grelot, *La Bible, parole de Dieu* pp. 317-27).

For those who admit a progress in revelation, a fulfillment in Christ of the divine promise contained in the Old Testament, a fuller sense is not only justified, it is required. This is more easily understood if we consider that the sacred author's intention is to teach truths regarding the mystery of man's salvation. The OT authors did not perceive clearly that this salvation would ultimately be found in Christ, but they conveyed this truth implicitly or virtually in various manners, as can be deduced from their partial but real contributions to such aspects of revelation as promise and fulfillment, prefiguration, the teleological inclination of history, the kingdom of God, and the Godward/Christward life of the people of God. Such is the wealth and depth of revelation that just as a poet's or a painter's attempt to capture the marvels of a spectacular scene always fall short of the reality, so the words to formulate the depths of revelation are rarely adequate to convey the meaning intended.

Documenting the Fuller Sense

Fuller meanings in the texts will obviously reveal themselves in greater number to the Christian reader of the OT, who sees in them latent references or anticipations of what God has wrought in Christ or in the Christian community. But within the Old Testament itself earlier texts certainly contain fuller meanings which later texts enable us to discover, as is made obvious by the way Israel reread its past. Ws 2:24, for example, marks a progress in the understanding of Gn 3, with the ascription to the devil of the origin of sin.

It is a documented fact that the disciples' understanding of Jesus grew during his own lifetime and afterwards, and this growth is obviously reflected in the NT texts. To give only one example, in St. Peter's confession at Caesarea the title "Son of the living God" ascribed to Christ referred at the time directly to his Messiahship, but the expression was apt for a deeper application, in the transcendent sense, which was revealed only later. The Holy Spirit would guide the apostles "into all the truth" (Jn 16:13), and teach the Church "all things" (Jn 14:26), also through different experiences like Pentecost, the sacramental life, the conversion of the Gentiles, the confrontation with the synagogue, and the persecutions. All these factors show that within the apostolic period there was room for a broader and deeper understanding of the earliest writings when they were used by later authors. This means, for example, that the words of Mark, can be read with a fuller sense in the light of the later gospels, if as it is claimed, Mark was written perhaps ten years before Matthew and Luke. This, of course, applies even more closely to John, a writing which embodies a more developed theological reflection on the mystery of Christ. Taking also into account the internal coherence of the mystery of salvation and the positive implications of the analogy of faith, it appears perfectly legitimate to consider as virtually contained in Biblical texts fuller meanings than those which literary criticism alone is able to discover. Although Scripture remains the norm of the Church's faith, it cannot fulfill this role properly in isolation from the apostolic tradition in which its authentic interpretation is to be found.

To illustrate by more concrete examples what we have said, we find in the Old Testament inchoative formulations of truths and experiences that will later be understood in a fuller sense than what the human author or his immediate readers could grasp. Adoptive divine filiation was attributed to Israel as the chosen people bound to God by a covenant (Ex 4:22), and even to the Israelites as individuals (Is 1:2). Only in the New Testament, however, would such filiation be fully implemented and revealed, through the participation in Jesus' own sonship (Rm 8:14-17). In a similar way, the psalmist called the Messianic King, God's "son" (Ps 2:7) in a manner which would be read in a fuller sense in the light of Christ's resurrection (Ac 13:33). The author of the *Miserere* (Ps 51) expressed his belief in the purification from sin through God's salvific grace, and Ezekiel foresaw the time when God's spirit would inhabit man's heart (36:25-27). All this would be fully realized in a new and unexpected way through the sacrament which configures the baptized to Christ (Rm 5:5; Ep 5:26). Since Jesus himself (Mk 10:45; 15:34) or the evangelists (Lk 22:37) have appropriated OT texts, like Ps 22 and Is 53, in connection with the Savior's sufferings, it can be assumed that they represented anticipating formulations of the future mystery of redemption, although their author understandably had only an obscure perception of this. It can also be sustained that OT statements regarding the Word, Wisdom, and the Spirit constitute intimations of what the NT would reveal concerning the Holy Trinity. In this regard it is instructive to read Heb 1-2 and the commentators' explanations concerning the use made there of the OT texts.

The fuller sense can be applied on more than one level, as is the case for Is 40:5, "And the glory of the Lord shall be revealed, and all flesh shall see it together:" interpreted figuratively the Sinai theophany (Ex 26:16f) and the prophecy or promise would be accomplished in Christ in different moments. According to the New Testament Jesus manifested God's glory already in his earthly life (Jn 1:4), through his miracles (2:17; 11:40), secretly at the Transfiguration (Lk 9:32; 1 P 1:16-18), and especially through his passion/resurrection (Jn 17:5). God's glory is reflected in the baptized, who participate in Christ's glorification (2 Cor 3:18), but the divine glory will appear fully at Christ's parousia (Mt 24:30). Although the exodus motif belongs rather to typology, it could be argued that a *sensus plenior* is also applied since in the typological rereading of the motif the terms *exodos* or its equivalents gradually received much broader applications (*see* Grelot, *La Bible parole de Dieu* 376f). Other concrete examples of the fuller sense are proposed by

Grelot in *Sens chrétien de l'Ancien Testament* 271-74.

Some Particular Views

For more than fifty years the existence and nature of a fuller sense have been discussed, more intensely between 1950 and 1955. Already in the first edition of *Institutiones Biblicae*, a book the Biblicum published in Rome in 1925, Fernandez used the expression *sensus plenior*, the newness and appropriateness of which would be recognized only gradually. The question can be considered, he wrote, whether God intended to convey *through the words* of the hagiographer a more abundant, fuller sense than that which the writer himself comprehended and wished to express. We do not mean, he explained, two different senses, but a certain broader sense, which the potentiality of the words contains, a sense not entirely unknown to the human writer. Then he quotes Thomas Aquinas, "Since the prophetic mind is an efficacious instrument, even true prophets do not know all that the Holy Spirit intends to convey through what they see, write, and report" (*Summa* 2-2, 173, a. 4). What is said of "prophecies," concluded Fernandez, applies also to certain doctrines which are insinuated in the Old Testament, as that of divine wisdom (Pr 8, Si 24, Ws 7-8). Several years later Bierberg discussed the existence of a *sensus plenior*, while Courtade observed that the inclination of history, the orientation of events surpasses the literal sense, without falling, however, in the spiritual or figurative sense. Dubarle agreed with this, adding a clarification: the literal sense includes all that the author has expressed, directly or indirectly, therefore not only the facts, but also their interpretation. The literal sense can be surpassed only with the help of the fuller revelation known through the New Testament.

Other authors discussed the need of the NT to discover the fuller sense (Turrado), particularly of Paul (J. Schmid). C.H. Dodd expressed the following view in 1952: "It would not be true of any literature which deserves to be called great, that its meaning is restricted to that which was explicitly in the mind of the author when he wrote. On the contrary, it is a part of what constitutes the quality of greatness in literature that it perpetuates itself by unfolding ever new riches of unsuspected meaning as time goes on" (p. 131). *A fortiori* can this be true of an inspired writer who plays a role in the unfolding of divine revelation. About the same time, writers, like de Tuya, were asking themselves if and how much a fuller sense can be reconciled with the doctrine of inspiration. This is much easier now that new dimensions have been given to the notion of inspiration, by P. Benoit as we have noted in the beginning of ch. 1, by Alonso-Schokel, Grelot, Vawter, and several authors we mention in the following bibliography (*see* Adinolfi, Burtchaell, Rahner, Smith, Vempeny). The dogmatic constitution *Dei Verbum* on divine revelation stated (n. 8) that the apostolic tradition "develops in the Church with the help of the Holy Spirit. For there is a *growth* in the understanding of the realities and the words which have been handed down." Using Augustine's similar formulation, *Dei Verbum* states: "God, the inspirer and author of both testaments, wisely arranged that the New Testament be hidden in the Old and the Old be made manifest in the New" (n. 16). Such declarations encourage research on the Scripture senses, including the fuller sense, as also other previous documents of the magisterium (*see* Braun).

In his published doctoral dissertation (1955), R.E. Brown had offered a comprehensive discussion of the *sensus plenior*, and stated that it must be a development of what is already said in the text (p. 145), that it flows from the text itself and is a deepening of its literal meaning (p. 149). Then it was Benoit's turn to grapple with the issue. He also sees "mysterious correspondences" between various texts, coupled with "successive deepenings," and for him the fuller sense is "the increase of objective signification which the words of the Old Testament receive when they are reused in the New Testament in the light of the typological fulfillment brought by Christ" (p. 188).

The debate over the *sensus plenior* took a new turn when R.E. Brown reviewed the whole argument in 1963 and expressed reservations on a notion he had previously defended. Soon afterwards Vawter proposed on the fuller sense "some considerations" which were meant to clarify some issues. Vawter expressed in particular the fear that if the *sensus plenior* is understood as a literal sense "we are asked to give up our traditional understanding of what is meant by the literal sense of Scripture." He claims that for Thomas Aquinas whatever God intends by the words of Scripture beyond the human writer's knowledge is a figured "thing," and for this reason a spiritual and not a literal sense. In the text of *Summa*, he quotes in n. 6 (Ia, q. 1, a. 10, ad 1), however, what Thomas is against is not an extension of the literal or historical sense, but the notion that equivocation can be found in Scripture out of which contrary doctrines could arise. The fuller sense is not strictly a new sense, it is a deeper understanding of the literal sense through a growth in revelation. Vawter would probably not agree with this, since for him "the question of a fuller literal sense is to be posed not in the comparison of two degrees of revealed knowledge but in the meaning of biblical words and texts" (p. 90). Other fears have been expressed by Protestant writers. For Protestants, writes J.M. Robinson (p. 16), there exists the danger that *sensus plenior* could be "a peg to hang new doctrines upon," presumably doctrines Protestants have already rejected or do not welcome. More specifically Amsler considers as an "abuse" the discovery in Gn 3:15 of a foundation for mariological developments (pp. 189-91).

According to J. Coppens, the *sensus plenior* results from prophetic intuition or the thrust of supernatural faith, as enriched over the course of time by a living tradition which serves as its authentic interpreter (p. 67). In his influential book *Les harmonies des deux Testaments*, published in 1949, Coppens had devoted more than thirty pages to the contribution of the fuller sense. Another prominent exegete of his time, E.P. Sutcliffe concluded thus in 1953 his study of the "plenary" sense: "As the books of the Old Law were intended not only for the Hebrews for whose immediate use they were written, but also for the new Israel, 'the Israel of God' (Gal 6, 16), whose members were to learn in its pages the gradual preparation for the New Covenant, what wonder is it that God so directed the human author's *choice of language* that future generations should see there 'the mystery of Christ, which in other generations were not known to the sons of men' (Ep 3, 4f), and so be enabled to recognize the hand of God guiding all things to their predestined end? This choice of language, the secret of which is revealed in the New Testament, shows in a very clear manner *the unity of the two Testaments*" (p. 343).

To guard against fanciful applications of the fuller sense, two main guidelines must be observed. Firstly, the development found must be in line with the original orientation of the text. Secondly, there must be a strict literary continuity, with distinctive words, indicating that the more recent author has deliberately chosen these words to convey his thoughts in continuation with the inchoative formulations found before him.

d) The Use of Biblical Typology

As we have noted (ch. 3, d) typology is a kind of prefigurement, and there is a difference between "figures" and "types." Another distinction has to be made, between typology and allegory (*see* Barr, Crouzel and Olsen), allegory being taken here in the sense Philo, for example, used it in his "allegorical" method for interpreting Scripture, a method adopted in part by some Alexandrian interpreters. While in typology the historical value of the text is presupposed, in allegory this has little importance and may even be offensive, because history in allegory is set aside to make room for the "spiritual" or "symbolical" sense, which, it is claimed, always lies behind the biblical text. "Thus while the Exodus story depicts Moses as the historical deliverer of Israel, sent by God to lead his people out of slavery into the freedom of the rule of God, allegory describes him as the possessor of knowledge and of the true philosophy, releasing the captured soul from the prison of sensual lust; the destruction of the Egyptian army represents the destruction of the passions" (Eichrodt 227). The *tupoi* or types, on the other hand, are persons, institutions, and events (1 Cor 10:11) of the Old Testament which are regarded as divinely established models or prerepresentations of corresponding realities in the NT salvation history (Heb 8:5). These latter realities are called "antitypes" in 1 P 3:21. They are of course more perfect than the types since the OT salvation history represents only, as it were, the preliminary stage, the preparation of what unfolds in the NT in a fuller and richer way. There is in other words an intensification of the process of salvation in the NT as it achieves its fulfillment. According to G.W. Grogan, a *typologist* like the author of Hebrews sees a divinely intended *correspondence* between two persons, events or institutions *in history* (p. 66). God is unchanging and the pattern of his action is predictable. On this is founded the "continuity of principle" which is basic in typology and is used in the NT. Thus Jesus can apply Is 6:9f to his listeners because they have the same attitude to the word of God as Isaiah's contemporaries, and God's judgment on them is consistent (Mk 4:11f). On the Vatican II guidelines for the interpretative use of typology, see Latakos' study.

The whole Bible can be seen to be constructed on typology, since the Old and the New Testaments are two realities that correspond to each other, each contributing to explain the other. The Old Testament, as a whole, writes Dubarle, is prophetic, since it reflects the forward movement of God's people towards the fulfillment of the divine word (p. 231). Like Grogan, so also von Rad insists on the requirement of history in typological exegesis. "The larger context into which we have to set the OT phenomena if they are to be meaningfully appreciated is not, however, a general system of religious and ideal values, but the compass of a specific history, which was set in motion by God's words and deeds and which, as the New Testament sees it, finds its goal in the coming of Christ. Only in this event is there any point in looking for what is analogous and comparable. And it is only in this way of looking at the Old and New Testaments that the correspondences and analogies between the two appear in their proper light" (vol. 2, p. 369). Persons, objects, institutions are not essentially, statistically, *quod se*, types; all depends on the *events* between Israel and God, and on what place all these events have in the great area of tension constituted by promise and fulfillment, which is so characteristic of Israel's whole existence before God (p. 371). "The coming of Jesus Christ as a historical reality leaves the exegete no choice at all; he must interpret the Old Testament as pointing to

Christ, whom he must understand in its light. This continual flow of reciprocal understanding is plainly laid down, both by the historical importance of the NT saving event and by the ceaseless movement of promise and fulfillment in the Old Testament" (p. 374). Also Lys strongly underlines the importance of history in typology.

It is known, however, and Ramlot recalls it, that typology exists within the Old Testament itself (1093f). Amsler finds several typological motifs of this kind: creation reenacted (Is 9:1; *see also* Reumann), new heavens and new earth (Is 61:16), new exodus (Is 2:11-16, Zc 10:10), second wandering in the wilderness (Ho 2:14f; 12:10), other desert miracles (Is 48:20f), new covenant (Jr 31:31-34), and the new David (often). (On the exodus theme in the Psalter *see* the beginning of the present chapter and Harvey's study.)

The Exodus Typology

Exodus typology is abundantly represented in the New Testament, particularly in John (*see* R.H. Smith), but also in other books (cf. Grelot 376). The Son of God was recalled from Egypt (Mt 2:15), as Israel had been, also called "my son" (Ho 11:1). The crossing of the Red Sea was reenacted in the miraculous crossing of the Jordan towards the promised land (Jos 3:15f). A new exodus through the desert took place with the return from the Babylonian exile (Is 40:3), but the true and definitive exodus will be from this earth to the eternal kingdom. John represented Jesus' redemptive mystery as a passage to the Father (13:1), while Luke tells us that at the Transfiguration they spoke of the *exodus* Jesus was to accomplish in Jerusalem (9:31). Paul saw the life of the baptized as an exodus experience (1 Cor 10:1-4), but only in Hebrews do we find a thoroughgoing application of the exodus motif to the Christian community: it is a pilgrim people on its way to the eternal rest (4:3-5) under the leadership of Christ (6:20), who as high priest entered first in heaven "perfected" by his personal sacrifice (5:9; 9:12).

The theme of the Paschal lamb also belongs to the exodus motif. It is the blood of the sacrificial Paschal lamb that protected the Hebrews against extermination (Ex 12:23), and it is in a Paschal context that Jesus instituted the Eucharist, the commemoration of his sacrificial death, as the Passover was a memorial of the deliverance from Egypt (Ex 12:14). Such is the connection of the saving mystery to the desert rite, and to its subsequent repetition in the Israelite Passover feast, that Paul could write: "Christ, our Paschal lamb, has been sacrificed" (1 Cor 5:7). It is easy to imagine how many applications of typology and the fuller sense can be discovered in the progressive revelation and in the varied experiences of the mystery of salvation (for the exodus typology *see* also the studies of Baudet, Daube, Harvey, and Huffmon).

Adamic and Paradisiacal Typology

In Rm 5:12-21 Paul compares antithetically Adam to Christ, by stating that as through the first man sin and death came to all men, in the same way grace and life abound through Jesus Christ. There he also declares explicitly that Adam "was a type of the one who was to come" (v. 14). The same notion expressly underlines a Pauline development on the resurrection (1 Cor 15:42-50). Elsewhere clear allusions point to the same Adamic typology. According to Gn 1:27f, God created man to his own image and gave him dominion "over every living thing that moves upon the earth." On the other hand, it is revealed truth that Christ "is the image of the invisible God, the first of all creation, in whom all things were created" (Col 1:15f; cf. Heb 1:1f). This implies that Christ who was born as son of Adam (Lk 3:38) had provided the model for Adam's creation in the image of God. Through his divinity Christ was first in the order of creation, as he was first as Savior in the order of redemption. Ps 8, referring to Gn 1, states that God has given dominion to man over all living beings. This again is alluded to in Ep 1:22: "And he has put all things under his feet and has made him the head over all things for the church . . ." But the priority of Christ, his preeminence, and his sovereignty extend over the whole creation, not over the living beings alone (1 Cor 8:6), for He is the Word through whom all things were made (Jn 1:3).

Already the Genesis texts suggested with the theme of the

paradise of Eden that man's beatitude, in union with God, was the purpose of creation. This design was soon foiled on man's part through the sin of Adam. But the ultimate restoration of man and his return to paradise were left as open possibilities with the promise that through the woman's seed, mainly through the Christ, mankind would eventually triumph over the powers of evil (Gn 3:15; Rm 16:20). The blessings for the future, which Israel received (cf. Ex 23:25f), must be linked with the messianic expectation, as Gn 49 seems to indicate, although immediately they were promised as rewards for the observance of the Law (Lv 26:3-12). The theme of the paradise regained in the *eschaton* becomes explicit in the prophetic teachings, especially in Is 11:6-9; 51:3; 65:17-25; Ezk 47:6-12; Jl 4:18; Zc 14:6-9.

The ancient oriental paradise myths either offered a very pessimistic presentation of human efistence, or tied man's destiny to the fatalistic astral mechanism of the cosmic cyclic return, as in the systems developed by Pythagoras (6th cent. B.C.), who also believed in the transmigation of souls. Two features that these speculations completely lack are proper to the Biblical conception. One is *salvation history*, the unfolding of which God designedly directs, and the other is the divine promise revealed to men, on which their hope for a return to paradise is founded. It appears from this that if the Biblical conception owes something to the oriental speculations, the content of the borrowing has been demythologized and adapted to fit into the revealed pattern of salvation (cf. Grelot 269f). The Adamic typology is one of the unveiling keys of this pattern, but the full knowledge of its implications and workings has not been communicated to men (cf. 1 Cor 13:12f).

The Exemplarism of Hebrews

Because of the literary, non-theological, similarities the Epistle to the Hebrews presents with the works of Philo, it has been said, perhaps rightly, that the writer of Hebrews was "a Philonian converted to Christianity" (Ménégoz 198). There is no consensus, however, on the nature and degree of dependence of Hebrews on

Philo. In my work *Priesthood* (Brill, 1973), I have collected some representative opinions (p. 261). For H. Chadwick, "the analogies are so near as to make a relationship of direct dependence much the simplest and most probably hypothesis" (p. 290). It is S.G. Sowers' conviction "that the writer of Hebrews has come from the same school of Alexandrian Judaism as Philo, and that Philo's writings still offer us the best single body of *religionsgeschichtlich* material we have for this N.T. Document" (p. 66). Still, Hebrews is fundamentally different from Philo in outlook and thought. Whereas Philo, for example, treats the OT allegorically, Hebrews interprets it with meticulous literalness and understands it as Messianic (Montefiore 6-9). Going even further, R. Williamson claims that the evidence points to the conclusion that "the writer of Hebrews had never been a Philonist, had never read Philo's work, had never come under the influence of Philo directly or indirectly" (p. 579).

The Letter to the Hebrews presents a prefiguration of its own. It resorts to *exemplarism* in discussing the relative values of the old dispensation as compared to the new (Grelot 266). Exemplarism figured among the symbolic formulations of religion in ancient oriental and classical cultures. There it expressed the belief that the earthly realities embedded in the movement of time were in fact imperfect reflections of their model found above, outside the limits of time. Occurrences in the world of deities, which the myths related to primordial history, have fixed once for all, it was thought, the features of all things terrestrial. This applied particularly to the sacred institutions for which extraterrestrial archetypes could be found in the mythic past. Generally speaking Biblical thought rejects this mythical interpretation. It sets in creation the absolute beginning of the world and knows no past history of happenings in the divine sphere, which would have been exemplars of what would take place here below.

The Epistle to the Hebrews employs exemplaristic prefigurement, but in a very distinctive way, without relying on mythical conceptions. Generally speaking Hebrews deals with Christ the High Priest, the Leader of the wandering people of God on their way to their rest (4:1-11), to their *katapausis (see* Hofius). For Hebrews the exemplar is in the future, not in the past, and this is in keeping with the biblical notion that history is moving towards the future. The mystery of Christ, whose advent takes place at the *eschaton*, is the exemplar to which sacred history as a whole can be referred. As compared to this archetype, set in the future (8:5), the OT realities appear as symbolic, "in parable" (11:19), as shadows (8:5), as copies (9:23), or "antitypes" (9:24) of the true reality of the mystery of Christ, the high priest of the sanctuary (8:2). Even Moses, about to erect the tent, was shown the model on which it would be patterned (8:6). The author does not explain what he means, but he is probably suggesting it was revealed to Moses that his cultic institution was provisional, symbolic, in view of the "true tent," which would be founded on Christ's sacrifice (*see* my *Priesthood* 197-204).

   In contrast to the conception of the eternal return, of the cyclic recurrence of all things, upheld, as we said, in ancient and oriental religions, we find in the Bible only one cycle, teleologically oriented towards the Christian event, polarized from the old to the new dispensation. Typology was part of this conception, and it assured the link between the two economies through the pattern of prefigurement and fulfillment.

The Contribution of the Fathers

   The contribution of the Fathers of the Church and other ancient Christian writers to typology and allegory well deserve to be treated in a special chapter. Patristic hermeneutics has been the object of numerous and excellent studies to which we refer our readers (for example Camelot, Clavier, Daniélou, de Lubac, den Boer, Ternant, *La Bible et les Pères*). The Greek writer Origen (185-252) and two Latin writers, Jerome (350-419) and Augustine (354-430) are towering figures of the history of Christian exegesis (*see* Vaccari), both for the literal meaning of the text (Jerome) and for its figurative meaning, which Origen and Augustine expounded in developments that have nourished Christian theology and mysticism for centuries, as the patrologies of B. Altaner and J. Quasten indicate. Good *Lexica*, like Lampe's, and the recent publication of *Biblia*

Patristica (see BibTB 1976, pp. 247f), make it easier to consult and better understand the vast early Christian literature which Migne made available in his time in the famed *Patrologia Graeca* and *Patrologia Latina*. Critical editions of the texts are now in course of publication in prestigious collections like the French *Sources Chrétiennes* and the German *Corpus Christianorum, Series Latina* (Brepols), *Corpus Scriptorum Ecclesiasticorum Latinorum* (Vienna), and *Die Griechischen Christlichen Scriftsteller der esten drei Jahrhunderte* (Berlin).

Bibliography for Section A

ALONSO-SCHÖKEL, L. *The Inspired Word. Scripture in the Light of Language and Literature*, tr. by Francis Martin (Montreal 1965).

AMSLER, S. "L'herméneutique néotestamentaire de l'Ancien Testament," in *L'Ancien Testament dans l'Eglise* (Neuchatel 1960), 91-99.

BARR, J. *Old and New in Interpretation: a Study of the Two Testaments* (London 1966).

BROCK, S.P. et al., eds., *A Classified Bibliography of the Septuagint* (Leiden 1973).

CLAVIER, H. *Les variétés de la pensée biblique et le problème de son unité*, Suppl. NT 43 (Leiden 1976).

CHILDS, B.S. *Biblical Theology in Crisis* (Philadelphia 1970).

COUSINEAU, A. "La présence de Dieu dans le Nouveau Testament," in *Après Jésus, autorité et liberté dans le peuple de Dieu* (Montréal 1977) 209-21.

DAUBE, D. *The Exodus Pattern in the Bible* (London 1963).

EICHRODT, W. *Theologie des Alten Testaments*, three vols. published in Leipzig between 1933 and 1939 (Engl. Tr. in two vols., 1961 and 1967: *Theology of the Old Testament*).

FLASHAR, M. "Exegetische Studien zum Septuagintpsalter," ZAW 32 (1912), three articles.

FOHRER, G. "Der Mittelpunkt einer Theologie des Alten Testaments," ThZ 24 (1968) 161-72.

GELIN, A. "Comment le peuple d'Israël lisait l'Ancien Testament," in P. Auvray, ed., *L'Ancien Testament et les chrétiens* (Paris 1951).

GESE, H. "Erwägungen zur Einheit der biblischen Theologie," ZThK 67 (1970) 417-36.

Idem., Zur biblischen Theologie. Alttestamentliche Vorträge (Munich 1977).

GRECH, P. "The Language of Scripture and its Interpretation, An Essay," BibTB 6 (1976) 161-76.

GRELOT, P. "Présence de Dieu et communion avec Dieu dans l'Ancien Testament," *Concilium* 40 (1968) 11-21.

HARVEY, J. "La typologie de l'Exode dans les Psaumes," ScEcc 15 (1963) 383-405.

Idem., "The New Diachronic Biblical Theology of the Old Testament (1960-1970)," BibTB 1 (1971) 5-29.

HASEL, G.F. "The Problem of the Center in the OT Theology Debate," ZAW 86 (1974) 65-82.

HERTZBERG, H.W. "Nachgeschichte alttestamentlicher Texte innerhalb des AT," in *Werden und Wesen des AT*, BZAW 66 (Berlin 1936) 110-21 (rereadings within the OT).

JACOB, E. "De la théologie de l'Ancien Testament à la théologie biblique. A propos de quelques publications récentes," *Rev.Hist.Ph.Rel.* 57 (1977) 513-18 (esp. Zimmerli, Gese, Clavier).

JASPER, F.N. "The Relation of the Old Testament to the New," ExpT 78 (1967) 228-35; 267-70.

JELLICOE, S. *The Septuagint and Modern Study* (Oxford 1968).

KLEIN, R.W. *Textual Criticism of the Old Testament. The Septuagint after Qumran* (Philadelphia 1974).

KRAFT, R.A. ed., *Septuagintal Lexicography*, two vols. (Missoula 1972).

KRAUS, H.-J. *Die biblische Theologie: Ihre Geschichte und Problematik* (Neukirchen 1970).

LAPOINTE, R. "Hermeneutics Today," BibTB 2 (1972) 107-54.

Idem, "Les traductions de la Bible sont-elles inspirées?" ScE 23 (1971) 69-83.

LE DÉAUT, R. "The Current State of Targumic Studies," BibTB 4 (1974) 3-32.

Idem., "Targumic Literature and New Testament Interpretation," *Ibid*. 243-89.

LYONNET, S.-SABOURIN, L. *Sin, Redemption and Sacrifice* (Rome 1970).

MC CASLAND, S.V. "The Unity of the Scriptures," JBL 73 (1954) 1-10: in the experience of a *divine presence* "is the deepest and most abiding unity of scriptures" (p. 10).

MC KENZIE, J.L. *Dictionary of the Bible* (Milwaukee 1965).

PANIKULAM, G. *Koinonia in the New Testament: a Dynamic Expression of Christian Life*, Analecta Biblica 84 (Rome 1979).

PIETERSMA, A. "The Greek Psalter. A Question of Methodology and Syntax," VT 26 (1976) 60-69.

SANDERS, J.-A. *Torah and Canon* (Philadelphia 1972).

SMEND, R. *Die Bundesformel*, Theologische Studien 68 (Zurich 1963).

SPERBER, A. "New Testament and Septuagint," JBL 59 (1940) 193-293.

SPRIGGS, D.G. *Two Old Testament Theologies*, Studies in Bibl. Theol. 30 (London 1974).

VACCARI, A. "De versione graeca Veteris Testamenti," in *Institutiones Biblicae*, vol. 1 (Roma 1951) 276-93.

DE VAUX, R. "Présence et absence de Dieu dans l'histoire d'après l'Ancien Testament," *Concilium* 50 (1969) 13-22 (the following article by D. McCarthy is on God's presence and the prophetic word).

VON RAD, G. *Old Testament Theology*, two vols. (London 1975).

ZIMMERLI, W. "Zum Problem der 'Mitte des Alten Testaments,' " EvT 35 (1975) 97-118.

Bibliography for Section B

ACHTEMEIER, ELIZABETH, "The Relevance of the Old Testament for _

Christian Preaching," in H.N. Bream *et al.*, eds. *A Light unto my Path: Old Testament Studies in Honor of Jacob M. Myers* (Philadelphia 1974) 3-24: "We should not expect to hear the Word of God from the OT except through Jesus Christ" (p. 23).

ALONSO-SCHÖKEL, L. *The Inspired Word. Scripture in the Light of Language and Literature* (Montreal 1965).

AMSLER, S. "L'herméneutique néotestamentaire de l'Ancien Testament," in *L'Ancien Testament dans l'Eglise. Essai d'herméneutique chrétienne* (Neuchatel 1960) 91-99.

ANDERSON, B.W. ed., *The Old Testament and Christian Faith* (New York 1969).

AUVRAY, P. ed., *L'Ancien Testament et les chrétiens* (Paris 1951).

BARRETT, C.K. "The Interpretation of the Old Testament in the New," in *Cambridge History of the Bible*, vol. 1 (London/New York 1970) 377-411; for a competent historical survey of "the exposition and exegesis of Scripture" *see Ibid.* vol 2, pp. 155-97.

BENOIT, P., ed., *How Does the Christian Confront the Old Testament?* (New York 1968).

BOX, G.H. "The Value and Significance of the Old Testament in Relation to the New," in A.S. Peake, ed., *The People and the Book* (Oxford 1925) 433-67.

BRIGHT, J. *The Authority of the Old Testament* (London 1967).

CAZELLES, H. *Ecriture, Parole et Esprit. Trois aspects de l'herméneutique biblique* (Paris 1970).

CHARLIER, C. *La lecture chrétienne de la Bible* (Maredsous 1950).

DAUBE, D. *The Exodus Pattern in the Bible* (London 1963).

DODD, C.H. *According to the Scriptures. The Substructure of New Testament Theology* (London 1957).

DONNER, H. "Das Problem des Alten Testamentes in der christlichen Theologie . . ." in H.J. Birkner, u.a., *Beiträge zur Theorie des neuzeitlichen Christentums*, Fs. W. Trillhaas (Berlin 1968) 37-52.

DRIVER, S.R. "The Permanent Religious Value of the Old Testament," *The Interpreter* 1 (1905) 10-21.

DUESBERG, H. " 'Il leur ouvrit l'esprit à l'intelligence de l'Ecriture' (Lc 24, 45)," *Concilium* 30 (1967) 97-104.

FITZMYER, J. "The Use of Explicit Old Testament Quotations in Qumran Literature and in the New Testament," NTS 7 (1960-61) 297-333.

GERHARDSSON, B. *Memory and Manuscript* (Uppsala 1961).

GRECH, P. "The *'Testimonia'* and Modern Hermeneutics," NTS 19 (1972f) 318-24.

Idem, "The Old Testament as a Christological Source in the Apostolic Age," BibTB 5 (1975) 127-45.

GUILLEMETTE, P. "Jésus et la Loi chez les synoptiques," dans *Après Jesus. Autorité et liberté dans le peuple de Dieu* (Montréal 1977) 73-95.

GUNNEWEG, A.H.J. "Uber die Prädikabilität alttestamentlicher Texte," ZTK 65 (1968) 389-413.

HIGGINS, A.J.B. *The Christian Significance of the Old Testament* (London 1949).

HOLTZ, T. "Zur Interpretation des Alten Testaments im Neuen Testament," TLZ 99 (1974) 19-32.

HUFFMON, H.B. "The Israel of God," *Interpretation* 23 (1969) 66-77.

KRAUS, H.-J. *Worship in Israel. A Cultic History of the Old Testament* (Oxford 1966).

KRINETZKI, L. "Das Verhältnis des Alten Testaments zum Neuen Testament. Seine Bedeutung für den Christen," in J. Schreiner, ed., *Wort und Botschaft* (Würzburg 1967) 343-58.

MANSON, T.W. "The Old Testament in the Teaching of Jesus," *BullJRLibr* 34 (1952) 312-32.

MARANGON, A. "Il senso cristiano dell'Antico Testamento," *AttiSett-Bibl* 20 (1970) 343-65.

MARCEL, P.C. "Our Lord's Use of Scripture," in C.F.H. Henry, ed., *Revelation and the Bible: Contemporary Evangelical Thought* (London 1959) 119-34.

MARSHALL, I.H. ed., *New Testament Interpretation: Essays on Principles and Methods* (Grand Rapids 1977).

MARTIN-ACHARD, R. *Essai biblique sur les fêtes d'Israel* (Geneve 1974).

MIRTOW, P. *Jesus and the Religion of the Old Testament* (London 1957).

MOWINCKEL, S. *The Psalms in Israel's Worship* I-II (Oxford 1962; on the Psalms and the Cult, esp. in Gunkel, Mowinckel, and Kraus, *see* L. Sabourin, *The Psalms* 34-48).

MURPHY, R.E. "Christian Understanding of the Old Testament," *Theology Digest* 18 (1970) 321-32.

PEDERSEN, J. "The Crossing of the Red Sea and the Paschal Legend," in *Israel, Its Life and Culture* III-IV (Copenhagen 1940) 728-37.

SANDERS, E.P. *Paul and Palestinian Judaism: a Comparison of Patterns of Religion* (Philadelphia 1977).

STUHLMACHER, P. "Neues Testament und Hermeneutik - Versuch einer Bestandsaufnahme," ZTK 68 (1971) 121-61.

VERMES, G. *Scripture and Tradition* (Leiden 1961).

VRIEZEN, T.C. *An Outline of Old Testament Theology* (Oxford 1970); on the original German edition of the book *see* Alonso-Schökel in *Biblica* 44 (1963) 210-16.

WENHAM, J.W. "Jesus' View of the Old Testament," in *Christ and the Bible* (London 1972) 11-37.

WRIGHT, A.G. "The Literary Genre Midrash," CBQ 28 (1966) 122-38.

Bibliography for Sections C and D

ADINOLFI, M. "La problematica dell'inspirazione prima e dopo la *Dei Verbum, Rivista Biblica* 17 (1969) 249-81. *See* NTA 14, p. 261.

ALONSO-SCHÖKEL, L. *The Inspired Word. Scripture in the Light of Language and Literature* (Montreal 1965).

AMSLER, S. "Prophétie et typologie," RThPh 3 (1953) 139-48.

ARTOLA, A. "La Inspiración según la Constitución 'Dei Verbum,' " *Salmanticenses* 15 (1968) 291-315.

BAKER, D.L. "Typology and the Christian Use of the Old Testament," Scot JT 29 (1976) 137-57; *see also* section 6 of his book *Two Testaments, One Bible*.

BARR, J. "Typology and Allegory," in *Old and New in Interpretation: a Study of the Two Testaments* (London 1966) 103-48.

BAUDET, R. "La typologie de l'Exode dans le Second-Isaie," in *Etudes Théologiques* (3rd centenary publication, Quebec 1963) 11-21.

BENOIT, P. "Les analogies de l'inspiration," in *Sacra Pagina*, vol. 1 (Gembloux 1959) 86-99.

Idem, "La plénitude des Livres Saints," RB 67 (1960) 161-96.

Idem, "Inspiration de la Tradition et inspiration de l'Ecriture," in *Mélanges M.-D. Chenu* (Paris 1967) 111-26.

BIERBERG, T. "Does Sacred Scripture have a *Sensus Plenior*?" CBQ 10 (1948) 182-95.

BRAUN, F.M. "Le sens plénier et les encycliques," RT 51 (1951) 294-304.

BROWN, R.E. *The Sensus Plenior of Sacred Scripture (Baltimore 1955).*

Idem, "The *Sensus Plenior* in the Last Ten Years," CBQ 25 (1963) 252-85.

Idem, "The Problems of the *Sensus Plenior*," EphThL 43 (1967) 460-69.

BULTMANN, R. "Ursprung und Sinn der Typologie als hermeneutischer Methode," in *Bultmann Exegetica* (Tübingen 1967) 369-80.

BURTCHAELL, J.T. *Catholic Theories of Biblical Inspiration since 1810. A Review and Critique* (New York 1969). On this book see CBQ 1970, pp. 260f.

CAMELOT, T. "L'exégèse de l'Ancien Testament par les Pères," in P. Auvray, ed., *L'Ancien Testament et les chrétiens* (Paris 1951) 149-67.

CAVALLETTI, S. "La tipologia dei Rabbini," in *Studi e Materiali di Storia delle Religioni* 37 (1967) 223-51.

CHADWICK, H. "St. Paul and Philo of Alexandria," BullJRylLibr 48 (1965-66) 290.

CLAVIER, H. "Esquisse de typologie comparée, dans le Nouveau Testament et chez quelques écrivains patristiques," *Studia Patristica* IV, T.U. (Berlin 1961) 28-49.

CONGAR, Y. "The Old Testament as a Witness to Christ," repr. in *The Revelation of God*, E.T. (London 1968), from *La Vie Intellectuelle* 17 (1949) 335-43.

COPPENS, J. *Les harmonies des deux Testaments: essai sur les divers sens des Ecritures et sur l'unité de la Révélation* (Tournai 1949).

Idem, "Le problème du sens plénier," ETL 34 (1958) 5-20.

Idem, "Levels of Meaning in the Bible," *Concilium* 10 (December 1967) 62-69.

COURTADE, G. "Les Ecritures ont-elles un sens plénier?" RecSR 37 (1950) 481-97.

CROUZEL, H. "La distinction de la 'typologie' et de l' 'allégorie,' " BullLitEcc 65 (1964) 161-74.

DANIÉLOU, J. *From Shadows to Reality: Studies in the Biblical Typology of the Fathers* (E.T., London 1960).

Idem, "Qu'est-ce que la typologie?" in P. Auvray, ed., *Op. cit.* 199-205.

DAUBE, D. *The Exodus Pattern in the Bible* (London 1963).

DELPORTE, L. "Les principes de la typologie biblique et les éléments figuratifs du Sacrifice de l'Expiation (Lév. 16)," ETL 3 (1926) 207-27.

DODD, C.H. *According to the Scriptures, the sub-structure of New Testament Theology* (London 1957).

DUBARLE, A.-M. "La lecture chrétienne de l'Ancien Testament," in P. Auvray, ed., *op. cit.,* 206-33.

EICHRODT, W. "Is Typological Exegesis an Appropriate Method?" in C. Westemann, ed., *Essays . . .* 224-44.

FERNANDEZ, A. "De sensu pleniori, consequenti, accomodato," in *Institutiones Biblicae* (1st ed. 1925, 6th ed. Rome 1951) 381-93.

GIBLIN, C.H. " 'As it is written . . .' - a Basic Problem in Noematics and its Relevance to Biblical Theology," CBQ 20 (1958) 327-53; 477-98; (would substitute "theological meaning" for "fuller sense").

GOPPELT, L. *Typos (Die typologische Deutung des Alten Testaments im Neuen)*, Gütersloh 1939.

Idem, "Typos . . ." *TDNT* 8 (1972) 246-59.

GRECH, P. "The Language of Scripture and its Interpretation: an Essay," BibTB 6 (1976) 161-76.

GRELOT, P. *La Bible Parole de Dieu. Introduction théologique à l'étude de l'Ecriture Sainte* (Paris 1965).

Idem, "L'inspiration de l'Ecriture et son interprétation," in *La révélation divine*, Unam Sanctam 70 (Paris 1968) 347-80.

GRIBOMONT, J. "Sens plénier, sens typique et sens littéral," ETL 25 (1949) 577-87.

HARVEY, J. "La typologie de l'Exode dans les Psaumes," ScEcc 15 (1963) 383-405.

HOFIUS, O. *Katapausis. Die Vorstellung vom endzeitlichen Ruheort im Hebräerbrief* (Tübingen 1970).

HUMMEL, H.D. "The Old Testament Basis of Typological Interpretation," *Biblical Research* 9 (1964) 38-50 (Not "fuller sense" but "fuller understanding").

KERRIGAN, A. "The Objects of the Literal and Spiritual Senses of the New Testament according to St. Cyril of Alexandria," *Studia Patristica* I, T.U. 63 (Berlin 1957) 354-74.

LAMPE, G.W. ed. *A Patristic Greek Lexicon* (Oxford 1961ff).

LARCHER, C. *L'actualité chrétienne de l'Ancien Testament d'après le Nouveau Testament* (Paris 1962) 489-513 (on typology).

LATAKOS, E. "La consideración tipologica de la Biblia en el Concilio Vaticano II," *Revista Biblica* 29 (1967) 129-39.

LUBAC, H. DE, *The Sources of Revelation* (New York 1968), in which the author presents his major work *Exégèse Médiévale. Les quatre sens de l'Ecriture*, 3 vols. (Paris 1959-64).

Idem, "Typologie et allégorisme," RecSR 34 (1947) 180-226.

LYS, D. *The Meaning of the Old Testament* (New York 1967) 55-73.

MAILHIOT, M.-D. "La pensée de saint Thomas sur le sens spirituel," *Revue Thomiste* 59 (1959) 613-63.

MÉNÉGOZ, E. *La théologie de l'épitre aux Hébreux* (Paris 1894).

MONTEFIORE, H. *A Commentary on the Epistle to the Hebrews* (London 1964).

MUÑOZ IGLESIAS, S. "Problemática del 'sensus plenior,' " *XII Sem.*

Bibl. Esp. (Madrid 1952) 224-59.

MURPHY, R.E. "Christian Understanding of the Old Testament," *Theology Digest* 18 (1970) 321-32.

OLSEN, G.W. "Allegory, Typology, and Symbol: the *sensus spiritualis*. Part I: Definitions and Earliest History," *Intern. Cath. Rev./Communio* 4 (1977) 161-79.

O'ROURKE, J.J. "Marginal Notes on the *Sensus Plenior*," CBQ 21 (1959) 64-71.

RAHNER, K. *Inspiration in the Bible* (New York 1961).

RAMLOT, L. "Prophétisme," SDB 8, cc. 1092-94.

REUMANN, J. "Creation, Continuing and New," in V. Vajta, ed., *The Gospel as History* (Philadelphia 1975) 79-110.

ROBINSON, J.M. "A Scripture and Theological Method: a Protestant Study in *Sensus Plenior*," CBQ 27 (1965) 6-27.

SCHMID, J. "Die attestamentlichen Zitate bei Paulus und die Theorie vom *sensus plenior*," *Biblische Zeitschrift* 3 (1959) 161-73.

SCHNEIDERS, S.M. "Faith, Hermeneutics, and the Literal Sense of Scripture," *Theological Studies* 39 (1978) 719-36.

SMITH, R.F. "Inspiration and Inerrancy," *Jerome Biblical Commentary* n. 66, pp. 499-514.

SMITH, R.H. "Exodus Typology in the Fourth Gospel," JBL 81 (1962) 329-42.

SOWERS, S.G. *The Hermeneutics of Philo and Hebrews* (Zurich 1965).

STEK, J.H. "Biblical Typology Yesterday and Today," *Calvin Theological Journal* 5 (1970) 133-63 (*see* NTA 15, p. 141).

SUTCLIFFE, E.P. "The Plenary Sense as a Principle of Interpretation," *Biblica* 34 (1953) 333-43.

TEMINO SAIZ, A. "En torno al problema del '*sensus plenior*,'" EstBib 14 (1955) 5-47.

TURRADO Y TURRADO, L. "Se demuestra la existencia del '*sensus plenior*' por los citas que el Nuevo Testamento hace del Antiguo?" *XII Sem. Bibl. Esp.* (Madrid 1952) 331-78.

DE TUYA, M. "Si es posible y en que medida un '*sensus plenior*' a la luz del concepto teólogico de inspiración," *Ibid.* 283-

329.

VACCARI, A. "Historia Exegeseos," in *Institutiones Biblicae* (Rome 1951) 510-67.

VEMPENY, I. *Inspiration in the Non-Biblical Scriptures* (Bangalore 1973).

VON RAD, G. *Old Testament Theology* (London 1975).

WILLIAMSON, R. *Philo and the Epistle to the Hebrews* (Leiden 1969).

WOOLLCOMBE, K.J. "The Biblical Origins and Patristic Development of Typology," in G.W.H. Lampe and K.J. Woollcombe, *Essays on Typology* (London 1957) 39-75.

GENERAL CONCLUSION

As Richardson recalls, God's saving activity in history is the theme of both Testaments, neither Testament alone completes the record of it, but each Testament testifies to the whole of God's saving work, not merely to a part of it. "The Old Testament is the kerygmatic record of God's saving action in that history which is completed in the New Testament" (p. 47). The Old Testament has to be represented on its own, according to its own intention, but with regard also to the New Testament, for which it contains both pre-understanding (Bultmann's *Vorverständnis*) and prefigurement. In the words of W. Zimmerli, the Old Testament is "the unconditioned assurance of the real historicity of Christ. It guards against every Christ-myth. As long as the Gospel is bound up together with the Old Testament, it will never permit itself to be singled out as a timeless element of proclamation" (p. 120). Since Yahweh is the Father of Jesus, whatever is said of him in the OT is relevant also for the NT faith and helps us to understand and to proclaim it. In addition, the Old Testament shows what kind of religious humanity there was before and without Christ, how destitute mankind was and what forbearance on God's part allowed it to survive, in view of the coming fulfillment. For Pannenberg "the connection between the Old and New Testaments is made understandable only by the consciousness of the one history which binds together the eschatological community of Jesus Christ and ancient Israel by means of the bracket of promise and fulfillment" (p. 323). For promise/fulfillment is a category rooted in history and prophecy and this guarantees that it corresponds to the essence of biblical thought and reflects the movement itself of salvation from its beginning to its ultimate goal.

In the present work we have proposed reflections on biblical themes, particularly adapted to illustrate the unity of the two Testaments, such as the notion of God, his law and kingdom, the covenant and the promise, the people of God. Then we have exposed the christological prefigurement of the Old Testament in the light of the New, as well as the Christward inclination of salvation history. Finally we have attempted to show how the reading of Scriptures responds to this Christward movement of salvation history and finds expression in the fuller sense of the texts, as well as in their typological dimension. Also biblical theology is involved in the process. "Only when Old Testament theology takes this final step to the threshold of the New Testament, only when it makes the link with the witness of the Gospels and the Apostles perfectly openly, and when it is able to make men believe that the two Testaments belong together, will it have the right to term itself a theological undertaking, and therefore 'Biblical theology.' If instead it analyzes the Old Testament in isolation, then, no matter how devotedly the work is done, the more appropriate term is 'history of the religion of the Old Testament' " (Von Rad, vol. 2, pp. 428ff).

When we speak of the unity of the two Testaments we understand in first place "Testaments" as the inspired written accounts of God's self-revelation, including his dealings with men, with his people in the framework of salvation history, and human response to the divine initiatives. Under this viewpoint Christ's role as factor of unity is obvious for the Christian believer, who accepts Christ's own claim that he came to fulfill the law and the prophets (Mt 5:17), and that "everything written about me in the law of Moses and the prophets and the psalms must be fulfilled" (Lk 24:44).

Under "Testaments" we can also understand the two dispensations and what they represented. To institutional Israel certainly belonged, although in varying degrees, the kings, the priests, the prophets, and the wise (cf. Jr 18:18). These four categories of leaders have also found their fulfillment in Christ, who appears in the New Testament as King-Messiah, high priest of the end-time economy (Heb 9:11), eschatological prophet (Jn 6:14), and as the incarnation of wisdom (cf. 1 Cor 1:30). Particular leaders, like

Moses and David, and individual figures, like the Suffering Servant or the Son of Man, also received fulfillment in the person of Christ, in a way not altogether expected.

The author of Hebrews saw that the time of the old cult had elapsed (8:13) and would be replaced by the era of the new tabernacle (8:2; 9:11), while John explained that the glorified humanity of Christ would be the new temple, the centre of the new worship (2:21). The Israelite feasts themselves would cede the place to Christian solemnities celebrated in the Church in worship of its Founder and Savior. Even Sabbath would have its counterpart in the Christian Sunday kept *the first day of the week* in remembrance of the Resurrection (Mk 16:2). As we have seen in connection with typology, the Old Testament as a whole, if understood correctly, can be considered as prophetic and figuratively (*typikos*) instructive, to use Paul's expression of 1 Cor 10:11. There is a new covenant (Mt 26:28), because there had been another covenant before, now replaced by a "better" covenant (Heb 8:6), with Christ as Mediator (9:15; 12:24). All this concurs to show that Christ is the cornerstone of the unity of the two Testaments in more than one way, although the purpose of this book has been to show that the Bible and all that it stands for finds in him the unity which true believers in the word of God are invited to recognize.

Taking into account what we have written in the beginning of chapter two on "Covenant and Testament," we suggest that the following Pauline text can illumine what we have been trying to say throughout the present study: "To this very day, when the old testament is read the veil remains unlifted; it is only in Christ that it is taken away" (2 Cor 3:14). In Christ, in fact, "in the fullness of time," is God's plan accomplished to bring into one all things in the heavens and on earth (Ep 1:10).

GENERAL BIBLIOGRAPHY
(a selection)

ALONSO-SCHÖKEL, L. *The Inspired Word. Scripture in the Light of Language and Literature* (Montreal 1965).

Id., "The Old Testament, a Christian Book," *Biblica* 44 (1963) 210-16.

AMSLER, S. *"L'Ancien Testament dans l'Eglise. Essai d'herméneutique chrétienne* (Neuchatel 1960).

Id., "Le dernier et l'avant-dernier. Les rapports entre le Nouveau et l'Ancien Testament," RecSR 63 (1975) 385-96.

ANDERSON, B.W. ed., *The Old Testament and Christian Faith* (New York 1969).

AUVRAY, P. *et al., L'Ancien Testament et les chrétiens* (Paris 1951).

BAKER, D.L. *Two Testaments, One Bible. A Study of some Modern Solutions to the Theological Problem of the Relationship between the Old and New Testaments* (Leicester, G.B., 1977).

BARR, J. *Old and New in Interpretation: A Study of the Two Testaments* (London 1966).

BARRETT, C.K. "The Interpretation of the Old Testament in the New," in *Cambridge History of the Bible*, vol. 1 (London/New York 1970) 377-411.

BAUMGÄRTEL, F. *Verheissung: zur Frage des evangelischen Verständnisses des Alten Testaments* (Gütersloh 1952).

Id., "The Hermeneutical Problem of the Old Testament," in C. Westermann, ed., *Essays on Old Testament Hermeneutics* (Richmond 1963) 134-59.

BEAUCHAMP, P. *L'un et l'autre Testament. Essai de lecture* (Paris 1976).

BENOIT, P. *et al.,* eds., *How Does the Christian Confront the Old Testament?* (New York 1968).

Id., "La plénitude de sens des Livres Saints," *Revue Biblique* 67 (1960) 161-96.

BLACK, M. "The Christological Use of the Old Testament in the New Testament," *New Testament Studies* (1971) 1-14.

BOX, G.H. "The Value and Significance of the Old Testament in Relation to the New," in A.S. Peake, ed., *The People and the Book* (Oxford 1925) 433-67.

BRIGHT, J. *The Authority of the Old Testament* (London 1967).

Id., Covenant and Promise. The Prophetic Understanding of the Future in Pre-Exilic Israel (Philadelphia 1976).

BRING, R. *Christus und das Gesetz. Die Bedeutung des Gesetzes des Alten Testaments nach Paulus und sein Glauben an Christus* (Leiden 1968).

Id., "Die Bedeutung des Alten Testamentes für die Christologie der Alten Kirche," in *Antwort aus der Geschichte*, Fs. W. Dress (Bonn 1969) 13-34.

BROWN, R.E. *The Sensus Plenior of Sacred Scripture* (Baltimore 1955).

Id., "The Problems of the *Sensus Plenior*," EphThLov 43 (1967) 460-69.

BRUCE, F.F. *This is That: The New Testament Development of Some Old Testament Themes* (Exeter 1968).

Id., ed., *Promise and Fulfillment*, Fs. S.H. Hooke (Edinburgh 1963).

BRUNNER, E. "The Significance of the Old Testament for Our Faith," in B.W. Anderson, ed., *op. cit.* 243-64.

BULTMANN, R. "The Significance of the Old Testament for the Christian Faith," in B.W. Anderson, ed., *op. cit.* 8-35.

Id., "Prophecy and Fulfillment," in C. Westermann, ed., *Essays* . . . 50-75.

CAMELOT, T. "L'Exégèse de l'Ancien Testament par les Pères," in P. Auvray, *et. al., op. cit.,* 149-67.

CARMIGNAC, J. "II Corinthiens III. 6,14 et le début de la formation du Nouveau Testament," *New Testament Studies* 24 (1977) 384-86.

CAZELLES, H., *Ecriture, Parole et Esprit. Trois aspects de l'herméneutique biblique* (Paris 1970).

CERFAUX, L. "L'exégèse de l'Ancien Testament par le Nouveau Testament," dans P. Auvray, *et. al., op. cit.* 132-48.

CHARLIER, C. *La lecture chrétienne de la Bible* (Maredsous 1950).

CHILDS B.S. *Biblical Theology in Crisis* (Philadelphia 1970).

Id., "A Tale of Two Testaments," *Interpretation* 26 (1972) 20-29.

CLAVIER, H. *Les variétés de la pensée biblique et le problème de son unité.* Suppl NT 43 (Leiden 1976).

CLEMENTS, R.E. *Prophecy and Covenant* (London 1965).

COPPENS, J. *Les harmonies des deux Testaments: essai sur les divers sens des Ecritures et sur l'unité de la Révélation* (2e édit., Tournai 1949).

Id., "Levels of Meaning in the Bible," *Concilium* vol. 10 (December 1967) 62-69.

CULLMANN, O. *Salvation in History* (London 1967).

DANIÉLOU, J. *From Shadows to Reality: Studies in the Biblical Typology of the Fathers* (London 1960).

DELGADO, A. "La unidad de las Escrituras," *Scripta Theologica* 4 (1972) 7-82, 279-354.

DEN BOER, W. "Hermeneutic Problems in Early Christian Literature," *Vigiliae Christianae* 1 (1947) 150-67.

DEQUEKER, L. "Old and New in the Bible. Guidelines for a Better Understanding of the Relationship between the Old and New Testaments," *Louvain Studies* 3 (1971) 189-205.

DIEM, H. "Die Einheit der Schrift," *Evangelische Theologie* 13 (1953) 383-405.

Id., "Jesus, der Christus des Alten Testaments," *ibid.* 14 (1954) 437-48.

DILLENBERGER, J. "Revelational Discernement and the Problem of the Two Testaments," in B.W. Anderson, ed., *op. cit.* 159-75.

DODD, C.H. *According to the Scriptures: the sub-structure of New Testament Theology* (London 1957).

DONNER, H. "Das Problem des Alten Testamentes in der christlichen Theologie. Ueberlegungen zu Begriff und Geschichte der altestamentlichen Einleitung," in H.J. Birkner u.a., *Beiträge zur Theorie des neuzeitlichen Christentum*, Fs. W. Trillhaas (Berlin 1968) 37-52.

DUBARLE, A.-M. "La lecture chrétienne de l'Ancien Testament," in P. Auvray, *et al., op. cit.* 206-33.

EICHRODT, W. "Is Typological Exegesis an Appropriate Method?" in C. Westermann, ed., *Essays* . . . 224-44.

EISSFELDT, O. "Ist der Gott des Alten Testaments auch der des Neuen Testaments?" in *Geschichtliches und Uebergeschichtliches im Alten Testament*, Theol. Studien und Kritiken 109, Heft 2 (Berlin 1947) 37-54.

FENSHAM, F.C. "The Covenant as Giving Expression to the Relationship between Old and New Testament," *Tyndale Bulletin* 22 (1971) 82-94.

FILSON, F.V. "The Unity between the Testaments," in M. Laymond, ed., *The Interpreter's One-Volume Commentary on the Bible* (Nashville 1971) 989-993.

FOHRER, G. "Der Mittelpunkt einer Theologie des Alten Testaments," *Theologische Zeitschrift* 24 (1968) 161-72.

FRANCE, R.T. *Jesus and the Old Testament: His Application of Old Testament Passages to Himself and His Mission* (London 1971).

GAEBELEIN, F.E. "The Unity of the Bible," in D.F.H. Henry, ed., *Revelation and the Bible: Contemporary Evangelical Thought* (London 1959) 387-401.

GALBIATI, E. "L'unita dei due testamenti," in T. Ballarini, ed., *Introduzione alla Bibbia* 2, 1 (Torino 1969) 8-12.

GELIN, A. "Comment le peuple d'Israël lisait l'Ancien Testament," in P. Auvray, et. al., *L'Ancien Testament et les chrétiens* (Paris 1951) 117-31.

GESE, H. "Erwägungen zur Einheit der biblischen Theologie," ZThK 67 (1970) 417-36.

GLEN, J.S. "Jesus Christ and the Unity of the Bible," *Interpretation* 5 (1951) 259-67.

GOGARTEN, F. "Theology and History," *Journal for Theology and the Church* 4 (1967) 35-81 (English Translation of an article published in 1953).

GOPPELT, L. *Typos. Die typologischen Deutung des Alten Testaments im Neuen Testament* (Darmstadt 1969). Also the art. "Typos, antitypos" in *TDNT* 8 (1972) 246-59.

GRECH, P. "The Old Testament as a Christological Source in the Apostolic Age," *Biblical Theology Bulletin* 5 (1975)

127-45.

GRELOT, P. *La Bible Parole de Dieu. Introduction théologique à l'étude de l'Ecriture Sainte* (Paris 1965), esp. pp. 231-301. There is an English Translation of this book (New York 1969), but the original French edition is used in our book.

Id., Sens chrétien de l'Ancien Testament. Esquisse d'un traité dogmatique (Tournai 1962).

GROGAN, G.W. "The New Testament Interpretation of the Old Testament: a Comparative Study," *Tyndale Bulletin* 18 (1967) 54-76.

HAHN, V. *Das wahre Gesetz: Eine Untersuchung der Auffassung des Ambrosius von Mailand vom Verhältnis der beiden Testamente* (Munster 1969).

HARVEY, J. "The New Diachronic Biblical Theology of the Old Testament (1960-1970)," *Biblical Theology Bulletin* 1 (1971) 5-29.

HESSE, F. "The Evaluation and the Authority of the Old Testament Texts," in C. Westermann, ed., *Essays* . . . 285-313.

HIGGINS, A.J.B. *The Christian Significance of the Old Testament* (London 1949).

Id., "The Old Testament and Some Aspects of New Testament Christology," in F.F. Bruce, ed., *Promise and Fulfillment*, Fs. S.H. Hooke (Edinburgh 1963) 128-41.

HOLTZ, T. "Zur Interpretation des Alten Testaments im Neuen Testament," *Theologische Literaturzeitung* 99 (1974) 19-32.

HUMMEL, H.D. "The Old Testament Basis of Typological Interpretation," *Biblical Research* 9 (1964) 38-50.

JASPER, F.N. "The Relation of the Old Testament to the New," *Expository Times* 78 (1967) 228-35, 267-70.

JENSON, R.W. "Die Kontinuität von Altem und Neuem Testament als Problem fur Kirche und Theologie heute," in H. Zeddies, ed., *Hoffnung ohne Illusion: Referate und Bibelarbeiten* (Berlin 1970).

KAISER, W.C. "The Centre of Old Testament Theology: the Promise," *Themelios* 10.1 (1974) 1-10.

KRAUS, H.-J. *Die biblische Theologie: Ihre Geschichte und Problematik* (Neukirchen 1970).

KRINETZKI, L. "Das Verhältnis des Alten Testaments zum Neuen Testament. Seine Bedeutung für den Christen," in J. Schreiner, ed., *Wort und Botschaft* (Würzburg 1967) 343-58.

KÜMMEL, W.G. *Promise and Fulfillment. The Eschatological Message of Jesus* (London 1957).

KUSKE, M. *Das Alte Testament als Buch von Christus. Dietrich Bonhoeffers Wertung und Auslegung des Alten Testaments* (Göttingen 1971).

KUYPER, L.J. "The Old Testament in the Church," *Reformed Review* 21.3 (1968) 9-25.

LAMPE, G.W.H. & WOOLLCOMBE, K.J. *Essays on Typology* (London 1957).

LARCHER, C. *L'Actualité chrétienne de l'Ancien Testament d'après le Nouveau Testament,* Lectio Divina 34 (Paris 1962).

LESTRINGANT, P. "L'unité de la Bible. Fondement théologique et religieux de la Réforme," in J. Boisset, éd., *Le problème biblique dans le Protestantisme* (Paris 1955) 45-69.

LINDARS, B. *New Testament Apologetic: The Doctrinal Significance of the Old Testament Quotations* (London 1961).

LOHFINK, NORBERT, *The Christian Meaning of the Old Testament* (London 1969).

LONGENECKER, R.N. "Can We Reproduce the Exegesis of the New Testament?" *Tyndale Bulletin* 21 (1970) 3-38.

LUBAC, H. DE *Exégèse Médiévale. Les quatre sens de l'Ecriture,* 3 vols. (Paris 1959-64).

Id., The Sources of Revelation (New York 1968), a presentation of the other work.

LUBSCZYK, H. "Die Einheit der Schrift. Zur herméneutischen Relevanz des Urbekenntnisses im Alten und Neuen Testament," in F. Hoffmann, u.a., eds., *Sapienter Ordinare*, Festgabe für E. Kleineidam (Leipzig 1969)

73-104.

LYONNET, S. *Il Nuovo Testamento alla luce dell'Antico* (Brescia 1972). This book is a development of an article published in *Nouvelle Revue Théologique* 87 (1965) 561-87.

LYS, D. *The Meaning of the Old Testament* (New York 1967).

MAC KENZIE, R.A.F. *Faith and History in the Old Testament* (Minneapolis 1963).

MANSON, T.W. "The Old Testament in the Teaching of Jesus," BullJRylLibr 34 (1952) 313-32.

MARANGON, A. "Il senso cristiano dell'Antico Testamento," *Atti Sett. Bibl. It.* 20 (1970) 343-65.

MARCEL, P.CH. "Our Lord's Use of Scripture," in C.F.H. Henry, ed., *Revelation and the Bible: Contemporary Evangelical Thought* (London 1959) 119-34.

MC CASLAND, S.V. "The Unity of the Scriptures," JBL 73 (1954) 1-10.

MC CULLOUGH, J.C. "Jesus Christ in the Old Testament," *Biblical Theology* 22 (1972) 36-47.

MC KENZIE, J.L. "The Value of the Old Testament," *Concilium* 10 (December 1967) 4-17.

Id., "The Significance of the Old Testament for Christian Faith in Roman Catholicism," in B.W. Anderson, ed., *op. cit.* 102-14.

MICHALSON, C. "Bultmann against Marcion," in B.W. Anderson, ed., *op. cit.* 49-63.

MILDENBERGER, F. *Gottes Tat im Wort. Erwägungen zur alttestamentlichen Hermeneutik als Frage nach der Einheit der Testamente* (Gütersloh 1964).

MILLER, M.P. "Targum, Midrash and the Use of the Old Testament in the New Testament," *Journal for the Study of Judaism* 2 (1971) 29-82. A bibliographical essay.

MIRTOW, P. *Jesus and the Religion of the Old Testament* (London 1957).

MOTYER, A. "Bible Study and the Unity of the Bible," in J.B. Job, ed., *Studying God's Word: An Introduction to Methods of Bible Study* (London 1972) 11-23.

MOULE, C.F.D. "Fulfillment-Words in the New Testament: Use and Abuse," *New Testament Studies* 14 (1968) 293-320.

MUÑOZ IGLESIAS, S. "Old Testament Values Superseded by the New," in P. Benoit *et al.*, eds., *op. cit.* 50-55.

Id., "Problemática del 'sensus plenior,' " *XII Sem. B. Esp.* (Madrid 1952) 224-59. Also an article on the typical sense in *ibid.* XIII (Madrid 1954) 301-24.

MURPHY, R.E. "The Relationship between the Testaments," CBQ 26 (1964) 349-59. Good review article.

Id., "Christian Understanding of the Old Testament," *Theology Digest* 18 (1970) 321-32.

O'COLLINS, G.G. "Revelation as History," *Heythrop Journal* 7 (1966) 394-406.

OESTERREICHER, J.M. *The Israel of God: on the Old Testament Roots of the Church's Faith* (Englewood Cliffs 1963).

PANNENBERG, W "Redemptive Event and History," in C. Westermann, ed., *Essays* . . . 314-35.

PREMSAGAR, P.V. "Theology of Promise in the Patriarchal Narratives," *The Indian Journal of Theology* 23 (1974) 112-22.

PROULX, R. "Une forme inédite de la présence de Dieu dans l'Ancien Testament," in *Après Jésus. Autorité et liberté dans le peuple de Dieu* (Montréal 1977) 199-208.

RAD, G. VON, "Typological Interpretation of the Old Testament," in C. Westermann, ed., *Essays* . . . 17-39.

Id., Old Testament Theology, 2 vols. (Study Edition, London 1975).

RICHARDSON, A. "Is the Old Testament the Propaedeutic to Christian Faith?" in B.W. Anderson, ed., *op. cit.* 36-48.

RIDDERBOS, N.H. "De Verhouding van het Oude Testament en het Nieuwe Testament," *Gereformeerd Theologisch Tijdschrift* 68 (1968) 97-110.

ROBINSON, J.M. "The Historicality of Biblical Language," in B.W. Anderson, ed., *op. cit.* 124-58.

ROWLEY, H.H. *The Unity of the Bible* (Philadelphia 1953).

RYLAARSDAM, "Jewish-Christian Relationship: The Two Covenants and the Dilemnas of Christology," *Journal of Ecumenical Studies* 9 (1972) 249-70.

SANDERS, J.A. "Torah and Christ," *Interpretation* 29 (1975) 372-90.

SCHMID, J. "Die Einheit der Testamente," *Judaica* 21 (1965) 150-66.

SCHMIDT, L. "Die Einheit zwischen Altem und Neuem Testament im Streit zwischen Friedrich Baumgärtel und Gerhard von Rad," *Evangelische Theologie* 35 (1975) 119-39.

SHIH, D.P. *The Unity of the Testaments as a Hermeneutical Problem* (Boston University Dissertation, 1971). See Diss. Abstracts Intern. vol. 32, p. 2186A.

SHIRES, H.M. *Finding the Old Testament in the New* (Philadelphia 1974).

SIEDL, S. "Das Alte und das Neue Testament. Ihre Verschiedenheit und Einheit," *Theologisch-praktische Quartalschrift* 119 (1971) 314-24.

SMEND, R. *Die Mitte des Alten Testaments*, Theologische Studien 101 (Zurich 1970).

SMITH, D.M. JR., "The Use of the Old Testament in the New," in J.M. Efird, ed., *The Use of the Old Testament in the New and Other Essays*. Studies in Honor of W.F. Stinespring (Durham, N.C. 1972) 3-65.

STAMM, J.J. "Jesus Christ and the Old Testament," in C. Westermann, ed., *Essays* . . . 200-10.

STEK, J.H. "Biblical Typology Yesterday and Today," *Calvin Theological Journal* 5 (1970) 113-62.

STRAMARE, T. "Quod in novo patet in vetere latet," *Bibbia e Oriente* 16 (1974) 199-210.

THOMAS, T.G. "The Unity of the Bible and the Uniqueness of Christ," *London Quarterly and Holborn Review* 191 (1966) 219-27.

VAN IERSEL, B. "The Book of God's People," *Concilium* 10 (December 1965) 25-38.

VAN RULER, A.A. *The Christian Church and the Old Testament*, E.T. unchanged from German 1955 edition (Grand Rapids, Mich. 1966).

VAN UNNIK, W.C. *"Hē kainē diathēkē—a* Problem in the Early History of the Canon," *Studia Patristica* IV, T.U. 79

(Berlin 1961) 212-27.

VAN ZYL, A.H. "The Relation between the Old and New Testaments," *Hermeneutica* (Pretoria 1970) 9-22 (text in Afrikaner).

VAWTER, B. "The Fuller Sense: Some Considerations," CBQ 26 (1964) 86-96.

VERHOEF, P.A. "The Relationship between the Old and the New Testaments," in J.B. Payne, ed., *New Perspectives on the Old Testament* (London 1970) 280-303.

VISCHER, W. *The Witness of the Old Testament to Christ* (London 1949, first published in German in 1934).

Id., "Everywhere the Scripture is about Christ Alone," in B.W. Anderson, ed., *op. cit.* 90-101.

VOIGHT, D.G. "Worin besteht das *Continuum* der beiden Testamente?" *Pastoralblätter* (Stuttgart 1967) 68-78. The *Continuum* rests in salvation history.

VRIEZEN, T.C. *An Outline of Old Testament Theology,* revd. E.T. (Oxford 1970).

WELCH, A.C. *The Preparation for Christ in the Old Testament* (Edinburgh 1933).

WENHAM, J.W. *Christ and the Bible* (London 1972).

WRIGHT, G.E. "History and Reality: the Importance of Israel's 'Historical' Symbols for the Christian Faith," in B.W. Anderson, ed., *op. cit.* 176-99.

Id., "The Unity of the Bible," *Scottish Journal of Theology* 8 (1955) 338-52.

Id., The Old Testament and Theology (New York 1969).

WESTERMANN, C. ed., *Essays on Old Testament Hermeneutics,* J.L. Mays edit. of this E.T. (Richmond, Virg. 1963).

Id., "The Way of the Promise through the Old Testament," in B.W. Anderson, ed., *op. cit.* 200-24.

Id., "Remarks on the Theses of Bultmann and Baumgärtel," in C. Westermann, ed., *op. cit.* 123-33.

WOLF, E. *Die Einheit des Bundes: das Verhältnis von Alten und Neuem Testament bei Calvin* (Neukirchen 1958).

WOLFF, H.W. "The Hermeneutics of the Old Testament," in C. Westermann, ed., *op. cit.* 160-99.

ZARAFA, P. "Christological Interpretation of the Old Testament," *Angelicum* 41 (1964) 51-62. Presents P. Grelot, *Sens chrétien de l'Ancien Testament.*

ZIMMERLI, W. "Promise and Fulfillment," in C. Westermann, ed., *op. cit.* 89-122.

Id., "Zum Problem der 'Mitte des Alten Testaments,' " *Evangelische Theologie* 35 (1975) 97-118.

SUBJECT INDEX